Filipino Care Workers in Israel

Diasporas in Asia and Beyond

As kaleidoscopes of Asia's colourful diversity and intricate connections, voluntary and involuntary diasporas carved new spaces for ethnic communities and cultures to take root and flower beyond one or more geopolitical borders. While Asia served as a point of departure for some, it was a stepping-stone for those in transition and a final destination for others. Voluntary or not, diasporas collectively learned to not only live and survive in foreign environments, but also to thrive by harnessing what hostlands had to offer. The heart of the Diasporas in Asia and Beyond book series is to explore diasporic experiences scattered in different parts of the world through rethinking 'Asia' as a unique experience for those arriving, as much as it is for those departing.

It accentuates Asia's transnational and/or cosmopolitan bonds with the world and vice versa by considering the diverse connections, both imagined and actual, that diasporas fabricated in the course of settling in or leaving Asia. The process of re-settlement, establishment, and growth of diasporic communities has produced complex dynamics: changing transimperial or transnational relationships with ancestral homelands, new forms of contestation and collaboration in markets, workplaces, political arenas, social spaces in Asian cities and beyond, conflict and competition with diasporic communities sharing the same heritage elsewhere in the world, and the rise of unprecedented polyglot cultures and hybrid identities that combine local, communal, national, and global experiences, as well as individual and communal pursuits past and present. The series welcomes monographs and edited volumes that focus on accounts and discourses situated in the margins of dominating colonial or national narratives, as well as diasporic experiences with negotiating and establishing spaces of their own that resulted in new forms of collaborations and divisions.

Series editors
Dr. Catherine Chan, University of Macau, China

Editorial Board
Prof. Tina Clemente, University of the Philippines Diliman, The Philippines
Prof. Daniel Goh, National University of Singapore, Singapore
Dr. Vivian Kong, University of Bristol, UK
Dr. Bernard Keo, La Trobe University, Australia
Dr. Francisca Lai, National Tsinghua University, Taiwan
Dr. Ka Kin Cheuk, City University of Hong Kong, China
Dr. Sophie Loy-Wilson, The University of Sydney, Australia

Filipino Care Workers in Israel

Migration, Trans-local Livelihoods and Space

Anna Lim

Amsterdam University Press

Cover photo: photo made by author

Cover design: Coördesign, Leiden
Lay-out: Crius Group, Hulshout

ISBN   978 94 6372 040 3
e-ISBN   978 90 4854 288 8
DOI   10.5117/9789463720403
NUR   740

© A. Lim / Amsterdam University Press B.V., Amsterdam 2025

All rights reserved. Without limiting the rights under copyright reserved above, no part of this book may be reproduced, stored in or introduced into a retrieval system, or transmitted, in any form or by any means (electronic, mechanical, photocopying, recording or otherwise) without the written permission of both the copyright owner and the author of the book.

Every effort has been made to obtain permission to use all copyrighted illustrations reproduced in this book. Nonetheless, whosoever believes to have rights to this material is advised to contact the publisher.

Table of Contents

List of Maps, Figures, and Tables	7
List of Abbreviations	9
Introduction	13
Women in Global Labor Market	16
Place-Making in Transnational Migration	19
Existing Studies in the Israeli Context	23
Locating My Research in Israel	26
Progressing Through the Chapters to Come	30
Bibliography	32
1. Between a "National Hero" and a "Global Servant"	39
Migrating from the Philippines to Work	40
Migration Journey to Israel	45
Foreign Workers in Israel	61
Bibliography	72
2. "Unsettled Settlers" in South Tel Aviv	79
Emergence of a Migrant Neighborhood	80
Mapping out Filipino Society	88
Bibliography	103
3. Flat as a Nodal Site in the Mobile Circuit	107
Organizing the Flat as a Shared Accommodation	108
Dynamic Construction of the Flat	115
Settlement of Transient Permanence	125
Bibliography	134
4. Networking Through Weekend Rituals	135
Mealtime Socialization: Dinner on Day-off	136
Birthday Celebrations: The Banquet and Exchange of Gifts	144
Paluwagan	150
Bibliography	155
5. Seeking a Shelter Behind Gate	157
Life in "Border Place"	158

Making Love in Liminal Phase	171
Paradox of Sheltering	176
Bibliography	185
Conclusion: Creating an "Imagined Community" in Displacement	189
Reflections on and Beyond Community and Boundaries	190
Intertwining Place Attachment and Mobility	192
Interplay of Migrant Agency and Structure	194
Bibliography	195
Acknowledgements	197
Bibliography	199
Index	217

List of Maps, Figures, and Tables

Maps

Map 1.	Israel	10
Map 2.	Southern neighborhoods of Tel Aviv	11

Figures

Figure 1.	Recruitment process flow	55
Figure 2.	Permits issued according to employment sectors (1996–2012)	63
Figure 3.	An Israeli employer and his Filipino care worker	71
Figure 4.	A view of Tel Aviv City from an apartment rooftop in *Neve Sha'anan*	82
Figure 5.	Levinsky Park on a Saturday afternoon (2011)	84
Figure 6.	Beds in Jane's flat	112
Figure 7.	Carriers in the room of Grace's flat	112
Figure 8.	Payment in detail for June 2010 in Jane's flat	114
Figure 9.	Payment in detail for August 2010 in Liza's Flat	115

Tables

Table 1.	Profiles of the flats from fieldwork	30
Table 2.	Deployment of OFWs by place of work and sex, 2022	42
Table 3.	Salary and brokerage fee of migrant care workers in Israel (2007–2019)	52
Table 4.	Status of temporary migrant workers, 2011–2021	64

List of Abbreviations

CBD	Central Business District
CBS	Central Bus Station
NIS	New Israeli Shekel
OFW	Overseas Filipino Worker
OZ	Ovdim Zarim
POEA	Philippine Overseas Employment Administration
ROSCA	Rotating Saving and Credit Association

Map 1. Israel

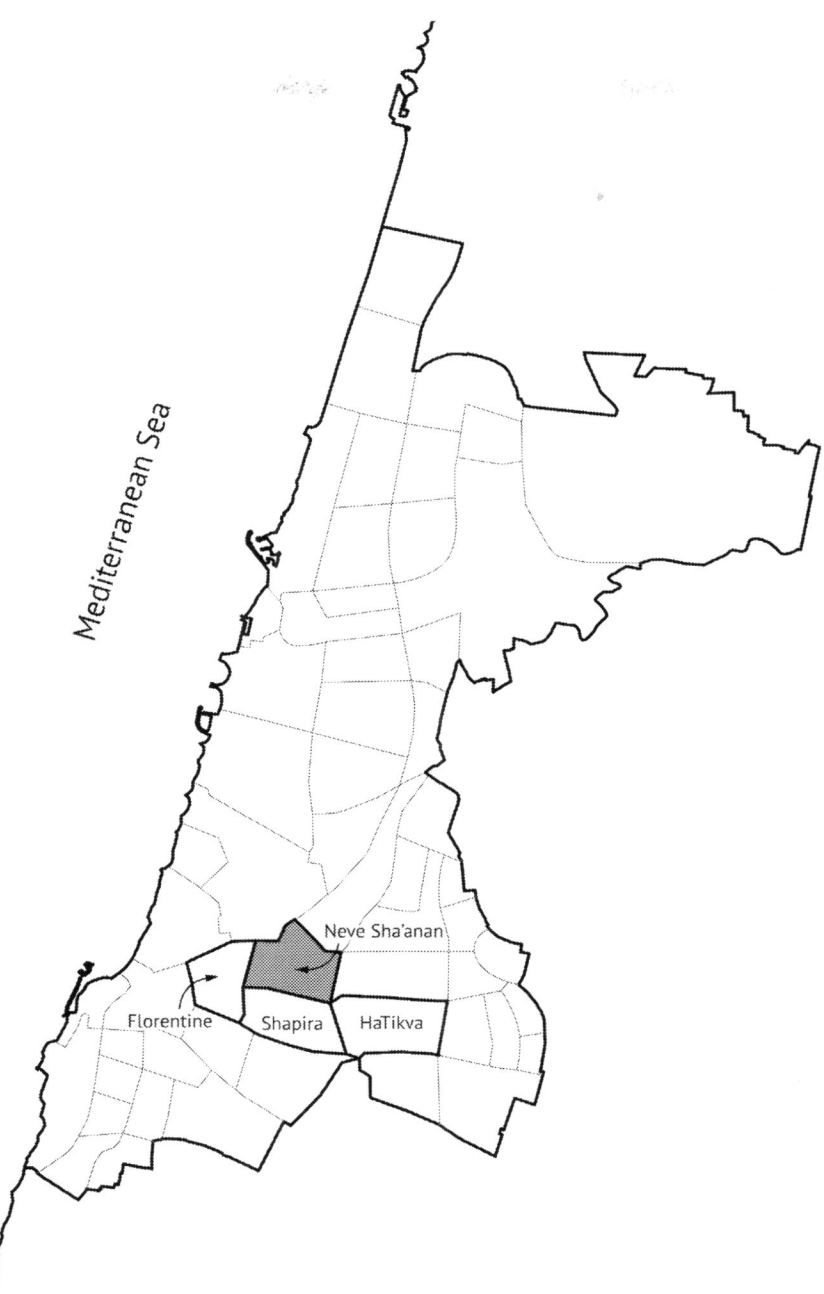

Map 2. Southern Neighborhoods of Tel Aviv

Introduction

Abstract: This introduction presents the aims and scope of the book by providing an overview of the theoretical frameworks and research methods. This book seeks to contribute to the growing body of literature on labor migration, space, community, and identities based on long-term ethnographic fieldwork. In line with recent studies, I explore "how Filipino migrant care workers build their own society in Israel," selecting a shared flat in the *Neve Sha'anan* neighborhood of Tel Aviv as the central conceptual space. Through the examination, I address how the flat is produced as a distinct migrant space through the place-making practices of the migrants, by which migrant lives and their needs in response to the wider society are constructed.

Keywords: Israel, Filipino care workers, feminization of labor migration, transnational migrant space, place-making, community

Upon moving as a graduate student to Tel Aviv in November 2008, one of the early scenes that drew my attention was that of elderly Israeli citizens walking arm-in-arm down the streets with their Filipino care workers. Pairs of elderly people and their shadow-like care workers, mostly women, could often be observed in public places such as small parks, streets, buses, and cafes in the daytime. It was striking for me to see migrant workers in the everyday sphere of life because South Korea, my country of origin, has not adopted a care-giving system employing migrant workers except Korean Chinese. Instead, overseas migrant workers in South Korea are mainly males employed most often as industrial factory workers who are rarely found in public places during the daytime hours of a typical weekday.

My initial curiosity expanded upon observing the Filipino migrants' regular movement to a particular area on weekends. Every weekend whenever I took a *sherut* (shared taxi) from the northern neighborhood of Ramat Aviv to the *Tachana Merkazit* (Central Bus Station) in the southern neighborhood of *Neve Sha'anan*, Tel Aviv, most of the other passengers were Filipinos carrying backpacks or other types of baggage.¹ During weekdays, however, I rarely witnessed this scene. At that time, I questioned why seemingly every weekend Filipinos gravitated toward the *Neve Sha'anan*, a place in which they were rarely seen during the week.

Shortly after noticing this pattern, I had the opportunity to befriend Angela, a Filipino woman in her early 30s, and to visit the flat that she co-rented with other Filipino care workers in the *Neve Sha'anan* neighborhood. It was a *Shabbat* (Jewish day of rest) evening in November 2008 that I met Angela for the first time.² We were waiting for the first bus at a bus stop near the Tel Aviv City Hall and exchanged email addresses after a short talk. She seemed interested that I had just arrived in Israel as a foreign student and Asian female of the similar age and that I had experiences as a Korean language teacher for Filipino women who married Korean men in South Korea. She had been interested in South Korea as a destination country for herself but so far had failed to find a job there.

Since that time, we had been in contact through SMS, and she invited me to her birthday party and on a Christmas trip. It was in preparing for that Christmas trip one night in December 2008, just one month after we had met, that I spent my first night in the Filipino apartment in the *Neve Sha'anan* neighborhood. When I arrived in the neighborhood, Angela asked me to help, and I moved her stuff with three of her friends to Jane's flat where she had just moved in. The Filipinos in the flat gave me a bunk on a two-story bed and cooked food for the trip while I was sleeping. The next morning at 4 a.m., most of the Filipinos in the flat and I went out to get on one of the seven buses parked near Levinsky Park, which brought us to the Holy places in Northern Israel. At that time, I didn't imagine that I would live in this apartment exactly one year later.

During my short Saturday night visit to her flat, which accommodated over 20 Filipinos, in the neighborhood of *Neve Sha'anan*, I encountered some interesting scenes that inspired this research. There were young Filipino men working as part-time couriers who picked up packages from other flats for shipment; Filipino women selling a variety of goods to other Filipinos;

---

1   The Hebrew phrase '*Tachana Merkazit*' refers to the Central Bus Station of Tel Aviv, which has functioned as transportation hub since 1993 when it replaced the Old Central Bus Station. Although the term 'Central Bus Station' is used throughout the book, I also employ the Hebrew term on occasion since the migrants use the Hebrew term rather than the English one.

2   *Shabbat* is the seventh day of the week, which starts at sundown on Friday and ends at sundown on Saturday evening. During this period, public transportation is limited due to a law that sharply curtails public transportation on *Shabbat*.

Filipinos eating Filipino food and chatting in *Tagalog* (the national language of the Philippines) or in their own dialects such as *Pangasinan* or *Ilocano*.[3] There were also grocery shops providing vegetables and products shipped from the Philippines, such as cosmetics, pills, clothing, and underwear.

These scenes on a Saturday night conjured up my own images of typical ethnic enclaves, such as Koreatown or Chinatown, in many American cities, which were differentiated from other parts of the cities. Although other ethnic groups including Chinese, Indians, and Africans were also widespread in the multi-ethnic region of *Neve Sha'anan*, the collective presence of Filipino women was distinctive, especially on weekends.

As a self-defined Jewish nation-state, Israel has actively encouraged the immigration of Jews from the Diaspora since its establishment in 1948. However, the recent wave of non-Jewish labor migrants into Israel has different characteristics and patterns from those of the preceding immigration waves that were based on ethnic absorption. Since the mid-1990s, Israel has become one of the world's major labor-importing countries. Non-Jewish temporary migrants from Asian and East European countries such as the Philippines, China, Thailand, Turkey, and Moldova have arrived in Israel to enter the low-wage job sector in the local labor market and have constituted a conspicuous minority of *Ovdim Zarim* (foreign workers) in the country.

The presence of labor migrants in Israel, as in many labor-importing countries, is legitimated solely by their laboring function as a temporary "workforce." For example, migrant workers in Israel are expected to work only in particular job sectors such as construction, agriculture, and elderly care, and return to their native country after a few years unless they choose to remain as undocumented workers or marry Israeli citizens to acquire permission for a permanent stay. It can be said that the stay of contract workers in Israel is short-term and precarious because their employment permits are issued and extended annually only under the agreement of their employers, which is called *Haseder hakvila*, a "binding arrangement."

Particularly, migrant care workers are employed only as live-in care workers and dispersed to local private households where they provide around-the-clock service for the elderly, while given a day-off on weekends. Considering their temporary status and live-in work conditions, it is not essential that the migrants rent a flat outside of their employers' homes.

---

3   The Philippines is a nation-state that is comprised of over a hundred different languages and thousands of islands. *Tagalog* is one of two official languages alongside English in the Philippines. Note, however, the dominant language spoken in a given region is the regional language such as Cebuano, Ilokano, Visayan, Pangasinan and others.

Moreover, the shared flat in *Neve Sha'anan*, locally known as a "dangerous urban slum," does not seem to provide a favorable living environment due to the high density and unsanitary conditions. Nevertheless, Filipinos co-rent flats with other Filipino migrants and spend their off-hours there, even though they come to their flats irregularly or just for a few hours on weekends.

Such attention to the particular life rhythms of Filipino care workers elicits questions such as: "What makes the migrants flock to their flats every weekend?" and "How do the migrants form their own society in a new environment and maintain it in spite of the constraints they face on a daily basis?" How do foreign workers create identities that support their lives in new locales? How is the uprooting effect of migration claimed in the lives of outsiders by finding a place and a common yet paradoxically distinct identity vis-à-vis other workers? These are questions addressed by my ethnography of Filipino care workers in Israel. They are also questions that build on and further develop the literature of space and place in identity formation. In what follows, I introduce my ethnographic research and position this work and its contributions in the literature on space and place in identity formation.

Women in Global Labor Market

One of the most prominent transformations during the 21st century is the increasing participation of women in the global labor market. During the 1970s, labor migration was largely dominated by male breadwinners, and women typically moved as part of a family linked with male migrants (Morokvasic, 1984). Since the early 1980s, however, women have entered the global labor market as paid laborers. Many of them have left their families behind in search of a better life abroad, rather than migrating as tied movers. Throughout the 1990s, for instance, approximately 60% of migrant workers from the Philippines were women (Martin, Abella, & Midgley, 2004). This trend has significant implications for both sending and receiving countries, as well as for the families and communities of migrant workers.

The notion of "feminization of migration," declared as a core dimension of the new age of migration and globalization, concerns gendered migration and the differences in male versus female migrant experiences (Castle & Miller, 2003). The term emphasizes not only the numerical dominance of female migrants but gender-differentiated labor, establishing gender as a crucial factor in understanding global labor migration. While male migrant workers are dominantly engaged in technical and production sectors, female migrant workers are employed most often as domestic helpers, nurses, care workers, or entertainers.

In line with this, research into labor migration has emphasized that women and men circulate differently in the global labor market, challenging a gender-blind perspective on migration and highlighting women as primary migrants (Kofman, 1999; Mahler & Pessar, 2006; Morokvasic, 1984). Domestic workers, especially female migrant workers, often face a range of challenges and vulnerabilities in their employment relationships, and their status as workers is often not fully recognized or protected by national legislation (Chammartin, 2005). This can leave them without legal recourse when their rights are violated or when they experience abuse or exploitation. Their gender and migration status can compound their vulnerability and marginalization, as they often face discrimination and additional barriers to accessing support and resources.

Given these circumstances, early studies of migrant domestic workers have highlighted these issues of vulnerability and marginalization in host societies (Longva, 1999). The underlying assumptions is that female domestic workers are doubly marginalized as a result of their dual position as women and as migrant workers (Piper, 2003, p. 22). More recently, scholars focus not only on domestic workers trapped in homes and their resultant isolation and vulnerability but also seek to highlight the agency of domestic workers within constrained employment contexts. By recognizing the ways in which domestic workers exercise their agency, researchers attempt to figure out the complex power dynamics at play in these employment relationships.

For instance, Constable (1997) draws on the experiences of Filipina domestic workers in Hong Kong and demonstrates how those migrants exercise their agency through everyday resistance, avoiding the pitfalls of overly binary notions of victim and agent. Similarly, Moukarbel (2009), in a study of Sri Lankan domestic workers in Lebanon, argues that workers resist the power and control exercised by their employers through behaviors such as lying, stealing, evasion, and foot dragging, rather than through confrontational actions.

Over the decades, sociological and anthropological studies of migrant work have associated the feminization of labor migration with the expansion of the "global care chain" (Ehrenreich & Hochschild, eds., 2003; Hochschild, 2000) and the increased capacity and expectations for women to act as primary breadwinners for their families (Sassen, 2000). The term "global care chain" refers to a series of personal links between people across the globe based on the paid or unpaid work of caring (Hochschild, 2000, p. 131).

By connecting the phenomenon to broader social, economic, and political processes, these scholars attempt to gain a more nuanced understanding of the experiences of female migrant workers.

Although transnational labor can bring economic benefits to migrants' families and the home country, their migration often means that families are separated. In the Philippines where women comprise almost two-thirds of the migrant labor force and most of them go abroad alone, mothering happens from a distance and women as wives live apart from their husbands (Parreñas, 2001, 2003). Studies have shown how this migration arrangement is particularly fraught for women who engage in "transnational motherhood" (Hondagneu-Sotelo & Avila, 1997; Parreñas, 2001; Piper & Roches, 2003).[4]

The gender balance of global migration flows triggers the so-called "international division of reproductive labor" (Parreñas, 2001), highlighting the issue of gender inequality in the global economy. The international division of reproductive labor draws attention to the gendered and globalized distribution of labor related to care work, including domestic work, caregiving, and sex work and to the inequalities and biases faced by women in these roles. These challenges to women's identities and self-preservation highlight the need for greater attention to gender and labor rights in the global economy and for policies that address the unique challenges faced by women in migration.

Nakano Glenn (1992) has further highlighted the "racialized division of reproductive labor" internationally, pointing to a racial hierarchy in the global labor market as well as a gender division. Gender relations are always mediated by other socially constructed categories such as class, age, race and ethnicity (Piper, 2003, p. 26–27). This creates a global labor market that is stratified along both gender and racial lines, with women of color and migrant women occupying the lowest rungs of this ladder. This means that the experiences of women in migration have been shaped not only by their gender but also by their other social identities and positionalities.

In a similar vein, several studies report a racial hierarchy of domestic workers in host countries (Hosoda, 2013; Moors et al., 2009; Sabban, 2004). Recent literature explores how domestic jobs can be seen as means through which asymmetrical, intersecting relations pertaining to gender, race, culture, class, and citizenship status are structured and negotiated (Pratt,

---

4   Parreñas (2001) describes that in the Philippines, transnational households are considered 'abnormal,' called 'broken homes,' and therefore viewed as a social and cultural tragedy. Transnational households are considered 'broken' because the maintenance of this household diverges from traditional expectations of cohabitation in the family.

1999). For example, Nagy (1998) emphasizes that nationality and gender are important axes of social and spatial differentiation in Qatar and that ethnicity and language occasionally are considered in recruitment decisions, becoming markers of stratification among migrant domestic workers. The existence of gender-specific job opportunities for migrant workers and the tendency of migration to sustain itself have produced male-dominated and female-dominated migratory linkages between certain countries.

The feminization of labor migration is particularly pronounced in the Philippines, Indonesia and Sri Lanka, where women have greater mobility than their counterparts in other Asian countries such as Pakistan and Bangladesh (Varia, 2011, p. 269). For instance, the 2021 Survey on Overseas Filipinos reports that 60.2% of Overseas Filipino Workers were women. In Israel, the majority of migrant care workers are Filipino women who have left their families behind in the Philippines to become breadwinners. In the larger Israeli society, Filipino women are a racial and ethnic minority. With rapid increase of female migration in domestic care work, the case of Israel contributes to ongoing debates on migration and gender, and the intersection of class, race and nationality in migrant laborer experiences.

In the ethnography to follow I build on these studies to demonstrate the agency, especially of female migrant workers, in creating community, mutual support, and identity through shared residence and weekend encounters with one another. In this case I pursue micro-resistance strategies replaced by the positive step of creating homes away from work sites through place-making practices. These new homes are communal flats, in which migrant workers emphasize safety and mutual belonging. Drawing on the place-making practices among the Filipino care workers in Israel, this study shows not only the ways in which migrants organize their lives but also conceptualizes the flat as constructed and experienced with the recognition of an increasingly interconnected transnational world, thereby underscoring the particular subjectivities of migrant workers.

Place-Making in Transnational Migration

Since the 1990s, there has been renewed interest in the issues of space and place in the social sciences, triggered to some extent by the spatial implications of globalization (Appadurai, 1995, 1996; Cresswell, 2004; Gupta and Ferguson, 1997; Harvey, 1990; Kearney, 1995; Lefebvre, 1991; Low & Lawrence-Zúñiga, 2003; Massey, 1994; McKay, 2006; Rodman, 1992). The "spatial turn" in the social sciences came with recognition of "the complex reality of places that are not simply settings for social action" (Rodman, 1992, p. 652). Overall, the spatial turn in the social sciences has led to a greater recognition of the importance of space and place in shaping social relations and identities and has challenged the assumption that social identities are rooted in fixed and bounded territories.

For example, Massey (1994) emphasizes the notion of "a global sense of place" and argues that globalization and time-space compression have compelled human geographers to rethink their definitions of place, arguing that "we can no longer regard places as separate and bounded entities; rather we must think of them as interlinked and open" (p. 156). As Lee and Li Puma (2002) also point out, places are being produced by "cultures of circulation," practices of evaluation, constraint, con-sociality and re-subjectivation that emerge with movements of people and exchanges of value. Places are neither static nor fixed but are subject to a social process (Friedmann, 2007).

To address my research questions focusing on how migrant Filipino women care takers create a sense of self and safety in Israel, it is necessary to review relevant studies of place and mobility in the perspective of transnationalism. Migration scholars have contemplated the dynamics of transnational ties and places, reconsidering the boundaries of nation-state in transnational movements of people (Levitt, 2001). The concept of transnationalism highlights the ways in which people and ideas move across national borders and create new forms of social and cultural identities, challenging the assumption that social identities are rooted in fixed, bounded territories.

Scholars of place and space highlight "the articulation of global/local dynamics in specific localities, challenging the binary dichotomy of local and global." Appadurai (1995), who developed "trans-locality" as a concept, critically points out that researchers must see locality "as primarily relational and contextual rather than as scalar" (p. 204). The conceptualization of "transnational social spaces" focuses on wider sociopolitical contexts and their interaction with concrete changes in peoples' everyday lives and places, incorporating transnational small groups, transnational circuits, and transnational communities (Faist, 2000).

This paradigm shift has been reflected in growing concerns over "transnational urbanism" (Smith, 2005), "cultural sites" (Olwig, 2009), "extended case methods" (Burawoy, 1998), "single-site ethnography" (Gielis, 2011), and "multi-sited ethnography" (Marcus, 1995). These scholars argue that spaces and places need to be examined both through their situated*ness* and their connected*ness* to a variety of other locales. For example, Smith argues that "transnational social relations are localized in single places, but at the same time are articulated with other places in trans-local communication circuits" (Smith, 2005). Following this concept, he suggests that we need to look at migrants' translocal place-making practices. The concept of "place-making" emphasizes the ways in which social actors actively shape and create places through their social practices and interactions.

Similarly, Gielis (2009) emphasizes the importance of place as an analytic lens for grasping migrant networks. In his research on home feelings of Dutch migrants living across the border in Germany, Gielis focuses on one particular house and addresses the simultaneous presence of various social networks in the single house and the migrants' feelings about home and belonging. According to Gielis (2009), "Although not all social networks are embedded in a single place, social networks are at least ascribed to and associated with certain places" (p. 275). In this way, places are filled with social meanings and inform identities for those in the ascribed or associated networks as in the Israeli case I develop.

It is noteworthy that there has been a growing body of literature that sheds light on the place-making practices of migrant domestic workers and highlights their agency in shaping the social and cultural meanings of particular places (Hondagneu-Sotelo, 2001; Lan, 2003; Mahler & Pessar, 2006; Oishi, 2005; Parreñas, 2000). While earlier scholarship focused on the nature of domestic work and unequal employment relations within the private realm (Arat-Koc, 1989; Bakan & Stasiulis, 1997; Cohen, 1991; Romero, 1992), more recent research has taken a step further to question community formation in diaspora and explore the construction of social spaces, taking into consideration migrants' own narratives and forms of subjectivity (Armenta, 2009; Law, 2001, 2002; McKay, 2006; Pande, 2012; Parreñas, 2000; Peralta, 2004; Wu, 2010; Yeoh & Huang, 1998).

Much of the scholarly discussion has focused on "public open places" in various host cities, such as Hong Kong (Law, 2001, 2002; Peralta, 2004), Singapore (Yeoh & Huang, 1998), and Taipei (Huang & Douglass, 2008; Lan, 2003), which are known as popular destinations for domestic workers in Asia. In the research with Filipino domestic workers in Singapore, Yeoh and Huang (1998) coined the term "weekend enclave," public spaces transformed by workers into community spaces that exist only on Sunday. The research of Filipino domestic workers by Peralta (2004), for instance, focuses on the public square in Hong Kong where domestic workers gather every Sunday. Peralta (2004) addresses the form, functions, and meanings of the weekly gathering at Statue Square to Filipino domestic workers and demonstrates how the Statue Square disrupts normative understanding of public space.

In a similar vein, some researchers pay attention to "closed private space" and describe how this private space serves as an escape route for freedom and autonomy in an oppressive environment (Bakan & Stasiulis, 1997; Cohen, 1991; Lan, 2003; Parreñas, 2001; Stasiulis & Bakan, 2005). In her research of Filipina domestic workers in Taiwan, for example, Lan explores how employers and workers negotiate social boundaries in the employer's house, shedding light on identity politics in the context of global migration. Other studies describe how the apartment workers co-rent in a host country provides them with "an intimate environment," where they can obtain privacy and time away from what are often 24 hour on-call obligations (Parreñas, 2001; Stasiulis & Bakan, 2005).

Scholars exploring these sites investigated how live-in domestic workers use public places or private homes to resist and negotiate their employment, transforming the urban landscapes of host countries. My book also addresses the ways in which migrant care workers negotiate their position in this case through the shared flat by practicing adaptive strategies for coping with restrictive work conditions. However, this ethnographic study selects the flat not only as an analytical lens for grasping various social networks that the migrants reestablish but also the formation of new value and meanings in the new environment.

Given the many regulations and circumscriptions placed on migrant life, it is important to address migrants' experiences, mobility, and complex social lives as productive in generating the flat and also as produced by the flat. By investigating how migrants create a distinctive and social space through the flat and its interconnections with wider social fields, this book redefines agency as the capacity of the marginalized and powerless to act in such a way as to cause or direct the course of events in a social milieu. Therefore, this study illuminates how the flat is constructed as a new key point of departure and arrival, in which the residents' attachment to the flat is transitional and impermanent (Isin & Rygiel, 2007).

This book further examines the flat in terms of both place attachment and mobility, through which migrants come to experience the flat. Clifford's account of the inter-wining concepts of roots and routes gives insight into understanding of the tension between the flat as a space of belonging and one of mobility or transformation as the flat develops into a meaningful social space: "'Roots' and 'routes' are not mutually exclusive. Rather, they are inter-wined, representing two different ways of regarding the relationship between people, culture, and place" (Clifford, 1997, p. 4). Both concepts are integrated in the migrants' ordinary experiences and in the making of the flat as a distinct social space, creating the role of the flat in imagining community.

Existing Studies in the Israeli Context

According to Kalir (2013), "Israel is an exemplary case of a state that, while extremely preoccupied with protecting its territorial borders and maintaining the ethno-national composition of its population, is nevertheless pushed by the forces of a global economy to open its labor market to migrant workers" (p. 312). In the mid-1990s the government recruited overseas workers, making the influx of "non-Jewish" migrants a significant feature of Israel society. Since 2005, asylum seekers and refugees from African countries have entered Israel in significant numbers, thus leading to research on those migrants (Paz, 2011; Sabar, 2010; Sabar & Kanari, 2006; Sabar & Posner, 2013; Yacobi, 2008, 2010).

The cases of Latino and African migrant women in domestic and service sectors who have entered the country unofficially are notable in research studies. For instance, Kemp et al. (2000) show how Latino and African migrant workers develop strategies of social and political participation in order to protect their interests despite their lack of political rights and resources, redrawing the limits of their membership in Israeli society. By doing this, the researchers highlight those migrants as political actors capable of individual and collective empowerment. They claim that migrant women come to have a sense of belonging by participating in religious activities based on churches. They further show that the migrant women subvert traditional conceptions of mothering through transnational mothering rhetoric.

Much literature focuses also on religious practices and a sense of belonging among migrant workers (Jackson, 2011; Kalir, 2009; Kemp & Raijman, 2003; Liebelt, 2011; Sabar, 2010). This research links religious faith and practices among domestic workers to the desire for a community with affective ties, one which enables the migrants to alleviate the effects of various forms of oppression or to reinvent personhood.

Kemp and Raijman (2003) explore how evangelical churches are established as alternative spaces for a new community of belonging among Latin American undocumented migrants. They argue that religion becomes a way of legitimizing the migrants' presence in a Jewish state, channeling their claims for inclusion in the host country. Kalir (2009) explores the phenomenon of the conversion to Christianity among Chinese migrant workers in Tel Aviv. He reveals how migrants' religious conversion to Christianity enables temporary migrant workers not only to have a space of belonging in Israeli society, but to accumulate cultural, symbolic, and social capital, impacting their lives upon their return to China.

The study of Filipino migrant care workers by Liebelt is also noteworthy for my study. Liebelt (2011) explores how Filipino care workers create social networks and construct their own identities, negotiating their marginal status and dealing often collectively with suffering and trauma. According to Liebelt, the migrants believe themselves as the servants of the "people of God" who care for the "Holy Land" and their narration proves their understanding of and belonging to Israel as a "new home." In another study (2012), she shows how Filipino migrant care workers create a communal life by parading icons of the Virgin Mary, crafting paper swans and consuming pork, and argues that care workers establish new subjectivities beyond ethnic or cultural identities, drawing on the concept of "aesthetic formation."

There is also a growing body of research that deals with digital behaviors for social networking and expressing identities among migrant workers (Babis, 2021; Brown, 2016; Golan & Babis, 2019). For instance, Brown (2016) demonstrates how migrant care workers negotiate and resist the gendered and racialized naturalization of their work by using the internet. She interprets the strategies migrants employ as a "diagnostic of power" that reveals the multiple tactics that migrants can take against structural violence. In her digital ethnography of Filipino care workers, Babis (2021) investigates how the migrant care workers construct their mourning practices on digital networks in different ways upon the death of their elderly employers and of a fellow Filipino migrant worker.

More recently, researchers have drawn attention to the rapid increase in the number of the children of migrant workers who were born in Israel and remain undocumented. Given that the existence of migrant workers' children challenges the Jewish character of the state, migration and citizenship debates have arisen. Research has developed concerning the ways in which the Israeli government and local society cope with the new minority of non-Jewish groups (Kemp, 2007; Kemp & Kfır, 2016; Shapiro, 2013). Based on her ethnographic research of the issue in Tel Aviv, Shapiro (2013) conceives those undocumented migrant workers and their children a "privileged underclass" in the local society to emphasize the paradoxes in migrant women's subjectivities and experiences.

As the presence of migrant workers became recognizable and the number of undocumented migrants dramatically increased in Israel, researchers dealt with the issue of the policies and the response of the local society (Batram, 1998; Kemp, 2007, 2010). Kemp and Raijman (2004) discuss the socioeconomic restructuring of Tel Aviv and incorporation strategies developed by the municipality with the influx of non-Jewish migrants. Illuminating the disjuncture between urban and national policies, they argue that the city of Tel Aviv is playing a central role in transforming migrants into "urban citizens" within the local society, interpreting their urban membership as the empowerment of migrant communities.

Bringing in the notion of ethical politics of care, Kemp and Kfir (2016) explore the bio-political contradictions within care migration policies and social mobilization, both of which raise public awareness of the situation of undocumented migrants, broadening the range of actors shaping the globalization of care. Willen (2007) delves into migrant "illegality," focusing on the undocumented migrants from West Africa and the Philippines in Tel Aviv. Based on her ethnographic fieldwork in the *Neve Sha'anan* neighborhood of Tel Aviv, Willen explores how "being illegal" shapes migrants' everyday experiences of being-in-the-world and sheds light on the subjective dimensions of a form of politically and socially abject status.

Broadening these studies, this book contributes to a detailed understanding of labor migration in Israel, drawing on the case of Filipino migrant care workers. I had chosen the shared flat as a field site to zoom in on everyday practices and boundary-making in the context of mobility. I aim to reveal the creative emergence of migrant space beyond resistance which shapes the migrants' lived experiences and mobile realities in the trans-local context of the weekend flat that Filipino migrant care workers co-rent. In this book I illuminate the flat located in *Neve Sha'anan* of Tel Aviv as the key site for the Filipino migrant lives and social networking and explore the ways in which the migrants conduct boundary-making practices and create a sense of place and identity for themselves, producing new forms of sociality through their dynamic interactions with the wider dimensions of society.

My study addresses the two major themes of space and community with reference to Filipino care workers in Israel and provides comprehensive insight into the dynamics of labor migration. Firstly, this study aligns with the growing body of research on transnational migrant space, underscoring the relevance of the migration research to broader discussions of space. Drawing on the place-making practices among the migrant care workers, this study shows not only the ways in which migrants organize their lives but conceptualizes the flat as constructed and experienced with the recognition of an increasingly interconnected transnational world, thereby underscoring the particular subjectivities of migrant workers. Furthermore, this study, taking up mobility and attachment as a lens of analysis, opens interesting avenues for understanding transnational migrant space, challenging the once sedentary paradigm of place.

Secondly, this study provides an account of boundary work, which is associated with research on community, network, and identity. While the Filipino migrants share national identity and status as working-class foreigners in Israel, their caretaking and migratory experiences are not usually shared. This study illuminates the flat both as a key source of community and support for the migrants offering self-defined boundaries in the new environment and as a locus for differences, in which the migrants negotiate degrees of difference and multiple social identities. This analysis disrupts traditional notions of place and community and provides useful insight into the complex construction and reconstruction of community and self through boundary-making practices among the migrants in the context of trans-locality.

Based on ethnographic research that is carried out in natural setting, this study attempts to trace the formation of flat-based community among Filipino migrant workers who have responsively interacted with the wider society. The evolving situation of the Filipino community in Tel Aviv provides a useful case study that demonstrates how temporary migrant workers occupy and produce urban spaces, experiencing place in different ways, and how different scales of belonging and boundary-making practices take place among the mobile subjects. This study deals also with the formation of Filipino society under the recruitment system called "binding arrangement" which had been in effect until 2021. As new hiring systems forbid the mediation of private agencies and brokers in the recruitment process, it is expected that the construction of flats may witness changes, since brokers previously had a decisive role for operating the shared flat.

Locating My Research in Israel

This book is an ethnographic account of migrant space and the interwoven experiences and social lives of Filipino migrant care workers in Israel. The study is based on 26 months of consecutive fieldwork from January 2010 to February 2012 and one month of follow-up field research during July 2015, as well as two months of research in January and February in 2018, mainly in the *Neve Sha'anan* neighborhood of Tel Aviv. During the fieldwork, I stayed in the flats that Filipino migrants co-rented to conduct participant observations and open-ended interviews.

Since 2014, I have also conducted online interviews with some informants who returned to the Philippines or moved to other countries for work, as well as with those staying in Israel. During this follow-up research, I conducted interviews with existing informants with the intent to trace changes in their legal and social conditions and the impacts of their migration and employment on their everyday lives. Furthermore, I met new informants who had recently arrived in Israel as care workers or who overstayed after giving birth to a baby. However, the main source for this book still comes from the consecutive fieldwork conducted between 2010 and 2012.

I selected the flats located in *Neve Sha'anan* of Tel Aviv as the central field site because the neighborhood is a hub in the migrants' route, both as an entry point and a stopover. Based on data gathered during this long-term fieldwork, I attempted to figure out how migrants produce distinct social spaces, patterned uniquely in space and time, through their dynamic interactions with surrounding spaces. In the initial stage of my fieldwork, I became a flatmate renting with the idea that I would be able to establish relationships with Filipino migrants and have access to them conveniently due to proximity. The six-month stay as a flatmate in Jane's flat, the first flat where I conducted preliminary research, helped me select "the flat" as the central conceptual space for my study, not only as a physical research site.

Firstly, the flat provides an entry point to Filipino migrant society, through which I was able to approach a considerable number of migrants who came to trust me and share information. My continuing involvement as a flatmate in various flats enabled completion of interviews and intense dialogues with Filipino migrant care workers, allowing me to observe their weekend lives in the privacy of their residential places. Secondly, the flat is the meeting place for the Filipino migrants who are dispersed during weekdays. It is the place where they gather and perform a variety of activities on a regular basis. Although there are several sites for social gathering such as Catholic or evangelical Christian churches and public parks, the flat is seen as the focal site and the basic social unit where the majority of migrants belong and form communities.

My research was conducted intensively during weekends when the migrants congregate in the flat. During weekdays, conversely, I had few opportunities to conduct research because the majority of my informants were live-in care workers.[5] Even though each flat where I stayed for my research had a few live-out care workers, my interviews with them were limited: many of them undertook part-time work after their legal work and went to bed fatigued. Nevertheless, my daily contact with them provided me with some opportunities to conduct one-on-one in-depth interviews, through which I gathered information that was harder to obtain from group interviews on weekends.

---

5 In the care sector, live-in care workers refer to those workers who live in their employers' houses and provide around-the-clock care service, while live-out care workers refer to those who live out of their employers' houses and daily commute.

My ethnographic approach builds upon the notion of multi-sited ethnography (Marcus, 1995). The major research site for this study is the flat, but the scope of the research expands to surrounding spaces. After developing more intimate relationships with my informants, I conducted interviews also in their employers' houses on normal weekdays. By following the places where my informants spent time, I was able to identify several sites in which their various social networks and activities were constructed, namely employers' houses, small parks close to the employers' houses, flats, churches, and public spaces in *Neve Sha'anan*. I regularly attended birthday parties and other social gatherings in various flats, churches, and public parks. I also traced the flats as my informants moved, since many of them constantly changed their places of residence within *Neve Sha'anan*.

Throughout my 26 months in the field, I stayed in four different flats. My movement from flat to flat took place in highly unpredictable and irregular circumstances. Over the course of fieldwork, however, I recognized that my movement from flat to flat was not unusual because many of the Filipino migrants were mobile during their stay in Israel. My own mobile practices in the field revealed the extent to which the migrants' movement was constitutive of their daily lives in the host society. Throughout the book and for the sake of convenience I call each flat according to the names of those Filipino migrants who formally established a contract with the landlord (see Table 1).

Initially, I spent six months from January to June 2010 in Jane's flat where Angela lived. Angela helped me move into the flat and initiate my research. During this phase, I became familiar with the particular conditions and structure of the flat as well as the general circumstances related to the *Neve Sha'anan* neighborhood. I recognized the significance of the flat in migrant life during this first six months, leading me to decide to pursue my fieldwork in flats. During the period of my stay in Jane's flat, there were 25 flatmates, most of whom were married women in their 40s and 50s, predominantly from *Pangasinan* province. Three of them were undocumented migrants.

Then I moved into Banessa's flat in July 2010, where I stayed for eight months. Angela moved into this flat and then she helped me move into the flat. During this time, there were 10 flatmates, most of whom were from the *Bisayas* province except three from *Pangasinan*. All of the flatmates were single women in their 40s or 50s, and all were documented workers. Next, I stayed in Liza's flat from March 2011 to December 2011 for 10 months. Among the twelve flatmates, eight were from *Ilocos* and four from *Baguio*. The majority of the flatmates were in their late 30s and 40s and married. I encountered two undocumented migrants during the period of my fieldwork here.

Finally, I stayed in Grace's flat from January to February 2012 for two months and again in July in 2015. This flat had 10 flatmates, and the majority of them were married women in their 40s and 50s. There were three undocumented migrants. During my most recent research in 2018, I stayed in May's flat for two months through the help of the existing informants. This flat was occupied by a couple, May and Albert, in one room and five Filipino women in their 30s in another room.

My informants arrived in Israel between 1995 and 2012. In terms of the gender ratio, most of the migrants I encountered during my fieldwork were women between 30 and 50 years old, which reflects the female-dominant proportion in the care sector. Women who married Israeli men were included in this research. In addition, Filipino neighbors, the friends of my informants, Israeli residents in *Neve Sha'anan*, Israeli employers, staff from job agencies, and real estate brokers who were engaged in the life of Filipino migrants were also included. The interviews were conducted in English, with the exception of some portions of the interviews in Hebrew. All of the names used in this book are pseudonyms to ensure the anonymity of the informants.

My personal experiences of being identified and set apart by informants during my fieldwork surely played an inevitable role in this study. As a Korean outsider and student I experienced marginality among the migrants. In the initial stage of my fieldwork, I had difficulty moving into a flat due to my different status despite the help of Angela as a "guarantor." My "outsider" status was further underscored by being a Protestant among the Filipinos, most of whom were Catholics. However, my gender status as female and similar age with them helped me to develop intimate relationships with the informants in the flat, which was a remarkably female-centered place. Besides, I was fortunate to be an Asian with migrant status like them, which clearly helped in this research by creating mutual perceptions of homogeneity.

Initially, I entered the first flat with the intent of developing relationships with Filipino migrants for the purpose of my research. However, they became more than research subjects because my status as a temporary migrant in Israel like them got entangled with theirs in some ways. Although I was not regarded as a full member of the flat community due to my different ethnic and social backgrounds, I was afforded an insider status by sharing the various flats and participating in communal activities. In these Filipino communities one becomes an outsider unless one lives in the flat and is embedded in the same complicated webs of obligation, engagement, and reciprocity for sustaining the flat through co-participation.

I explore herein the formation of a distinct migrant space using three inter-related themes that offer new perspective on migrant experiences.

Firstly, I challenge the view of an ethnic group as a social unit for research and draw more attention to the dynamic processes of community building among the Filipino migrants with different social and ethnic backgrounds. Secondly, I take mobility and attachment as foci of analysis and open up interesting perspective on the transnational migrant space, challenging a sedentary paradigm of palace. Finally, I draw on dialogic interactions between agents and the wider social structures in which they are embedded to address how small subsets of migrants construct temporary "imagined communities."

	Jane's Flat	Banessa's Flat	Liza's Flat	Grace's Flat	May's Flat
Period of My Stay	JAN 2010 – JUNE 2010 (6 months)	JUL 2010- MAR 2011 (9 months)	APRIL 2011- JAN 2012 (10 months)	FEB -MAR 2012 JUL 2015 (3 months)	JAN-FEB 2018 (2 months)
No. of Residents On Average	25	10	12	10	7
No. of Male Residents	3	1 (Palestinian Egyptian)	4	0	1
No. of Undocumented	2	0	4	2	(1)
Major Place of Origin	Pangasinan	Bisayas	Illocos	Batangas	Batangas Manila
Age of Residents	late 30s, 40s	40s	late 30s, 40s	40s, 50s	30s, 40s
Religion	Half of the flatmates are church-goers (Catholic)	Generally Secular Catholic	Generally Secular Catholic	Generally Secular Catholic: 2 Catholic church-goers / 1 Protestant church-goer	Secular Catholic
Main informants	Angela, Judy, Tom, Sarah	Banessa,Nerlose, Jasmine, Mary, Analyn, Peggy	Joy, Liza, John, Ella, Jennifer, Gary, Maya	Grace, Sally, Lisa, Ana, Sani, Jenny	May, Albert
Notes			More than half of the flatmates are couples		

Table 1. Profiles of the Flats from Fieldwork

Progressing Through the Chapters to Come

Chapter 1 looks at the process and structural mechanisms that facilitate the flow of people between Israel and the Philippines at both macro and micro levels. I first characterize the emigration flow from the Philippines, within the state-led labor export system which manufactures Filipino workers as "national heroes" in global demand. Secondly, I provide empirical descriptions of the ways in which Filipino migrants decide to migrate to Israel and explore how the migrants are channeled into the Israeli labor market, drawing attention to the informal operations of intermediary networks in initiating and sustaining the Filipino migrant flow to Israel. Finally, I overview the Israel migration regime and labor policies, within which Filipino migrants are employed as contract care workers and their legal/social statuses are shaped.

Chapter 2 investigates how Filipino migrant workers are socially and spatially segregated in Israel, transforming the marginalized and stigmatized urban periphery into the dynamic center of a migrant economy and network formation. I first provide the urban setting and landscape of the *Neve Sha'anan* neighborhood of South Tel Aviv where shared flats have sprouted up and discuss how the concentration of foreign populations in the neighborhood produces a stigmatized space of Otherness. Secondly, I provide a broad picture of the formation of Filipino society in the ethnically diverse neighborhood. I first describe the ways in which Filipino migrants are transplanted into the neighborhood upon arrival by emphasizing the role of migrant networks and explore how the stigmatized urban periphery is transformed into the "capital of the foreign workers."

Chapter 3 elucidates the construction of the flat that involves seemingly contradictory spatial processes of fixity and fluidity. I investigate how the flat is organized and managed as a shared accommodation and elucidate the formation of new social forms, further investigating the inter-relations between different social forms and hierarchical order within the flat. Then I illuminate how the coexistence of incompatible differences becomes the key driving force in migrants' mobility. I trace the trajectory of the flat-based networks through migrants' mobility, examining the ways in which the migrants realize their movement and transform "flat" spaces into places of identity. Through this, I demonstrate how the flat remains an eternal space of settlement, serving as a nodal site in the migrants' mobile circuit, drawing on the notions of place attachment and mobility, through which migrants come to experience the flat.

Chapter 4 delineates the formation of a spatial-temporal community among Filipino migrants. The flat becomes a key source of community with self-defined boundaries and support for the migrants. The shared flat provides the migrants with a holiday place away from their workplace, enabling them to enjoy freedom and autonomy, where they feel at home. In the absence of their existing network of support and their welfare system in their country of origin, the migrants develop support networks based on place attachment. In this chapter I discuss how weekly events—the communal dinners, birthday parties, and *paluwagan* ("rotate saving association")—function as a mechanism to unite heterogeneous migrants with different backgrounds and identities into a coherent community with a distinctive social order.

Chapter 5 further delineates the boundaries between the flat and its outside surroundings, drawing special attention to the lived experiences of illegality and extramarital relationships. It explores how the migrants transform the flat into a shelter, collectively responding to the precarious and often hostile environments surrounding them. I illustrate how the flat becomes a fortified space through two major exclusionary practices among flatmates: the access regulation and the mutual enforcement of anonymity. Through the investigation, I demonstrate that the process of making shelter entails physical and social segregation between social groups, reinforcing boundaries between inside and outside of the flat and creating a paradoxical situation inside the flat, in which one's privacy and security are likely to be threatened by insiders even while internal solidarity is promoted.

Bibliography

Appadurai, A. (1995). The production of locality. In R. Fardon (Ed.), *Counterworks: Managing the diversity of knowledge* (pp. 204–225). New York. https://doi.org/10.4324/9780203450994

Appadurai, A. (1996). *Modernity at large: Cultural dimensions of globalization*. University of Minnesota Press.

Arat-Koc, S. (1989). In the privacy of our own home: Foreign domestic workers as solution to the crisis in the domestic sphere in Canada. *Studies in Political Economy, 28*(1), 33–58. https://doi.org/10.1080/19187033.1989.11675524

Armenta, A. (2009). Creating community: Latina nannies in a West Los Angeles park. *Qualitative Sociology, 32*, 279–292. https://doi.org/10.1007/s11133-009-9129-1

Babis, D. (2021). Digital mourning on Facebook: The case of Filipino migrant worker live-in caregivers in Israel. *Media, Culture & Society, 43*(3), 397–410. https://doi.org/10.1177/0163443720957550

Babis, D. (2022). Inclusion and beauty pageants? The Filipino migrant worker community in Israel. *Gender, Place & Culture, 29*(5), 625–648. https://doi.org/10.1080/0966369X.2021.1887090

Bakan, A. B., & Stasiulis, D. (1997). Foreign domestic worker policy in Canada and the social boundaries of modern citizenship. In A. B. Bakan & D. Stasiulis

(Eds.), *Not one of the family: Foreign domestic workers in Canada* (pp. 29–52). University of Toronto Press.

Batram, D. V. (1998). Foreign workers in Israel: History and theory. *International Migration Review, 32*(2), 303–325. https://doi.org/10.1177/019791839803200201

Brown, R. H. (2016). Multiple modes of care: Internet and migrant caregiver networks in Israel. *Global Networks, 16*(2), 237–256. https://doi.org/10.1111/glob.12112

Burawoy, M. (1998). The extended case method. *Sociological Theory, 16*(1), 4–33. https://doi.org/10.1111/0735-2751.00040

Castles, S., & Miller, M. J. (2003). *The age of migration*. Guilford Press.

Chammartin, G. M. (2005). Domestic workers: Little protection for the underpaid. *Migration Information Source*, Migration Policy Institute.

Clifford, J. (1997). *Routes: Travel and translation in the late twentieth century*. Havard University Press.

Cohen, R. (1991). Women of color in white households: Coping strategies of live-in domestic workers. *Qualitative Sociology, 14*(2), 197–215. https://doi.org/10.1007/BF00992194

Constable, N. (1997). *Maid to order in Hong Kong: Stories of Filipina workers*. Cornell University Press.

Cresswell, T. (2004). *Place: A short introduction*. Blackwell Publishing Ltd.

Faist, T. (2000). *The volume and dynamics of international migration and transnational social spaces*. Oxford University Press.

Friedmann, J. (2007). Reflections on place and place-making in the cities of China. *International Journal of Urban and Regional Research, 31*(2), 257–279. https://doi.org/10.1111/j.1468-2427.2007.00726.x

Gielis, R. (2009). A global sense of migrant places: Towards a place perspective in the study of migrant transnationalism. *Global Networks, 9*(2), 271–287. https://doi.org/10.1111/j.1471-0374.2009.00254.x

Gielis, R. (2011). The value of single-site ethnography in the global era: Studying transnational experiences in the migrant house. *Royal Geographical Society, 43*(3), 257–263. https://doi.org/10.1111/j.1475-4762.2011.01020.x

Glenn, E. N. (1992). From servitude to service work: Historical continuities in the racial division of paid reproductive labor. *Journal of Women in Culture and Society, 18*(1), 1–43.

Golan, O., & Babis, D. (2019). Digital host national identification among Filipino temporary migrant workers. *Asian Journal of Communication, 29*(2), 164–180. https://doi.org/10.1080/01292986.2018.1541097

Harvey, D. (1990). Between space and time: Reflections on the geographical imagination. *Annals of the Association of American Geographers, 80*(3), 418–434. https://doi.org/10.1111/j.1467-8306.1990.tb00305.x

Hochschild, A. R. (2000). Global care chains and emotional surplus value. In W. Hutton & A. Giddens (Eds.), *On the edge: Living with global capitalism* (pp. 130–146). Jonathan Cape.

Hondagneu-Sotelo, P. (2001). *Domestica: Immigrant workers cleaning and caring in the shadows of affluence*. University of California Press.

Hondagneu-Sotelo, P., & Avila, E. (1997). "I am here but I'm there": The meanings of Latina transnational motherhood. *Gender and Society, 11*(5), 548–71. https://doi.org/10.1177/089124397011005003

Hosoda, N. (2013). Kababayan solidarity? Filipino communities and class relations in United Arab Emirates cities. *Journal of Arabian Studies, 3*(1), 18–35. https://doi.org/10.1080/21534764.2013.802945

Huang, L., & Douglass, M. (2008). Foreign workers and spaces for community life: Taipei's little Philippines. In A. Daniere & M. Douglass (Eds.), *The politics of civic space in Asia* (pp. 67–87). Routledge.

Isin, E. F., & Rygiel, K. (2007). Of other global cities: Frontiers, zones, camps. In H. Wimmen (Ed.), *Cities and globalization: Challenges for citizenship*. Saqi Books.

Jackson, V. (2011). Belonging against the national odds: Globalisation, political security and Philippine migrant workers in Israel. *Global Society, 25*(1), 49–71. https://doi.org/10.1080/13600826.2010.522982

Kalir, B. (2009). Finding Jesus in the Holy Land and taking him to China: Chinese temporary migrant workers in Israel converting to evangelical Christianity. *Sociology of Religion, 70*(2), 130–156. https://doi.org/10.1093/socrel/srp027

Kalir, B. (2013). Moving subjects, stagnant paradigms: Can the "mobilities paradigm" transcend methodological nationalism?. *Journal of Ethnic and Migration Studies, 39*(2), 311–327. https://doi.org/10.1080/1369183X.2013.723260

Lan, P. (2003). Negotiating social boundaries and private zones: The micropolitics of employing migrant domestic workers. *Social Problems, 50*(4), 525–549. https://doi.org/10.1525/sp.2003.50.4.525

Law, L. (2001). Home cooking: Filipina migrant workers and geographies of the senses in Hong Kong. *Ecumene, 8*(3), 264–283. https://doi.org/10.1177/096746080100800302

Law, L. (2002). Defying disappearance: Cosmopolitan public spaces in Hong Kong. *Urban Studies, 39*(9), 1625–1645. https://doi.org/10.1080/00420980220151691

Lee, B., & LiPuma, E. (2002). Cultures of circulation: The imaginations of modernity. *Public Culture, 14*(1), 191–213. https://doi.org/10.1215/08992363-14-1-191

Lefebvre, H. (1991). *The production of space*. Wiley-Blackwell.

Levitt, P. (2001). *The transnational villagers*. University of California Press.

Liebelt, C. (2011). *Caring the "Holy Land": Filipina domestic workers in Israel*. Berghahn Books.

Liebelt, C. (2012). Consuming pork, parading the virgin and crafting origami in Tel Aviv: Filipina care workers' aesthetic formations in Israel. *Ethnos, 78*(2), 255–279. https://doi.org/10.1080/00141844.2012.655302

Longva, A. N. (1999). Keeping migrant workers in check: The kafala system in the Gulf. *Middle East Report*, (211), 20–22. Middle East Research and Information Project, Inc. www.jstor.org/stable/3013330.

Low, S., & Lawrence-Zuniga, D. (Eds.). (2003). *The anthropology of space and place*. Blackwell Publishers Ltd.

Mahler, S. J., & Pessar, P. R. (2006). Gender matters: Ethnographers bring gender from the periphery toward the core of migration studies. *Center for Migration Studies of New York, 40*(1), 28–63. https://doi.org/10.1111/j.1747-7379.2006.00002.x

Marcus, G. E. (1995). Ethnography in/of the world system: The emergence of multi-site ethnography. *Annual Review of Anthropology, 24*, 95–117. https://doi.org/10.1146/annurev.an.24.100195.000523

Martin, P., Abella, M., & Midgley, E. (2004). *Best practices to manage migration: The Philippines*. https://doi.org/10.1111/j.1747-7379.2004.tb00247.x

Massey, D. S., Goldring, L., & Durand, J. (1994). Continuities in transnational migration: An analysis of nineteen Mexican communities. *American Journal of Sociology, 99*(6), 1492–1533.

McKay, D. (2006). Translocal circulation: Place and subjectivity in an extended Filipino community. *The Asia Pacific Journal of Anthropology, 7*(3), 265–278. https://doi.org/10.1080/14442210600979357

Moors, A., Jureidini, R., Ozbay, F. & Sabban, R. (2009). Migrant domestic workers: A new public presence in the Middle East?. In S. Shami (Ed.), *Publics, politics and participation: Locating the public sphere in the Middle East and North Africa*, 177–202. SSRC Books.

Morokvasic, M. (1984). Birds of passage are also women. *International Migration Review, 18*(4), 886–907. https://doi.org/10.1177/019791838401800401

Moukarbel, N. (2009). Not allowed to love?: Sri Lankan maids in Lebanon. *Mobilities, 4*(3), 329–347. https://doi.org/10.1080/17450100903195409

Nagy, S. (1998). "This time I think I'll try a Filipina": Global and local influences on relations between foreign household workers and their employers in Doha, Qatar. *City & Society, 10*(1), 83–103. https://doi.org/10.1525/city.1998.10.1.83

Oishi, N. (2005). *Women in motion: Globalization, state policies, and labor migration in Asia*. Stanford University Press.

Olwig, K. F. (2009). A proper funeral: Contextualizing community among Caribbean migrants. *Journal of the Royal Anthropological Institute, 15*(3), 520–537. https://doi.org/10.1111/j.1467-9655.2009.01571.x

Pande, A. (2012). From "balcony talk" and "practical prayers" to illegal collectives: Migrant domestic workers and meso-level resistances in Lebanon. *Gender & Society, 26*(3), 382–405. https://doi.org/10.1177/0891243212439247

Parreñas, R. S. (2000). Migrant Filipina domestic workers and the international division of reproductive labor. *Gender & Society, 14*(4), 560–580. https://doi.org/10.1177/089124300014004005

Parreñas, R. S. (2001). *Servants of globalization: Women, migration and domestic work*. Stanford University Press.

Parreñas, R. S. (2003). The care crisis in the Philippines: Children and transnational families in the new global economy. In B. Ehrenreich & A. R. Hochschild (Eds.), *Global woman: Nannies, maids and sex workers in the new economy* (pp. 39–54). Metropolitan Books, Henry Holt and Company.

Peralta, M. T. S. (2004). *From where are you back home?: Ethnography of Filipino domestic workers spending Sundays at Satatue Square*. Ph.D. Thesis. The University of Southern California.

Philippine Statistics Authority. (2021). *Survey on overseas Filipinos*. https://psa.gov.ph/content/2021-overseas-filipino-workers-final-results

Piper, N. (2003). Bridging gender, migration and governance: Theoretical possibilities in the Asian context. *Asian and Pacific Migration Journal, 12*(1–2), 21–48.

Piper, N., & Roces, M. (2003). Introduction: Marriage and migration in an age of globalization. In N. Piper & M. Roces (Eds.), *Wife or worker? Asian women and migration* (pp. 1–22), Rowman & Littlefield Publishers Inc.

Population and Immigration Authority. (2019). *Data on foreigners in Israel: Report*. https://www.gov.il/BlobFolder/reports/foreign_workers_status_2019/he/sum_2019.pdf

Pratt, G. (1999). From registered nurse to registered nanny: Discursive geographies of Filipina domestic workers in Vancouver, BC. *Economic Geography, 75*(3), 215–236.

Rodman, M. C. (1992). Empowering place: Multilocality and multivocality. *American Anthropologist, 94*(3), 640–656. https://doi.org/10.1525/aa.1992.94.3.02a00060

Romero, M. (1992). *Maid in the U.S.A*. Routledge.

Sabar, G. (2010). Israel and the "Holy Land": The religio-political discourse of rights among African migrant labourers and African asylum seekers, 1990–2008. *African Diaspora, 3*(1), 43–76.

Sabar, G., & Kanari, S. (2006). "I'm singing my way up": The significance of Music amongst African Christian migrants in Israel. *Studies in World Christianity, 12*(2), 101–125. https://doi.org/10.3366/swc.2006.0017

Sabar, G., & Posner, R. (2013). Remembering the past and constructing the future over a communal plate: Restaurants established by African asylum seekers in Tel Aviv. *Food, Culture & Society, 16*(2), 197–222. https://doi.org/10.2752/175174413X13589681351692

Sabban, R. (2004). Women migrant domestic workers in the United Arab Emirates. In S. Esim & M. Smith (Eds.), *Gender and migration in Arab States: The case of domestic workers* (pp. 86–107). International Labour Organization.

Sassen, S. (2000). Women's burden: Counter-geographies of globalization and the feminization of survival. *Journal of International Affairs*, 503–524. https://doi.org/10.1163/157181002761931378

Shapiro, M. (2013). *The politics of intimacy: An ethnography of illegalized migrant women and their undocumented children in Tel Aviv, Israel*. Ph.D. Thesis. York University.

Smith, M. P. (1992). (2005). Transnational urbanism revisited. *Journal of Ethnic and Migration Studies, 31*(2), 235–244. https://doi.org/10.1080/1369183042000339909

Stasiulis, D., & Bakan, A. (2005). *Negotiating citizenship: Migrant women in Canada and the global system*. University of Toronto Press.

Wu, P. (2010). How outsiders find home in the city: ChungShan in Taipei. In H. Jeffrey (Ed.), *Insurgent public space: Guerrilla urbanism and the remaking of contemporary cities* (pp. 134–146). Routledge.

Yacobi, H. (2008). *Irregular migration to Israel: The sociopolitical perspective*. Cooperation project on the social integration of immigrants, migration, and the movement of persons (CARIM).

Yacobi, H. (2010). "Let me go to the city": African asylum seekers, racialization and the politics of space in Israel. *Journal of Refugee Studies, 24*(1), 47–68. https://doi.org/10.1093/jrs/feq051

Yeoh, B., & Huang, S. (1998). Negotiating public space: Strategies and styles of migrant female domestic workers in Singapore. *Urban Studies, 35*(3), 583–602. https://doi.org/10.1080/0042098984925

1. Between a "National Hero" and a "Global Servant"

Abstract: This chapter looks at the process and structural mechanisms that facilitate the flow of people between Israel and the Philippines at both macro and micro levels. Filipino migrants decide their destination based on various push-pull factors along the lines of individual migrants' life course, gender, and the economic/social capitals in a trajectory of the changing global market. I provided empirical data on the migration process from the Philippines to Israel under the institutionalized network of recruitment system that involves the intervention of an intricate web of licensed agencies, informal agents or sub-agents and personal networks, requiring the applicants to pay a much higher brokerage fee. Such a complex migration pattern of Filipino migrants to Israel has developed within legal regulatory frameworks, while creating a black market.

Keywords: Philippines, OFWs, recruitment system, migrant process, migrant networks

In this chapter, I draw a detailed picture of the migration process of Filipino migrant workers to Israel and investigate how the Filipino migrants are placed in Israeli households as paid care workers under the Israeli regime. I first describe the emigration flow from the Philippines within the state-led labor export system and illuminate what motivates the migrants to head for Israel. Then I specify how Filipino migrants are channeled into the Israeli households as care workers within the institutionalized networks of the migration industry, drawing attention to a wide range of formal and informal intermediaries in initiating and sustaining Filipino migrants' flow into Israel. Finally, I describe the work conditions and status of migrant care workers in the Israeli migration regime based on my fieldwork data.

In 2018, the Israeli government signed the first of its Bilateral Labor Agreements with Philippine government in the care-giving sector. In 2021,

---

Lim, Anna. *Filipino Care Workers in Israel: Migration, Trans-local Livelihoods and Space.* Amsterdam: Amsterdam University Press, 2025.
DOI: 10.5117/9789463720403_CH01

the Population Immigration and Border Authority, a government agency which operates under the Israeli Ministry of the Interior, implemented agreements by hiring Filipino care workers without the involvement of private recruitment agencies. However, this chapter focuses on the process before the new arrangement.

Migrating from the Philippines to Work

The Philippines is currently the world's largest exporter of labor next to Mexico and is the highest per capita exporter of labor in Southeast Asia. The Philippines has had a long history of both temporary and permanent international migration. During the American colonial period, Filipinos moved to the United States to work in agriculture, food processing, and service sectors (Sri Tharan, 2009). After independence in 1946, most out-migration from the Philippines was directed to the United States, Canada, and other European countries for permanent migration. In the 1960s, Filipino migrants heading to these countries were largely composed of professional workers such as nurses, doctors, and technicians.

Since the 1970s, however, "temporary" labor migrants based on contracted positions have dominated the flow of emigrants from the Philippines (Smart et al., 1985, p. 29–30). The oil boom in the 1970s demanded a huge increase of laborers in the Gulf States, especially in the construction sector spurred by increasing wealth. Thus, the Gulf States began recruiting contract workers from outside the region and Filipino males were sent to the region as temporary construction workers on a large scale (De Haas, 2010). Twelve percent of the Filipino migrant workers who left the Philippines in 1975 were deployed to the Gulf States and 87% in 1987, coinciding with the construction boom. In addition, the closure of labor markets in Western Europe caused by the oil price shock led migrant workers to search for job opportunities in the Gulf States (see Kapiszewski, 2006).

Despite the decrease in oil prices and the Gulf Wars through the 1990s, however, the number of Filipino workers in the Gulf States did not decline. Rather, the Gulf States still remain their top destination. In 2022, a total of 1.96 million Filipino workers were deployed as land-based or sea-based workers. Saudi Arabia (23%), the UAE (13.7%), Kuwait (7.7%), Hong Kong (6.1%), and Qatar (5.8%) were the top five destination countries for Overseas Filipino Workers (OFWs hereafter) in 2021 (Philippines Statistics Authority, 2021). An increasing demand for domestic labor in Gulf States has become one of the major reasons that the area has remained top destinations for OFWs.

In the 1970s, Filipino women also started migrating for overseas labor as domestic workers, particularly to Hong Kong, but on a smaller scale (Gibson, Law & McKay, 2001, p. 368). Since the 1990s, however, the labor export from the Philippines has been dominated by women responding to the increasing demand for domestic workers, nurses and entertainers (Ball, 2004). Women have come to comprise the majority of the annual deployment of new hires from the Philippines, accounting for as much as 60% (Guerrero, 2012, p. 275). In 2022, 57.8% (1.13 million) of the total OFWs deployed were females, most of whom were engaged in domestic work, and the largest number of OFWs was in the age group of 30 to 34 years old, which accounted for 23.4% of the total OFWs (Philippine Statistics Authority).

Notably, the distribution of OFWs reveals highly gendered patterns, with female workers deployed primarily as service and domestic sector occupations, being categorized as unskilled work, and male workers engaged in construction and production sectors considered skilled (Tyner, 2000). Among the total female OFWs, who deployed in 2022, 69.8% were engaged in elementary occupations, which include the performance of simple and routine tasks such as cleaning and cooking, while 28% of male workers worked as machine operators and assemblers (Philippine Statistics Authority).

The destinations of Overseas Filipino Workers have diversified over the decades. However, the occupation of OFWs was linked to specific destinations. For instance, female workers migrate mainly to the Gulf States, Hong Kong, Singapore, and Italy as domestic workers, while men migrate mainly to the Gulf States as construction workers and to South Korea, Japan, and Taiwan as factory workers. South Korea and Japan are also destination countries for entertainers. Care workers or health care assistants have gone overwhelmingly to Israel, Saudi Arabia, Taiwan, and Singapore, with the top destination being Israel. Of the total OFW deployed as care workers in Israel 85.3% were recently females (Philippine Statistics Authority).

Place of Work	Both Sexes	Male	Female
Number (in thousands)	1,963	828	1,135
Total	100	100	100
Africa	1.0	2.1	0.2
Asia	80.8	64.9	92.4
East Asia	17.8	18.3	17.4
Hong Kong	6.1	0.5	10.2
Japan	2.9	4.7	1.6
Taiwan	4.5	5.1	4.0
Other Countries in East Asia (including China and South Korea)	4.3	7.9	1.7

Place of Work	Both Sexes	Male	Female
Southeast and South Central Asia	8.2	7.8	8.6
Malaysia	1.4	1.1	1.7
Singapore	5.0	4.5	5.3
Other Countries (including Brunei, Cambodia, and Indonesia)	1.2	2.2	1.6
Western Asia	54.8	38.9	66.4
Kuwait	7.7	1.9	11.9
Qatar	5.8	4.2	7.0
Saudi Arabia	23.0	19.8	25.4
UAE	13.7	10.0	16.3
Other Countries (Bahrain, Israel, Lebanon and Jordan)	4.6	3.1	5.8
Australia	2.9	5.4	1.0
Europe	9.0	16.3	3.7
North and South America	6.3	11.3	2.7

Table 2. Deployment of OFWs by Place of Work and Sex, 2022
Source: Philippine Statistics Authority

The current flow of labor emigration started with the formulation of the 1974 Philippine Labor Code under the dictatorial Marcos regime in a trajectory of economic crisis. By the early 1970s, the accumulation of debts and the high rate of unemployment in the Philippines had been aggravated by worldwide recession (De Guzman, 2003). The Marcos regime instituted the 1974 Labor Code for promoting overseas employment and systematically sent Filipinos for overseas work. Unlike the earlier group of migrants who sought an opportunity for permanent residency in the host country, this later group, originally bound by temporary contracts abroad, became known as Overseas Filipino Workers (OFWs), becoming the preferred version of migration with the insertion of "Filipino," adding a national projection as befits "new heroes" (De Guzman, 2003).

The Labor Code regarded overseas employment as "an important strategy to absorb excess domestic labor" and "the institutionalization of government participation in overseas employment" (Asis, 1992, p. 71). Under these circumstances, OFWs became key to the Philippines' economic strategy and were regarded as active development agents, making up a significant portion of the country's GDP (Tyner, 2000, p. 64). The inflows of remittances to the Philippines amounted to USD 6 billion in 2000 but rose to USD 30.1 billion in 2019 at an average growth rate of about 10% per year, being ranked third in the total remittances after India and China (*Bangko Sentral ng Pilipinas*, 2020).

Over the years, the Philippine economy increasingly depended on overseas labor markets not only to relieve the unemployment problem and financial crisis but also as a staple of the national income through remittances (Solomon, 2009). Many families rely on the overseas remittances for basic necessities such as food, housing, and education. The remittances have become a dependable and necessary income source both for the country's survival and for the households (Cruz, 2008, p. 361), even though there is a pessimistic view that perceives migration and its accompanying remittances as an "illness" that weakens the economy, increasing the dependency on remittances (Asian Development Bank, 2009).[1]

The most significant turning point in Philippine emigration history is the establishment of the Philippines Overseas Employment Administration (POEA) in 1982. POEA dispatches delegations to several labor importing countries to secure job opportunities for OFWs. In 1989, for example, POEA organized marketing missions to Hong Kong for job opportunities on news of that territory's national labor shortage (Tyner, 2000). A growing number of female workers was deployed also to Taiwan during the 1990s, following its liberalization of migrant worker policies, as well as an overall commodification of domestic economies and the increased demand for domestic workers (Tyner, 1999, p. 683). In 2004, when information technologies and electronic sectors reopened in Taiwan, POEA ventured again to Taiwan to export labor force to the manufacturing industry.

POEA is generally responsible for the supervision of the deployment of OFWs under the best possible terms by dealing with licensing and regulation of private recruitment and placement agencies, and marketing for OFWs and the placement of workers in government-to-government hiring in cooperation with those private agencies. The mission of POEA extends also to the educating, training, recruiting and deploying OFWs (Carlos, 2010). POEA seeks to enhance the quality and effectiveness of its pre-departure orientation seminar for household workers and care workers by partnering with leading non-government organizations (NGOs) (Sri Tharan, 2009, p. 189). A notable example is a care worker course, created to cater to the requirements of the overseas labor markets. The Philippine Training, Education and Skills Training Agency (TESDA) offers the course through accredited schools and grants a "certificate" to its graduates (Carlos, 2010, p. 8).

---

1   Many scholars argue that structural problems such as unemployment, inflation, an expanding foreign debt, and sharpened social inequality in the Philippines are symptoms of the dependency relation with United State economic imperialism, in which a "growth-through-borrowing" philosophy was actively promoted, and the Philippines constantly used loans to address economic crises (Guevarra, 2009; San Juan Jr., 2010).

In recognition of their contribution to the national economy, OFWs have often been celebrated as "heroes of the nation," by which the state promotes the process of emigration and attempts to incorporate OFWs as part of the nation (Rodriguez, 2002). In a 1988 speech given to a group of Filipino domestic workers in Hong Kong, the former president Cory Aquino used the term *mga bagong bayai* (modern-day heroes) and in the following year, declared December as the "Month for Overseas Filipinos."[2] Although the idea of "a national hero" has long been associated with hegemonic masculinity of Filipino sea fares, the government, needing to address both male and female migrants, has used the term to be less gender-specific, honoring the economic contributions of both men and women to their families and the country.

Within this context, the labor migration apparatus and structures in the Philippines have been developed into a highly institutionalized and complex agglomeration of government, private, and non-government organizations (Ball, 1997; Tyner, 2000). The involvement of the private recruitment sector has clearly enabled the sending country to develop new markets and greatly expand labor exports (Lim & Oishi, 1996, p. 39). With the government setting and implementing the recruitment and deployment rules, the private sector facilitating the training and recruitment, and the society motivating and inspiring the labor force to target overseas work, the Philippines has been relatively successful in mobilizing its resources to capture a considerable part of the overseas labor market (Carlos, 2010, p. 8).

The Philippine Government capitalized on newly emerging employment opportunities and has strongly responded to the changing global labor market through marketing. In the process of labor brokering or labor diplomacy, gendered representations of occupations and workers has taken place by its aggressive marketing strategy of female workers as a cheap and docile but skilled labor force and of male workers as professional construction workers and sea farers (Ball, 1997; Choy, 2003; McKay, 2007). Ezquerra (2009) points out that the Philippine government portrays Filipino domestic workers as elite servants, reinforcing the marketing and commodification of Filipino women, and this strategy falls into an essentialization of Filipino women through their racialization and feminization (p. 68).

Using the notion of "feminization of survival," Sassen (2000) notes that "households and whole communities are increasingly dependent on women for their survival" (p. 506). It is within this context that Filipino migrants,

---

2   In 1988, Proclamation NO. 276 declared December of every year as "Month of Overseas Filipinos."

who are presented as a marketable commodity with special value by the Philippine government, have been channeled into the Israeli labor market as contract care workers and provide around-the-clock services in local private households.

Migration Journey to Israel[3]

The Israeli government has so far refused to sign bilateral agreements with the Philippine government to regulate recruitment and employment conditions, thereby enabling profit-seeking private agents to dominate this field (Kemp & Raijman, 2014, p. 615). This was the case in the Philippines-Israel migration system until 2021. Within the privatized recruitment system, actual recruitment procedures were complex, taking on a variety of configurations including formal, informal, or hybrid arrangements for profit (Hernández-León, 2005). In 2018, the Israeli government finally signed a bilateral agreement with the Philippines with respect to the care sector after a series of negotiations, and in 2021, the hiring of Filipino care workers in Israel became governed by the new arrangement. In this chapter, however, I deal with the recruitment process of Filipino care workers who entered Israel before the current agreement.

Migration Decision-Making
When I first met Angela at a bus stop in 2008, her age was 31. Angela turned 30 years old in 2007 when she decided to move to Israel as a care worker. Before coming to Israel in 2008, Angela had worked in Taiwan as a factory worker for five years during her 20s. Although she was permitted to work two more years, she returned to the Philippines because the salary of factory workers in Taiwan decreased at that time.[4] She returned to Manila and opened a small restaurant with the money she earned in Taiwan, but soon closed the restaurant when she found it was not profitable. Then she applied for work in South Korea as a factory worker. After applying, she spent a year waiting for a reply but failed to obtain work there because, in her belief, the factory owners preferred men and younger applicants, and she was already over 30 years old.

---

3   This section is adapted from my article, Lim (2015). Networked mobility in the migration industry: Transnational migration of Filipino care workers to Israel. *Asian Women*, 31(2), 85–118.
4   According to Angela, many manufacturing factories in Taiwan began relocating to China in the mid-2000s, seeking cheaper labor.

Then Angela wanted to join her aunts in Canada and work as a care worker, but when she discovered that the entry conditions were strict, requiring job experience as a care worker and a financial guarantee, she gave up the plan. At that time, one of her relatives returned from Israel and informed Angela about the job opportunities in that country. Angela did not hesitate to make up her mind when she heard from one of her hometown friends that she had a cousin who worked in Israel as a care worker and agent, a mediator between job applicants and agencies. Finally, Angela came to Israel as a care worker through Mark, the cousin of her hometown friend. Although she had never considered working as a care worker abroad, she believed that a caregiving was a different job from any domestic work that requires cleaning and cooking for a family.

In 2012, when Angela had accumulated four years of experience as a care worker in Israel, she initiated her migration to Canada by contacting an agency and preparing the necessary documents. During the course of my fieldwork, I witnessed Angela visiting the Canada Embassy in Tel Aviv several times for job interviews. In spite of all her efforts, however, she failed to obtain a work permit. When I visited *Neve Sha'anan* in 2015, she had just come back from a one month-vacation, during which she married and then returned to Israel alone. In 2017, she went to the Philippines again, to give birth to a baby. After her "vacation" finished, she came back to Israel alone again, leaving her baby to her husband and mother-in-law.

Although Angela married a Filipino man from a middle-class family and has her child, she is still working in Israel as a care worker, struggling to migrate to Canada as a care worker. According to Angela, her husband, who has a stable job, asked her to return home. But she told me that "I cannot imagine what my life would be like if I go back to the Philippines." As she originally planned to move to Canada and finally get permanent residency there, Angela did not stop applying for jobs to Canada and continued to build her career as a care worker. Meanwhile, she helped her two sisters move to Israel as care workers. She said, "I don't expect they will pay back to me as I sent them a big money for their tuition fee, allowances, and brokerage fee. Instead, I hope they would support our parents, sharing the burden with me."

Like Angela, the majority of my informants had worked in different labor-importing countries and planned to migrate to another country in the future, searching for a better life for their family and certainly for themselves. As elaborated in the story of Angela, the lives of individual migrants and their families are not evolving in a vacuum. The changes in a migrant's life course may result in significant changes also to the family in the Philippines, while the migrant experiences transformations in their roles and relationships along with a sequence of live events and transitions.

In a study of domestic workers in Hong Kong, Constable (1997) explained that many of the domestic workers exhibited a great degree of ambivalence about returning home not only because of the disappearance of an income source but also due to their insecurities about fitting back into a society that would not be able to provide them with the wages and lifestyle to which they had grown accustomed. This is also evident in my fieldwork data. Like Angela, Mary, a Filipino woman in her early 30s, plans to migrate to Canada. She came to Israel in 2009 shortly after her marriage in the Philippines. Now that she has already been in Israel for almost four years, the maximum period of her visa, she has begun to consider her next destination, hopefully Canada. Mary confesses, "I love my husband but I will not go back to the Philippines. We [Filipinas] already tasted here a better quality of life. I don't want to live in the Philippines."

Gradually increasing numbers of Filipino women go abroad, seeking employment particularly in domestic work, and Filipino migrant women were often represented either as "heroines of national development" or as "new slaves of a globalized capitalist system." When I asked Filipino informants what made them decide to leave their own family and country behind, many of them simply answered "I had no choice." At the same time, they continued to say proudly that they contributed to improving their family members' quality of life, and their family members relied totally on the remittances they sent. Over the course of my fieldwork, however, it became clear to me that this ambiguous answer underlined migrants' agency in deciding upon and continuing their mobility.

While some liberal democratic states, such as Canada and Australia, facilitate the transition of temporary labor migrants to permanent settlement, the majority of receiving countries accept temporary migrants only within strict functional limits, enforcing exclusionary policies on them, namely restricted durations of migration and ineligibility of family reunification. Under these circumstances, the migration of OFWs tends to fall under the rubric of "circular migration" (Oishi, 2005: Parreñas, 2010), although some of them attempt to settle permanently or semi-permanently by overstaying their visa or marrying a local citizen. In this perspective, Barber (2000) describes Filipino domestic workers in particular as a "provisional diaspora," noting that many of these migrant workers take on sequential overseas contracts, often with a vision of returning to their "homeland" or finding some final home away from home (Yeoh & Huang, 2000).

As illustrated in Angela's experiences, factors such as age, gender, and industry preferences can limit job opportunities. The informants who had worked in Asian and Gulf countries as domestic workers during the 1980s and 1990s explain that they went to those countries because it was easy for them to go there as a "nanny." Jenny, who was born in 1967, married at the age of 18 and gave birth to two sons. Leaving her sons to one of her sisters who runs a grocery store in Manila, Jenny went to Singapore as a nanny in 1997 and came back home after four years. But after a year she left her family again, moving to Hong Kong as a domestic worker. Jenny, who had worked also in Kuwait and Dubai as a housemaid for four years, stated, "The salary is very low there, but I had no money for brokerage fees, and I just wanted to go abroad. My monthly wage was less than USD 200 at that time. The agency paid the brokerage fee for me and deducted it from my salary."

It was her elder sister, Jane, who helped her move to Israel as a care worker. While her elder brother worked as an engineer in Saudi Arabia during the 1990s, Jane also went to Saudi Arabia in her 20s and worked as a domestic worker for 11 years. She moved to Israel as a care worker after the termination of her contract in Saudi Arabia and helped Jenny to find job in Israel. According to Jenny, "Salary in Dubai and Hong Kong was very low (approximately USD 250) and everything was not good there. But here [in Israel] I am satisfied with my salary and work conditions." Jenny said she would go back to Manila after her working visa in Israel expires because she is "now too old to work as a domestic worker." At that time, she was 42 years old.

In practice, Hong Kong and several Gulf countries have been the primary destination countries for Filipino women despite low wages. This is not only because those countries employ migrant domestic workers on a large scale but because the entry conditions for domestic workers are loose and the migration cost is cheap, enabling cross-border movement of unskilled female labor. Those cases illustrate the economic circumstances that often set the stage for the decision to migrate. However, the migrants' decisions to migrate to Israel is often a combination of individual choice based on a various push-pull factors.

According to a survey from the Philippines Statistics Authority (2018), an overwhelming majority of OFWs were between 20 and 39 when they first migrated. Forty-five percent of them are married, while 39% of them are single (Tabuga et al., 2021, p. 7). The migration profiles of the informants who have overseas labor experience can be summed up as follows: Females who are currently in their 40s and 50s and have worked as housemaids in Hong Kong, Singapore, and Gulf countries such as Kuwait, Dubai and

Saudi Arabia during the 1980s and 1990s; males who are in their 40s and were factory workers in South Korea or construction workers in the Gulf during the late 1990s and early 2000s; and males and females in their 30s who worked for local companies in the Philippines or as factory workers in Taiwan during the 2000s. Because many of them plan to eventually migrate to Canada where migrant care workers are accepted under relatively liberal labor policies and permanent residency, they tend to see their career as a care worker in Israel as a steppingstone toward Canada.[5]

In her research on Filipino care workers in Israel, Liebelt (2012) points out that migrant workers decide and move on within a global hierarchy of desirable destination countries, according to the great differences between nation states with regard to the salaries and the legal entitlements migrants can claim, the costs and risks migrants are faced with in order to enter, and their overall subjective and imaginative attractiveness. My research provides detailed empirical data based on in-depth interviews with Filipino care workers and shows how the destination is selected by the migrants based on various push-pull factors along the lines of individual migrants' life course, gender, and the economic/social capitals in a trajectory of the changing global market.

The migrants decide upon their destination countries within their capability regarding the capitals they have, responding to the conditions demanded by the host countries such as job experience, age, gender, English proficiency level, level of education, and brokerage fee. Grace's expression sums up this reality: "If I have a college degree, of course I will not go there (Typically those countries that employ domestic workers such as Hong Kong, Singapore and Gulf countries). I am going to look for another opportunity. Most of them said it's like a stepping stone, just as a stepping stone" (Lim, 2015).

As indicated in the case of Grace and Angela, unskilled workers attempt to climb a hierarchy of potential destinations, engaging in "a stepwise migration, which involves individual migration journeys based on short-term, multi-year overseas contracts in a series of countries organized according to a socially- and personally-constructed destination hierarchy" (Paul, 2011). While the host countries regulate and restrict the entrance of migrant workers, requiring stringent migration requirements, "migrant workers

---

5 After a period of 3,900 hours of employment, which must be completed between a minimum of 22 months and a maximum of four years, foreign live-in care workers can apply for permanent residency in Canada (Hawthorne, 2010). Pratt (1999) documented the plight of live-in care workers, some of whom were nurses, in their struggle to become permanent residents in Canada, while losing their self-esteem and confidence as a professional nurse.

accumulate migration-related capital, increase their savings and gain the necessary work experiences to qualify for jobs in more preferred countries during their stay abroad and attempt to expand their destination options" (Paul, 2011, p. 1843).

According to my informants, Israel is regarded as one of the more desirable destination countries for unskilled female labor due to the higher wages, relatively favorable work conditions, and the positive job image of care workers as semi-professionals. The majority of my informants differentiated a care worker job from other types of domestic work jobs, stigmatizing the job category of domestic workers as the labor of inferiors (Boyle, 2002, p. 536–537). The regulations for employment specify that anyone at least 24 years of age can apply for the job, but most of the informants argue that those who are less than 30 are not employed because they believe that such a job as a care provider is unsuitable for those in their 20s who lack birth and rearing experiences. More strikingly, the age restriction for migrant care workers in Israel is looser than in other destination countries hiring domestic workers, so that even women in their 40s who lack job experiences are able to apply for jobs.

Conversely, the opportunity to work in Israel is relatively scarce for the migrants due to quota controls and entry conditions that require applicants to have a college degree and be fluent English speakers. Particularly, the exorbitant brokerage fee turns out to be a major obstacle for Filipino workers desiring to enter Israel (see Table 3). In the Israeli context, which requires applicants to pay an exorbitant brokerage fee as a condition for entry, the access to financial resources serves as a crucial factor in their decision-making process to work in Israel. Sally represents one example of how Filipino migrants decide to migrate to Israel under shifting conditions.

The Case of Sally
Sally is a 43-year-old single mother who has a 24-year-old son. Before coming to Israel, she worked for a small company in Manila until 2000 when the company closed due to the financial crisis. As a woman of age 32 at that time, she had difficulty in finding a new job in the Philippines. According to Sally, many companies in the Philippines tend to push female employees to leave their jobs when they reach the age of 30. Like many other Filipinos do, Sally decided to seek a job opportunity abroad and attempted to apply for a factory job in Taiwan, together with her ex-coworker in her mid-20s. According to my informants, regardless of age and gender, obtaining work overseas as a factory worker is very desirable to OFWs since they can earn a relatively high salary and make extra money doing overtime work as well during their restricted stay.

However, Sally was not even allowed to submit an application due to age limit restrictions for such workers, whereas her ex-coworker successfully migrated to Taiwan as a factory worker. Shortly after, she was approached by a broker on the street, who was looking for "young and pretty women" to recruit as entertainers in Japan.[6] As a woman over 30 without any special job skill, Sally had limited options for migration. A single mother, she had to support her family, especially her son, and she decided to go abroad for work when faced with unemployment during a local economic crisis.

However, Sally was blocked from entering Taiwan as a factory worker due to her age and gender, whereas she would have been welcome to enter Taiwan as a domestic worker and Japan as an entertainer, as the only restriction on such positions is that the applicant be a woman.[7] Through the information she received from her sisters in Israel, though, Israel emerged as a desirable destination country where she could earn a high salary and maintain her self-esteem as a care worker, not as a nanny. The most decisive factor in her migration decision, finally, was the offer of financial support from her sisters who were working in Israel as care workers.

When supply exceeds demand, there is fierce competition among the applicants, and this makes the recruitment system a lucrative business, forcing potential migrants to use the services (Martin, 2007). Although the law permits agencies to collect brokerage fees of no more than the amount equivalent to one-month wage for migrant care workers, the brokerage fee typically exceeds the sum of their one-month wage. Significantly, the brokerage fee is determined by the country of origin and gender. The brokerage fee for Filipino care workers has increased each year in Israel and reached up to USD 6,000 in late 2000s and USD 10,000 in late 2010s (see Table 3).[8] According to the data from *Kava LaOved* (2013), the brokerage fee that Filipino care workers pay is relatively lower than that of other Asian workers from Sri Lanka, Nepal, and India, and male care workers pay higher brokerage fees for all countries of origin.

---

6 The term Japayuki was coined in a Japanese document. In 1981, the Japanese government started issuing "entertainer visas" (Tyner, 2004). In 1997, the 28,500 Filipina entertainers in Japan accounted for 95% of all female OFWs in that country and 99% of all Filipino female entertainers in the world (Tyner, 2004, p. 165).
7 According to my informants, the monthly wage for foreign care workers in Taiwan is known as around USD 500, and the brokerage fee is between USD 1,500 and USD 3,000, while the monthly wage of factory workers in Taiwan is around USD 750.
8 Raijman and Kushnirovich (2012, p. 88) argue that the reason for the steep rise in recruitment fees is related to the Ministry of the Interior's 2005 decision to extend the period migrant workers were allowed to stay in Israel from 27 to 63 months, and brokers saw this extension as an opportunity to demand higher fees from workers.

	2007	2008	2009	2010	2011	2013	2015	2017	2019
Salary (NIS)	2,800	3,000	3,400	3,600	4,100	4,300	4,650	5,000	5,300
Brokerage Fee(USD)	6,000	6,500	6,700	7,110	8,500	9,100	10,688	12,000	13,000

Table 3. Salary and Brokerage Fee of Migrant Care Workers in Israel (2007–2019)
Source: Kav LaOved (2013) and Author's Interview Data. NIS (New Israeli Shekel)

Migrant care workers with limited access to migration resources are required to find an employer and pay their brokerage fee before they enter Israel. Although the Israeli law prohibits the placement agency from requiring any direct or indirect fees from the employee (Lobel, 2001, p. 125), it has become an accepted practice that the agencies collect a higher amount underground. According to my informants, most were not capable of paying the brokerage fee when they applied and had to seek funds either from their family members or a private agent. Therefore, those who have access to financial capital as well as network connections to reduce the costs, risks, and uncertainty of migration are more likely to migrate to Israel.

In particular, the potential migrants' family members in Israel increase the likelihood of cross-border movement in the ways that they willingly resolve the migrants' financial problems in migrating to Israel where the brokerage fee for migrant care workers is unbearably expensive. As indicated in the case of Sally, migrants rely on their networks to gain direct or indirect access to economic resources for realizing their migration, representing one example of using social ties to gain social and financial aids for overseas migration.

Indentured Mobility Through Networks

State policies play a pivotal role in determining the direction, extent, and character of cross-border migrant flow (Castle & Miller, 2003). However, the state is not the only compelling factor in shaping migrant trajectories. In order to fully understand the dynamics of Filipino migratory flows to Israel, it is worth illuminating the migration process from the migrants' point of view, drawing on the lived experiences of Filipino migrants without losing sight of the state control over the process. Relying on interviews and fieldwork, I will explore how the migration flow from the Philippines to Israel is shaped, focusing on the linkages between state policies and the operations of the migration networks at a micro-level. I will then describe how the migrants realize their migration projects within the institutionalized networks of the migration industry.

Recruitment Processes

Kemp and Raijman (2014) delve into the intersection of state policies, private brokers, and local employers in Israeli contexts by adopting a meso-level analysis and attempt to identify the mechanisms, actors, and relational patterns at play at the labor importing end, giving insight into the role of state policies and regulations as the initial conditions for the development of a labor trafficking industry. Their examination reveals how systemic features of official labor migration schemes embedded in neo-liberal logics of governance and institutionalized power relations can become powerful catalysts of trafficking in labor taking place first and foremost within the realm of legal labor migration (Kemp & Raijman, 2014, p. 607). The study gives insight into the role of state policies and regulations as the initial conditions for the development of a labor trafficking industry.

In the Philippine-Israel migratory corridor, three key stakeholders are generally involved in the recruitment process of care workers: placement agencies in Israel, recruitment agencies in the Philippines, and the migrant workers. The governments' role is essentially to define the responsibilities for each stakeholder and to develop a regulatory framework to ensure that each stakeholder fulfills its responsibility through enforcement and licensing policies. The Manpower Contractors Act of Israel (1996) states that "in the triangular relationships between the agencies, user-employers and employees, the placement agencies in Israel are the legal employer" (Lobel, 2001, p. 124).[9] In this framework, in order to formally employ a migrant care worker, licensed agencies in Israel and the Philippines must be involved in the entire process of recruiting care workers, even when user-employers find a care worker through word-of-mouth.

To be permitted to employ a migrant care worker, an older adult has to be completely dependent in the physical and instrumental activities of daily living, and those who employ care workers must hold a permit to give legal status to their care workers. In these cases, the migrant care workers are employed by the care recipient, not the welfare system, although a private nursing agency is usually involved in this caregiving arrangement. The agency connects the care recipient and the migrant care worker and provides some supervision of the appropriateness and quality of the delivered care.

Generally, the Filipina care workers are given the official 63-month resident permit and can keep their visas within that period, even in the

---

9   The private agencies in the host countries are usually referred to as placement agencies or man-power agencies. In this book, I refer to the private agencies in Israel as "placement agencies" and those agencies in the Philippines as "recruitment agencies."

rare event that their employers pass away. The migrant care workers are entitled to a visa permit given for a year at a time, which must be extended annually with their employers' consent. In other words, the care worker is bound to a particular employer who holds an employment permit. Under this binding system, the termination of employment relationship results in the loss of visas, regardless of the reason that the workers leave their employers and the duration of their stay in Israel.

The official recruitment procedure involves the process of recruitment and screening and is undertaken by licensed agencies in both sending and receiving countries. Once the applicants decide to migrate, they submit the required documents to a licensed recruitment agency in the Philippines for verification from the Department of Foreign Affairs in the Philippines (DFA). The verified documents are transmitted to a placement agency in Israel with the approval of the Philippine Overseas Labor Office (POLO), located in the Philippine Embassy in Israel. Following this, the placement agency submits the paperwork together with the documents from a potential employer to the Israeli Ministry of the Interior. Upon approval, these documents are transmitted to the Israel Embassy in the Philippines, where the applicants receive their work visa and signs labor contracts. Finally, the applicants participate in orientation seminars prior to their departure.

The case of Analyn illustrates the official recruitment process from the migrant's point of view. Analyn decided to go to Israel in 2004 when she heard about a care worker job from an agent who approached her on the street in her hometown. She then visited a recruitment agency in Manila guided by the agent and submitted the required documents to apply for a care worker position in Israel. As part of the process she underwent an interview and then participated in a two-week language course for Hebrew and a job training course for care workers, including instruction on house cleaning, cooking, and care of the elderly. After that, she was interviewed by the Israeli Embassy in Manila and waited another seven months until the agency arranged an employer for her. Analyn paid USD 4,200 for her brokerage fee, which included her flight ticket and document processing fees.

However, my research data indicate that the actual recruitment procedures are more complex than this official procedure due to the intervention of an intricate web of licensed agencies, informal agents or sub-agents and personal networks, requiring the applicants to pay a much higher brokerage fee. While the intervention of licensed agencies is mandatory for managing the document procedure, the role of the agent as a recruiter is distinctive. Although the local agencies in the Philippines advertise openings by posting job orders on their websites or running ads in newspapers, it is the agent

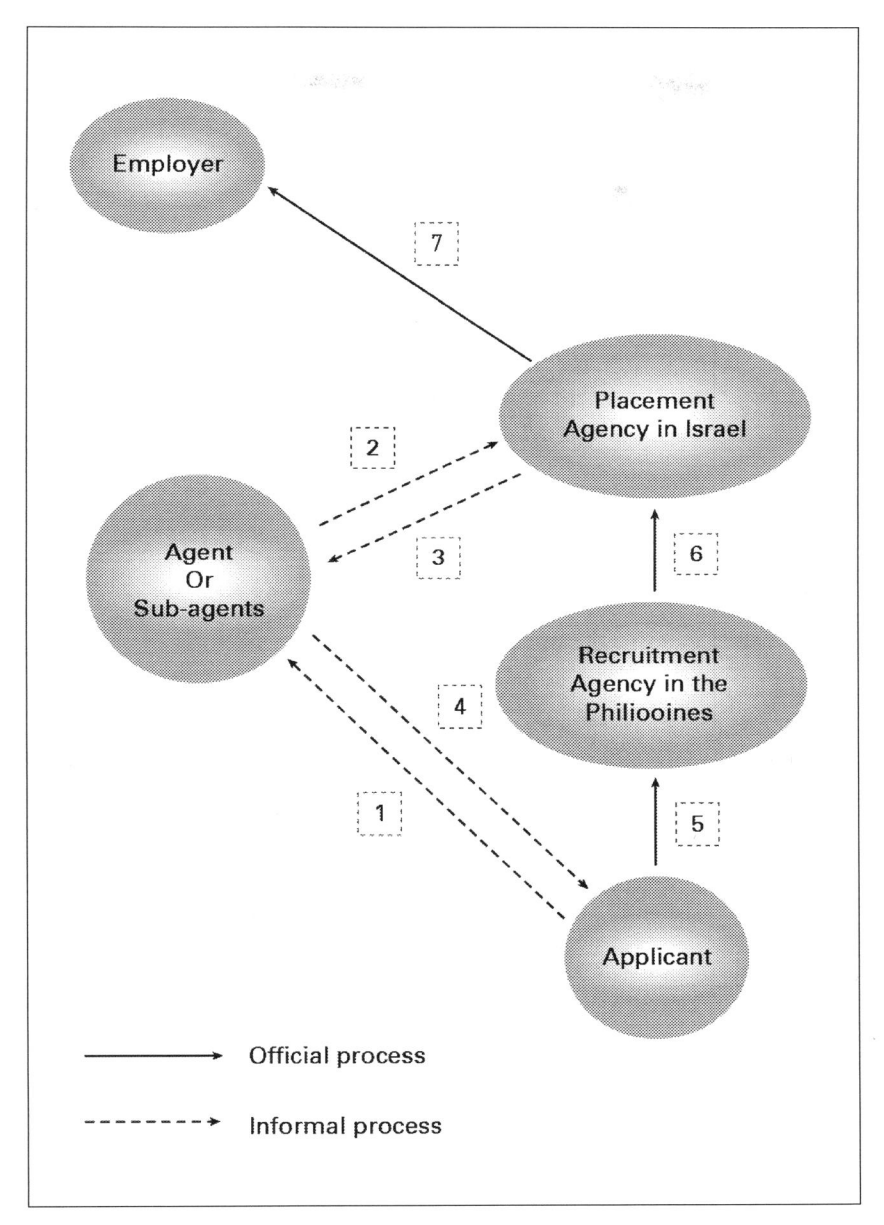

Figure 1. Recruitment process flow

who practically recruits care workers from the Philippines and links them to the placement agencies in Israel.

Usually, the agent is a Filipino woman currently working as a contract care worker or a former care worker who married an Israeli man. An agent is connected with several placement agencies in Israel as a freelance broker and is involved in all stages of the migration process, providing the agencies with promising care workers. Sub-agents are those persons who work for agents, helping the agents find applicants, either in Israel or in the Philippines (see Figure 1).

The power of an agent is produced in the niche of the Israeli labor system that stipulates that "the issue of working visa must be secured prior to the entry of the migrants to the receiving country" and "the legal recruiter is the placement agency in Israel." Once the applicants are connected to an agent, the agent then forwards the applicant's resume to a specific placement agency in Israel that conducts an under-the-table recruitment. When the placement agency decides to enroll the applicant, agents instruct the applicant to apply through a certain recruitment agency in the Philippines, which is affiliated with the placement agency in Israel.

In sum, the applicants apply to placement agencies in Israel through an informal channel beforehand and then officially apply through the licensed agencies only after their recruitment is pre-determined through the agents. Then the placement agencies match the applicants with potential employers in Israel, issuing a working visa for them. By this, it is obvious that the legitimate agencies hire migrant care workers through illegal employment practices.

Most importantly, the majority of my informants report that the operation of the agents guaranteed the success of their movement to Israel by securing their employment and shortening the recruitment process to three months, while the process without the intervention of agents takes almost one year like Analyn's case. In actuality, it is very common to see agents in the Philippine–Israel care worker migration system. Many of the informants emphasize the significant role of agents in actualizing their labor migration and still believe that without agents they might not have succeeded in migrating to Israel.

For example, Roger, a Filipino care worker, argues, "If you don't have an agent, it takes time. [It is] very hard. But if you find an agent here in Israel, the process goes fast." According to Analyn, rumors circulate among Filipino migrants that placement agencies have now begun rejecting applicants without the intermediation of agents. As a sub-agent, Angela's role is to mediate between an applicant and an agent like Mark, who works with several placement agencies that are eligible to legally recruit migrant care workers in Israel. The testimony of Angela gives us a view into how agents operate in the recruitment system:

> If the placement agency fails to match the applicant with an employer, the agent tries to look for a job through another agency. Sometimes, the

employer doesn't wait [through the long procedure for empowerment and cancels the process]. They prefer a Filipina [who is already] in Israel to a newcomer who doesn't speak Hebrew. Then what will you do? To find an employer for the applicant is now my job [sub-agent's job]. That's the normal case. The applicants cannot choose [their job] because there are a lot of applicants. If the applicants don't have an agent, it's very hard. It's impossible [to find a job for them]. It is the agent who communicates with the agencies in the Philippines and Israel. The applicant doesn't communicate directly with the agency. [There are] Always agents. The agencies never communicate even with the sub-agent like me because they don't know me.[10]

When agents are not "at hands," applicants employ different strategies to get in contact with them, mainly through their personal networks. As a sub-agent, Angela's role is to mediate between an applicant and Mark who works with several placement agencies that are eligible to legally recruit migrant care workers in Israel. As indicated in Angela's statement above, placement agencies are reluctant to "indirectly" recruit Filipino care workers through the recruitment agencies, due to the potential risk of migrant desertion upon arrival.

Instead, the placement agencies employ agents, who screen the applicants beforehand and undertake the responsibility for all follow-up problems relevant to the applicants. Therefore, agents and their network of sub-agents are required to be what Angela calls a "guarantor." In this sense, agents and sub-agents do not attempt to recruit "strangers" but those who are within their extended networks. Angela continues to explain:

> It was me who connected Nelrose's sister, Jasmine, with the agent, Mark. It took only three months. If I didn't know Nelrose, I would not "help" her because the agencies don't want to recruit strangers. The agency needs a guarantor like me. I am the guarantor. Right now I have an applicant, Suzan. She is my cousin. The agency in Israel will not call Suzan. Instead, they will call me. They collect their fee directly from me, not from her. If the process goes wrong, I am responsible for it. If Suzan doesn't pay her fee, I have to pay for her. [It's] a little bit dangerous [job]. That's why I recruit only someone I know.

In the same way that agents and subagents attempt to recruit care workers within the circle of their own networks, applicants tend to perceive the

---

10   In this book, I incorporate informants' words without changing.

agents or sub-agents as trustable networks in their uncertain journey to Israel. As an agent, Mark recruited Angela as a reliable resource for labor through his cousin, Jenny, because Angela is one of Jenny's close friends from her hometown. Angela also came to Israel through an agent, Mark, who was also a cousin of her close friend. According to Angela, she decided to come to Israel because she trusted Mark as an acquaintance, who was guaranteed by one of her close friends. In this sense, agents and sub-agents within the migrants' network circles can be regarded as "migrant social capital," enabling the prospective migrants to secure information or other forms of assistance from current migrants to reduce the cost and risks of migration (Garip, 2008).

Migration Indebtedness
As Tyner (2000) points out, "paradoxically, the complex networks binding origin countries and destination countries are invisible" (Goss & Lindquist, 1995, p. 337), but this invisible migration network serves the key role in creating and sustaining the global labor circuits. In a study of the Mexico-U.S. migratory system, Hernández-León (2005) proposes the concept of the "migration industry," which includes legal, illegal, formal and informal services, and regards it as an ensemble of businesses and services which facilitate and sustain international migration. In this way, the agents and sub-agents are part of the "migration industry," which creates an intricate and costly infrastructure (Hernández-León, 2005, p. 13).

The privatization of the labor recruitment system under the state regulatory scheme shapes the entry of migrant labor to the labor market through which the influx of Filipino care workers is perpetuated. As Xiang and Lindquist (2014) argue, migration should be imagined as a multi-faceted space of mediation occupied by commercial recruitment intermediaries, formal and informal bureaucrats, NGOs, migrants, and technologies.

Due to their multiple roles in the recruitment process, significantly, agents are located at the intersections of private actors and systems, in which the distinction between social networks and profit-oriented brokers becomes blurry, while placement agencies, which are authorized by government, depend on informal agents who utilize their own network ties to recruit potential migrants. Relevant actors, such as agencies, agents, sub-agents, and personal networks, are separated from one another but perform complementary functions to realize a migration.

This is especially evident in the agents' and sub-agents' role as moneylenders. In addition to the role as a guarantor and intermediary, the agents and sub-agents also serve as moneylenders who prepay the brokerage fee for the migrants in the forms of a loan. According to my interviews with the informants, the intervention of agents in the recruitment process enables those who are not capable of paying the brokerage fee to migrate to Israel, and the possibility of access to economic resources drives the potential migrants to decide about migration.

The agent working as a care worker in Israel directly or indirectly collects fees from the applicant in the Philippines through personal cash delivery or a money transfer system. The precise division of profits between agencies in Israel and in the Philippines remains unknown, but estimates range from 50% to 70% of the fees paid go to the placement agencies in Israel (*Kav LaOved*, 2008), which coincides with what Angela states. Angela explains that the majority of a fee goes to the Israeli placement agencies, while roughly USD 1,700 of the fee goes to the recruitment agency in the Philippines for the payment of the flight and document-processing. The agent takes USD 500 from the total amount the applicant paid. As a sub-agent, Angela receives USD 200 per head from Mark.

The agent directly pays the fee from his or her own pocket to the Israeli agency. This insures the agent will take responsibility for all the troubles that arises in the process. For this reason, they often describe their agent as "a trustee helper" who serves as "a safety net," as a direct and quick passage to Israel. Such "patron-client networks" between migrant workers and their agents play a critical role in creating and perpetuating the migratory flows from the Philippines to Israel. It was from Grace that for the first time I heard of an agent as a moneylender. In a case where an applicant borrows money from the agent, as shown in the case of Grace, the agent directly pays the fee from his or her own pocket to the Israeli agency.

The Case of Grace
Grace came to Israel in 2009 when she was 30 years old as a single woman. Before coming to Israel, Grace worked in South Korea as a factory worker. Upon returning to her hometown, she began looking for job opportunities abroad again. At that time, Suzan, one of her local friends, encouraged Grace to go to Israel by providing her detailed information about a care worker job, work conditions and how to apply. When Grace responded to the news, Suzan introduced her to Evelyn, Suzan's cousin who was on vacation from Israel where she was working as a care worker and also as an agent.

Suzan presented Grace with two offers: firstly, she would manage the recruitment procedure quickly so that Grace could come to Israel within a few months; secondly, she would lend money to Grace for the migration costs. As Grace had no finances for migration at that time, she was very enthusiastic and proceeded with the migration process. From the moment that both sides agreed go ahead with the plan, an 8% interest rate on the USD 5,000 loan began to accrue. Two months later Grace received a text from Evelyn in Israel, saying, "Okay, now you have a visa."

However, the intervention of agents in the recruitment process results in the indebted mobility among migrants who must ultimately pay the excessive illegal brokerage fee. For each payment on her salary day, Grace paid some amount for the principle and interest at a rate of 8%. Grace paid Rosa USD 500 from the principal and USD 400 for the interest after subtracting from her first salary. The next month, she had a balance of USD 4,500 and USD 360 for interest on the USD 4,500. Sometimes she paid only USD 200 because she had to send money back to her family in the Philippines. However, she couldn't keep repaying her debt after she quit her job. Grace says, "I still have USD 1,000 to pay her, but I don't have money. She is working inside the *tachana*, but I didn't contact her, and she didn't also call me. Maybe she knows that I paid her enough. Yah, it's more. I paid already a lot of money."

It is noteworthy that such a complex migration pattern of Filipino migrants has developed within legal regulatory frameworks, while creating a black market. The emergence of a black market can be summed up as follows: It is illegal for migrant care workers to work as agents because they are restricted to work only in the care sector for a single employer. Any kind of part-time work that migrant care workers participate in is illicit. Nonetheless, the system persists. The placement agencies create an underground route in the employment process, which takes place outside the formal route, by hiring the informal and illicit agents. Finally, the placement agencies collect an illicit fee that violates the laws because the fee greatly exceeds the sum of the workers' one-month wage.

In this chapter, I provided empirical data on the migration process from the Philippines to Israel under the recruitment system that involves the intervention of a placement agency. In July 2021, the first batch of care workers from the Philippines within the new framework was deployed in Israel. The purpose of the new arrangement was to regulate the recruitment process, prohibiting the collection of illicit fees by private agencies and regulating also the increasing number of undocumented residents from the State's perspective. Future research should address the new forms of hiring and recruitment and their governance as these will by now have significant influence on the migration patterns and migrant experiences.

Foreign Workers in Israel

This section addresses labor migration in Israel, providing a general description of the employment and relevant government policies, and offers an overview of the labor policies and employment conditions related to care work. I also describe how the restrictive policies paradoxically resulted in the rapid increase of a large population of the undocumented. Finally, I describe the work conditions and status of migrant care workers, highlighting the Filipino migrants' experiences in the Israeli migration regime.

Influx of Non-Jewish Migrants
Since its establishment in 1948, Israel has been a country of immigration, experiencing several large waves of Jewish immigration. As a Jewish and democratic state, Israel's immigration regime is based on the Jewish/non-Jewish distinction. The Jewish immigration to Israel, articulated as "the ingathering of the exiles," was legally sanctioned in 1950 through the Law of Return and this still forms the basis of the Israeli immigration regime today automatically granting fundamental rights of citizenship only to Jews. The status of non-Jewish migrants in the country are determined by the 1952 Entry to Israel Law and the 1954 Prevention of Infiltration Law. In this ethno-national framework, up until the 1990s there was virtually no mass immigration of non-Jews to Israel except the last wave of immigration from the former Soviet Union.

Since the mid-1990s, migrant workers from Asian and East European countries have arrived in Israel to enter the low-wage job sector in the local labor market. By 1967, Israel already had a highly stratified labor market, in which Palestinian citizens worked at the lowest levels (Batram, 1998, p. 305). After the occupation of the West Bank and Gaza Strip as a result of the 1967 War, the Israeli economic boom saw an urgent need for workers, especially in the construction and agriculture sectors, and the Israeli government began to employ Palestinian workers as a convenient and profitable solution to the shortage of workers and as a means to deepen the economic "integration" between Israel and the Occupied Territories (Rosenhek, 2006, p. 3).

Up until the late 1980s, the agriculture and construction sectors relied heavily on this low-wage labor from the Occupied Territory. Around 110,000 Palestinian workers in the 1980s made up 25% of Israeli agricultural jobs and 45% of construction jobs (Jackson, 2011, p. 56). Following the outbreak of the *Intifada* (1987–1993), the Gulf War (1991) and the Oslo Peace Process (1993), however, the Israeli government closed the crossing points between the Occupied and Israel territories (Ellman & Laacher, 2003).[11] The border closure resulted in a severe labor shortage, particularly in the construction and agricultural sectors (Rosenhek, 2003, p. 242). Employers' associations in those two sectors faced with the crisis demanded the recruitment of cheap migrant labor. Although the Israeli government initially opposed that solution and proposed instead diverse programs to attract Israeli workers (see Rosenhek, 2003, p. 241), it finally authorized the recruitment of migrant workers.

Throughout the 1990s, some migrants to Israel overstayed on a tourist or pilgrim visa for work. These visiting workers were mainly from Ghana and Nigeria (Sabar, 2010, p. 49). However, in 1993 the government decided to officially hire migrant workers on a large scale.[12] Generally, the migrant workers were recruited in particular job sectors by nationality, reinforcing the segmented Israeli labor market. According to Batram (1998), in 1996, 75,600 workers—75% of all documented workers—were employed in the construction sector in which labor was predominantly performed by Rumanians, Turkish, and Chinese workers, while 7% of laborers, primarily Filipinos, were employed in the caregiving sector for the chronically sick and elderly.

However, since 2002 the main sector of permits per employment has shifted from construction to the elderly caregiving sector. The government sets a maximum quota for employment permits in construction and agriculture. But in the caregiving sector, unlike the others, quotas are not set, making the elderly care sector the largest sector for the employment of low-paid migrant workers in Israel. As of 2020, the number of migrant workers with permits stands at 98,200, and most of them are employed in three main sectors: caregiving (57%), agriculture (23%) and construction (15%) (OECD, 2020). The Philippines and Thailand are one of the major sources of labor flows to Israel.

It is important to note that an increasing number of asylum seekers and refugees from African countries have entered Israel since 2005 and participate in the local labor market as the cheapest workforce. Surrounded by Arab and Muslim countries, Israel's prosperity and democratic structure act as significant pull factors for migrants. These asylum seekers, fleeing political persecution and economic crisis in their home countries, have become a conspicuous minority in Israel, together with migrant workers.

---

11   The first *Intifada* of the Palestinians in the Occupied Territory ran from about 1987–1993, and ended with the signing of the Oslo Accords, which provided steps leading to the establishment of a Palestinian State (Ellman & Laacher, 2003).

12   The "Foreign Workers Law" (1991) defines a "foreign worker" as "a worker who is not a citizen or a resident of Israel." (Population and Immigration Authority, 2016).

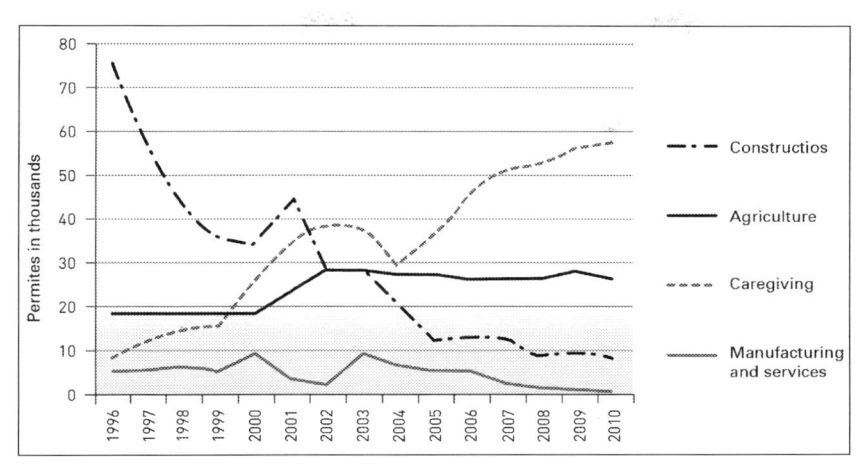

Figure 2. Permits issued according to employment sectors 1996–2012
Source: Kemp and Raijman (2014, p. 612)

As of June 2016, an estimated 42,147 asylum seekers reside in Israel, the majority of whom are Eritrean (30,595) and Sudanese (8,232) (Nakash et al., 2017, p. 261).

Most of these asylum seekers have temporary protection in the form of "2A5 conditional release visas," which are renewable every three months, but they live under the constant threat that protection will be revoked. Many of them now reside in Tel Aviv, where they have found accommodation and established their lives. Since the end of 2008 when the government began granting temporary protection to Eritreans and Sudanese, some asylum seekers have opened small businesses including restaurants, internet shops, and clothing stores catering to an African clientele in *Neve Sha'anan*.

Migrant Policies and Regulations

The binding system structures the status of migrant workers in Israel. In this system a visa is issued on behalf of a worker and attached exclusively to a designated employer (Drori, 2009, p. 45). Within the arrangement, migrant workers may not work for another employer, even on rest days or after regular working hours. The employment permits must be extended annually "under the agreement of their employers," which grants the employers control over their employees. Until the Foreign Workers Law was revised in 2011, the workers had extremely limited access to redress when they stayed over 51 months, the maximum period of contract. If the employer agrees upon an employment contract annually, the worker can continue working indefinitely for the same employer.

In 2011, there were two amendments to the Law, providing more options for workers to move from one employer to another. Firstly, the extension of a care workers' employment may extend beyond 63 months, the maximum period of legal work, even when the worker has not been employed by the employer for at least one year. Secondly, the transfer of migrant workers in the sector between employers is allowed (Nathan, 2012). In spite of such reform allowing intra-sector mobility between employers and agencies, indentured labor still stands as the core of the migrant labor policy in Israel. Workers who lose their work due to dismissal, quitting or an employer's death must find a new legal job within at most 90 days.

Migrant workers did not gain the right for family reunification. Migrant workers are not allowed to obtain work permits if their spouse or close relatives are working in Israel. That is, married couples are not expected to come to Israel together, "nor [do] children born in Israel and to non-Israeli parents receive any form of citizenship or residency rights" (Willen, 2003). In case migrant workers give birth to a child, they have to decide if they will leave Israel within three months or send the child to their home country. In actuality, no-family policies have contributed to the increase of overstay and the formation of new groups of migrant workers' children since many mothers have decided to remain in Israel with their child without permits.

The aim of the binding system is to maximize surveillance over labor migrants' entrance into the country and their activities in the labor market, while minimizing the state's responsibility for the ways in which they are recruited, the terms of their employment, and their living conditions (Raijman & Kemp, 2016, p. 5). However, this arrangement paradoxically has yielded the emergence of an increasing population of undocumented workers (Kemp & Raijman, 2003, p. 13–15). Significantly, there has been a rapid increase of overstay by workers whose permits have expired or whose contract with their employer has been broken voluntarily or in-voluntarily.

Year	Legal	Illegal	Total
2011	74,778	14,118	88,896
2013	71,352	15,366	86,718
2015	77,192	15,915	93,107
2018	98,214	16,230	114,444
2020	98,188	18,136	116,324
June 2021	100,199	19,858	120,057

Table 4. Status of Temporary Migrant Workers, 2011–2021
Source: The OECD Expert Group on Migration 2020–2021 (Nathan, 2021)

In Israel, migrant workers without work permits were few as early as the late 1970s, but the Ministry of the Interior found about 1,500, who had overstayed their visas, including family members from Yugoslavia, Turkey, and the Philippines. According to the Officials at the Central Bureau for Statistics of Israel, there were at least 50,000 who entered on tourist visas and overstayed, while some entered on forged passports. In actuality, Israel has attracted large numbers of foreign visitors from various countries through Holy Land pilgrimages and tourism (Liebelt, 2010). Although there are cases of tourists who overstayed and became undocumented migrants, the majority of undocumented workers in Israel entered Israel as documented workers and overstayed their work visa. At the end of June 2021, the total number of migrant workers who entered Israel legally was 120,057. Of these, 100,199 had a valid visa and 19,858 were without a valid visa (Nathan, 2021).

In 2002, when the number of migrants without permits rapidly increased and the unemployment rate was high, the Israeli government decided to implement the "Close the skies" policy to reduce the numbers of migrant workers and deport those without permits (Kemp, 2010, p. 7). Under the regulation, recruitment of new migrant workers in the construction and agriculture sectors was prohibited, while this regulation was not applicable to the care sector. Simultaneously, a deportation campaign was systemically implemented with the aim of reducing the undocumented population. In 2002, the Immigration Police Department was officially inaugurated, deploying Immigration Police. This unit was replaced by the *OZ* (Hebrew abbreviation for *Ovdim Zarim*, meaning foreign workers) Unit under the direction of the Ministry of the Interior in 2009.

Initiating a mass deportation campaign, the government refrained from deporting women and children, but soon it declared that it would deport families, including children, and finally deported 1,300 migrant workers and their families in 2003 (Ruth, 2003). While the number of undocumented workers has fluctuated under shifting policies over the decades, there has been no noticeable drop in the number of migrant workers in the country. Between 1995 and 2008, about 76,100 migrant workers without permits were deported, but the share of migrant workers with and without permits has still gradually increased.

Over the decades, the citizenship of migrant workers' children has also become a critical issue. In Israel, the Law of Return (1950) and the Citizenship Law (1952) embody citizenship based on *jus-sanguinis*, by automatically granting citizenship to Jews while excluding the non-Jew population. Under the law that signifies and embodies the ethnic foundation of the state, the majority of the children of migrants are classified as "illegal residents" and expected to be deported. There is no accurate data, but in the educational system about 1,500 undocumented children were registered in 2016 (Nathan, 2021, p. 67).

In response to the government's restrictive policy, Israeli NGOs and various civil organizations mobilized actions against the deportations and asserted the right to stay in Israel for the undocumented children. Advocating for their legal status, activists emphasized cultural assimilation and social belonging, rather than humanitarian action (Kemp & Kfır, 2016). In 2003, for instance, ACRI (Association for Civil Rights in Israel) launched a petition against the Ministry of the Interior when it announced the deportation of undocumented children who were born in Israel and spoke Hebrew as "Israeli in every way" (Paz, 2016, p. 22).

Finally, the Ministry of the Interior granted some children who met requirements permanent residency permits. In 2005, the government legalized 562 children of the 862 requests that were filed (Nathan, 2012, p. 2), granting renewable temporary residency for their parents and siblings. Since then, the government has intermittently granted permanent residency status to the children of migrant workers who were born in Israel and speak Hebrew. Although implemented as an ad hoc decision, the legalization policies opened up a path to new opportunities for many children at certain points in their lives.

Significantly, the city of Tel Aviv has developed incorporating strategies over several decades that contrast with the state-led migration policy that excludes the foreign population (Kemp & Raijman, 2004). In 1998, the Municipality of Tel Aviv organized the Forum for Foreign Workers and in the following year established MESILA (Aid and Information Center for the Foreign Community in Tel Aviv-Jaffa) to provide social welfare services such as education and health to those foreign residents with and without permits. In 2001, the children of migrant workers and refugees were integrated into the Israeli educational system. By 2019, there are 10,000 children without paper in Israel, and the majority live in Tel-Aviv (approximately 6,500) (Population and Immigration Authority, 2019).

Social Status of Migrant Care Workers
Israel, which has witnessed rapid growth of the elderly population, has also seen increased demands for long-term care in the face of only a small proportion of nursing care institutions for senior citizens who need long-term care.[13]

---

13 When the State of Israel was established in 1948, people over the age of 65 represented only 4% of the population, but the age group has annually increased, accelerating the average

Under these circumstances, the Community Long-Term Care Insurance Law (LTCIL) was implemented in 1988 (Brodsky & Naon, 1993). According to the laws, citizens over the age of 65 or younger adults who suffer from disability may require the service with basic daily living tasks or receive subsidies for services from the National Insurance (*Bituach Leumi*). To cope with the shortage of indigenous home care workers and avoid institutionalization, the Israeli government decided to employ migrant care workers (Ayalon, 2009).[14]

Migrant care workers are required to work on a live-in basis in the house of their employer, while given a day-off on weekends. In the Israeli labor market, live-out care workers are primarily Israeli citizens, while live-in care workers are primarily migrants. Israeli workers are largely unwilling to provide round-the-clock care (Ayalon & Ohad, 2013).[15] Migrants are dispersed to local private households, where they provide around-the-clock service for the elderly. In many cases, migrant care workers live with their employers since the family members of the elderly live in a separated household and sometimes come to visit, especially on Friday and Saturday for family gathering on *Shabbat*. Migrant care workers often recognize the adult children of their elderly employer as a kind of employer as well because they practically manage the employment and work conditions.

Domestic work is described as "an intimate labor that involves embodied and affective interactions in the service of social reproduction" (Borris & Parreñas, 2011, p. 7) or "a commoditized form of intimacy" (Constable, 2009). Care giving is performed as invisible labor in private houses where care worker and care recipient live together and their relationships are often established as intimate partners. For example, most of my Filipino informants who had established a good relationship with their employer called their employers *yima* (mother) or *abba* (father), making employment relations pseudo-family ties.

As many researchers have already pointed out, however, being "part of the family" contributes to blurred boundaries between professional and personal care, and requires many home-care workers to perform emotional duties and other extra work without additional pay (Aronson & Neysmith,

life expectancy. In 2018, 11.8% of Israel's population were over 65 years old, and 41% of senior citizens were 75 years of age (United Nations, 2020).

14 Institutional care costs USD 2,500–4,000 compared with the cost for foreign workers (USD 700–1,000 per month). Foreign workers are cheaper than homecare workers who are Israeli citizens (Iecovich, 2007, p. 107–108).

15 Live-out care workers are primarily Israeli citizens, with a substantial portion of the workers coming from the former Soviet Union as part of the large immigration wave of Jews in the early 1990s (Ayalon & Ohad, 2013, p. 16).

1996). Employers are the major group with whom the care workers daily interact in their migrant life, and the employers' house is the place that care workers spend the majority of their time in Israel.

By law, in Israel, employers are required to offer their care workers an accommodation and food. They typically deduct a sum amount of money from the workers' wage for their living expenses such as food and beverages, water, gas, electricity and national insurance.[16] Although the care workers are given their own room or a sofa for accommodation, the live-in situation still results in restrictions on the care workers' privacy, as they do not have the same rights or freedom to space as their employers in the private household. During visits to my informants' workplace, I paid attention to surveillance cameras, installed for the safety of the elderly who particularly suffered from Alzheimer's. My informants often asked me to stay in limited areas, out of the angles, and we stayed in the kitchen for interviews.

The job requirements for live-in care workers are usually ambiguous and unlimited as the work is not specified in a time schedule, nor easy to be standardized. Many researchers have argued that even when the job description of a care worker is well defined, the private and circumstantial nature in which the job is performed often changes the requirements, and the worker is asked to perform additional tasks in the absence of adequate financial compensation (Aronson & Neysmith, 1996). According to the Filipino informants, they are employed as care workers, but cleaning the house is included in their daily work, and in some cases cleaning and cooking are their major work. They explained that they mop the floor in the morning, while some of them take care of the grandchildren of their employers on a regular basis.

This was the reason that Angela wanted to migrate as a factory worker rather than domestic worker. During my fieldwork, Angela sometimes told me how she missed life in Taiwan where she worked as a factory worker. The manufacturing company where she worked housed more than 500 Filipino workers who did not know each other previously in a seven-story building. Angela was at the company's dorm, sharing one room with other three more Filipinos, thus she didn't feel lonely, nor did she get bored. Although the job was tough, according to Angela, she enjoyed having free time after her work in the evening to socialize with her roommates and others. They

---

16   According to the data of January 2013, the amounts deducted from the workers' monthly salary are as follows: Jerusalem area (190.09 NIS), Tel Aviv (216.30 NIS), Central Israel/Haifa (144.25 NIS), South (128.20 NIS), North (117.97 NIS) and bills for water, gas, and electricity (77.92 NIS) (*Kav LaOved* website).

went to shopping malls, parks, restaurants, disco bars and video rooms that accommodate 10 people at a time. They also went fishing or dating with fellow Filipino workers.

It is noteworthy that the indentured legal status of migrant care workers is heightened in the live-in work situation, especially after the period of 63 months since their entry into Israel. As several researchers argue, the collapsed boundary between the Filipino migrants' sense of public and private space within the context of their employers' houses often leads to exploitative working conditions (Bakan & Stasiulis, 1997; Cohen, 1991; Lan, 2003; Stiell & England, 1997). Specific experiences of migrant care workers from my fieldwork help in understanding the ambiguous features of domestic work caused by live-in situations and the asymmetrical employment relations.

In particular, those who have already fulfilled the minimum period of a contract are more likely to voluntarily accept burdensome requests in order not to create conflict with their employers. Judy's case exemplifies the ambiguous job requirements of live-in care workers under the given conditions of their vulnerable legal status. Judy had been working as a live-in care worker since 2005 for five years, and her major task was supposed to be to serve an elderly man. However, she was forced to babysit a two-year-old granddaughter of her employer three days a week and clean the house for two hours every day.

Judy is well aware of the fact that this is unfair, but she has been performing such tasks without complaining. She was afraid of being discharged if she rejected the work given to her because her contract had already exceeded the maximum period. Judy states, "The old man asks me, and he has my visa. What can I do? It's really tough, but I am doing it because I have no choice." In Judy's expression, "we try to be nice to our employer if it is almost four years that we stayed in Israel. If they don't want me abruptly, I cannot stay here anymore."

Nerlose's case is also worthy of attention. During the dinner time on a Friday night, I heard her complain that her monthly salary, 2,900 NIS (approximately USD 780), was less than the minimum wage (4,300 NIS as of 2012). This salary was to cover her intense labor in the big house where she cleaned for several hours a day, in addition to serving the elderly. In the past she visited her agency whenever she had complaints with regard to her workplace, but now that she had exceeded her minimum contract, she doesn't complain any more. Jasmin, another flatmate who was sitting next to Nerlose to support her, states, "Nerlose cannot complain again because it's her last visa. Negotiation is impossible. So she must be careful. Other

Filipinos don't want to make any trouble. For me, I am not afraid because I will not hide. I will just go back to the Philippines."

It seems that the Filipino care workers have ambivalent attitudes with respect to these additional tasks. They accept some tasks without complaining as a matter of course and they accept others because of the fear of being dismissed in the case that they don't do what is asked of them. John, a 56-year-old live-in care worker, starts his daily work by changing the cloth of his employer and never fails to clean the house. He thinks that his work is not hard as much as he earns and even feels guilty when he just sits next to his employer on the bed. At the same time, he believes that if he doesn't clean the house, he will be dismissed.

> I told them I will clean the house because I don't have many things to do there. It is common sense that a care worker cleans the house because I think it's my house, especially I am a live-in. And I get high salary, but not so much work, then I feel a kind of guilty. If you say no when your employer asked you to clean, maybe you will be fired.

Laura, a 48-year-old live-in care worker, also performs domestic work in her employer's house. Sometimes she feels even that she does odd jobs more than care work. It is hard for her to say "no" when her employer's family asks her help. Laura says that she feels sorry when she has nothing to do on the chair while her employer takes a nap. The requested work piles up especially during Passover, one of the biggest Jewish holidays. On the Passover holiday, Laura got a sudden call from her employer, asking her to come for work. Although she was to be paid for the labor, she didn't want to work on the holidays, but she soon left her apartment, saying that "I have no choice." When I asked her why the care workers unwillingly clean house, she answered that "If I don't do that, my employer will release me." In this way, she is in a standby condition in response to employer's spontaneous requests.

Extra work to be done on the off-day is another issue that may cause conflicts between employers and employees. Usually, the daily work of live-in care workers finishes only when their employers go to bed at night. Ella had established a good relationship with her first employer, who allowed her to call him *abba* and his wife *yima*. But the only problem was that her employer didn't want her to have off-days while Ella yearned for an off-day on weekends. The only thing that the care worker can do, in this case, is to find someone who substitutes for her as a part-timer or to be dismissed. Finally, Ella's employer dismissed her and hired another Filipino care worker. Since then, Ella has been working part time as a live-out care worker for a

Figure 3. An Israeli employer and his Filipino care worker

14-year-old Israeli girl who is mentally challenged and cleaning the house of her employer's younger sister twice a week.

The majority of the migrants have a regular day-off on weekends, in which they are allowed to leave the employer's houses. However, many of the migrants claim that they are actually given 26 hours or less than that for their day-off. Some of them have no guaranteed time off due to the poor health conditions of their employers. Both live-in and live-out care workers agree that each has its own advantage and disadvantage. Nonetheless, it seems that minimizing contact with employers by becoming a "live-out" has been identified as the most successful strategy for domestic day workers to gain autonomy and flexibility in arranging the procedure and pace of work (Romero, 1992, p. 152).

Migrant workers in Israeli households are expected to recognize their cultural difference from their employers as well as social status differences. Although an emotional attachment can be found between employers and employees in the "labor of emotion," employers have different social and demographic features from their migrant care workers and the interactions between the social groups may enhance the boundaries that divide them.

Considering that an employer's house is a microcosm of social inequality in global economy (Lan, 2003), the specific working conditions and labor policies of the host society impact the process in which Filipino migrant workers engage to build their own society. The formation of an enclave is stimulated not only by internal factors such as common ethnic identity, class, language and culture, but also by such external factors as labor policies, employment relations, and social prejudice, evidenced in segregation of the migrant group from the host society and other groups.

Bibliography

Aronson, J., & Neysmith, S. M. (1996). You are not just in there to do the work: Depersonalizing policies and the exploitation of home care workers' labor. *Gender & Society*, *10*(1), 59–77. https://doi.org/10.1177/089124396010001005

Asian Development Bank. (2009, December). *Remittances in Asia: Implications for the fight against poverty and the pursuit of economic growth.* https://www.adb.org/sites/default/files/publication/28397/economics-wp182.pdf

Asis, M. (1992). The overseas employment program policy. In G. Battistella & A. Paganoni (Eds.), *Philippine labour migration: Impact and policy* (pp. 68–112). Scalabrini Migration Center.

Ayalon, L. (2009). Family and family-like interactions in households with round-the-clock paid foreign carers in Israel. *Ageing & Society*, *29*(5), 671–686. https://doi.org/10.1017/S0144686X09008393

Ayalon, L., & Ohad, G. (2013). Live-in versus live-out home care in Israel: Satisfaction with services and care workers' outcomes. *The Gerontologist*, *55*(4) 628–642. https://doi.org/10.1093/geront/gnt122

Bakan, A. B., & Stasiulis, D. (1997). Foreign domestic worker policy in Canada and the social boundaries of modern citizenship. In A. B. Bakan & D. Stasiulis (Eds.), *Not one of the family: Foreign domestic workers in Canada* (pp. 29–52). University of Toronto Press.

Ball, R. E. (1997). The role of the state in the globalization of labour markets: The case of the Philippines. *Environment and Planning A: Economy and Space*, *29*(9), 1603–1628. https://doi.org/10.1068/a291603

Ball, R. E. (2004). Divergent development, racialised rights: Globalised labour markets and the trade of nurses: The case of the Philippines. *Women's Studies International Forum*, *27*(2), 119–133. https://doi.org/10.1016/j.wsif.2004.06.003

Bangko Sentral ng Pilipinas. (2020). Banko Sentral Pilipinas Dato. https://www.bsp.gov.ph/SitePages/Default.aspx

Barber, P. (2000). Agency in Philippine women's labour migration and provisional diaspora. *Women's Studies International Forum*, *23*(4), 399–411. https://doi.org/10.1016/S0277-5395(00)00104-7

Batram, D. V. (1998). Foreign workers in Israel: History and theory. *International Migration Review, 32*(2), 303–325. https://doi.org/10.1177/019791839803200201

Borris, E., & Parreñas, R. S. (2010). *Intimate labors: Cultures, technologies, and the politics of care.* Stanford Social Sciences.

Boyle, P. (2002). Population geography: Transnational women on the move. *Progress in Human Geography, 26*(4), 531–543. https://doi.org/10.1191/0309132502ph384pr

Brodsky, J., & Naon, D. (1993). Home care services in Israel-implications of the expansion of home care following implementation of the community long-term care insurance law. *Journal of Cross-Cultural Gerontology, 8*(4), 375–390. https://doi.org/10.1080/0141987042000337858

Carlos, M. R. (2010). *Filipino careworkers in ageing Japan: Trends, trajectories and policies.* A Paper to be presented at the conference Migration: A World in Motion, 18–20. February 2010, University of Maastricht, Netherlands.

Castles, S., & Miller, M. J. (2003). *The age of migration.* Guilford Press.

Choy, C. C. (2003). *Empire of care: Nursing and migration in Filipino American history.* Duke University Press.

Cohen, R. (1991). Women of color in white households: Coping strategies of live-in domestic workers. *Qualitative Sociology, 14*(2), 197–215. https://doi.org/10.1007/BF00992194

Constable, N. (2009). The commodification of intimacy: Marriage, sex, and reproductive labor. *Annual Review of Anthropology, 38,* 49–64. https://doi.org/10.1146/annurev.anthro.37.081407.085133

Cruz, G. T. (2008). Between identity and security: Theological implications of migration in the context of globalization. *Theological Studies, 69*(2), 357–375. https://doi.org/10.1177/004056390806900207

De Guzman, O. (2003). Overseas Filipino workers, labor circulation in Southeast Aisa, and the (mis)management of overseas migration programs. Kyoto Review of Southeast Asia, (4). Retrieved from http://kyotoreview.org/issue-4/overseas-filipino-workers-labor-circulation-in-southeast-asia-and-the-mismanagement-of-overseas-migration-programs

De Haas, H. (2010). The internal dynamics of migration processes: A theoretical inquiry. *Journal of Ethnic and Migration Studies, 36*(10), 1587–1617. https://doi.org/10.1080/1369183X.2010.489361

Drori, I. (2009). *Foreign workers in Israel: Global perspective.* SUNY Press.

Ehrenreich, B., & Hochschild, A. R. (2003). *Global woman: Nannies, maids and sex workers in the new economy.* Henry Holt and Company.

Ellman, M., & Laacher, S. (2003). *Migrant workers in Israel: A contemporary form of slavery.* Euro-Mediterranean Human Rights Network (EMHRN), Copenhagen & Paris, June 2003. www.euromedrights.net.

Ezquerra, S. (2009). *The regulation of the south-north transfer of reproductive labor: Filipino women in Spain and the United States.* Ph.D. dissertation, University of Oregon.

Garip, F. (2008). Social capital and migration: How do similar resources lead to divergent outcomes?. *Demography, 45*(3), 591–617. https://doi.org/10.1353/dem.0.0016

Gibson, K., Law, L. & McKay, D. (2001). Beyond heroes and victims: Filipina contract migrants, economic activism and class transformation. *International Feminist Journal of Politics, 3*(3), 365–386. https://doi.org/10.1080/14616740110078185

Goss, J., & Lindquist, B. (1995). Conceptualizing international labor migration: A structuration perspective. *International Migration Review, 29*(2), 317–351. https://doi.org/10.1177/019791839502900201

Guerrero, S. H. (2012). Gender and migration: Focus on Filipino women in international labor migration. *Review of Women's Studies, 10*(1/2), 275–298

Guevarra, A. R. (2009). *Marketing dreams, manufacturing heroes: The transnational labor brokering of Filipino workers.* Rutgers University Press.

Gupta, A., & Ferguson, J. (1997). Beyond culture: Space, identity, and the politics of difference. In A. Gupta J. & Ferguson (Eds.), *Culture, power, place: Explorations in critical anthropology* (pp. 1–29). Duke University Press.

Hawthorne, L. (2010). How valuable is two-step migration?: Labour market to outcomes for international student migrants to Australia. *Asian Pacific Migration Journal, 19*(1), 5–36. https://doi.org/10.1177/011719681001900102

Hernández-León, R. (2005). The migration industry in the Mexico–U.S. migratory system. *UCLA CCPR Population Working Papers.* http://www.paper.ccpr.ucla.edu/index.php/pwp/article/view/PWP-CCPR-2005-049

Iecovich, E. (2007). Live-in and live-out homecare services and care recipient satisfaction. *Journal of Aging and Social Policy, 19*(2), 105–122.

Jackson, V. (2011). Belonging against the national odds: Globalisation, political security and Philippine migrant workers in Israel. *Global Society, 25*(1), 49–71. https://doi.org/10.1080/13600826.2010.522982

Kav LaOved. (2013). *Black money, Black labor: Collection of brokerage fees from migrant care workers in Israel.* Retrieved from https://www.kavlaoved.org.il/wp-content/uploads/sites/3/2014/05/Black-Money-Black-Labor.pdf

Lan, P. (2003). Negotiating social boundaries and private zones: The micropolitics of employing migrant domestic workers. *Social Problems, 50*(4), 525–549. https://doi.org/10.1525/sp.2003.50.4.525

Liebelt, C. (2010). Domestic workers' struggles and pilgrimages for a cause in Israe. *The Asia Pacific Journal of Anthropology, 11*(3–4), 245–267. https://doi.org/10.1080/14442213.2010.511632

Liebelt, C. (2012). Consuming pork, parading the virgin and crafting origami in Tel Aviv: Filipina care workers' aesthetic formations in Israel. *Ethnos, 78*(2), 255–279. https://doi.org/10.1080/00141844.2012.655302

Lim, A. (2015). Networked mobility in the migration industry: Transnational migration of Filipino care workers to Israel. *Asian Women, 31*(2), 85–118. https://doi.org/10.14431/aw.2015.06.31.2.85

Lim, L. L., & Oishi, N. (1996). International labor migration of Asian women: Distinctive characteristics and policy concerns. *Asian and Pacific Migration Journal, 5*(1), 85–116. https://doi.org/10.1177/011719689600050010

Lobel, O. (2001). Class and care: The roles of private intermediaries in the in-home care industry in the United States and Israel. *Harvard Journal of Law and Gender, 24*, 89–140.

Martin, P. (2007). Managing labor migration in the 21st century. *City & Society, 19*(1), 5–18. https://doi.org/10.1525/city.2007.19.1.5

McKay, D. (2007). Sending dollars shows feeling: Emotions and economies in Filipino migration. *Mobilities, 2*(2), 175–194. https://doi.org/10.1080/17450100701381532

Nakash, O., Nagar, M., Shoshani, A. & Lurie, I. (2017). The association between perceived social support and posttraumatic stress symptoms among Eritrean and Sudanese male asylum seekers in Israel. *International Journal of Culture and Mental Health, 10*(3), 261–275. https://doi.org/10.1080/17542863.2017.1299190

Nathan, G. (2012). *The OECD expert group on migration (SOPEMI) report, immigration in Israel 2011–2012.* KRIF, Jerusalem, Israel.

Nathan, G. (2021). *The OECD expert group on migration SOPEMI annual report 2020–2021.* Research and Information Center, Israeli Parliament (Knesset).

OECD. (2020). *International migration outlook 2021.* https://www.oecd-ilibrary.org/social-issues-migration-health/international-migration-outlook-2021_29f23e9d-en

Oishi, N. (2005). *Women in motion: Globalization, state policies, and labor migration in Asia.* Stanford University Press.

Paul, A. M. (2011). Stepwise international migration: A multistage migration pattern for the aspiring migrant. *American Journal of Sociology, 116*(6), 1842–1886.

Paz, A. I. (2016). Speaking like a citizen: Biopolitics and public opinion in recognizing non-citizen children in Israel. *Language & Communication, 48*, 18–27. https://doi.org/10.1016/j.langcom.2016.01.002

Paz, Y. (2011). *Ordered disorder: African asylum seekers in Israel and discursive challenges to an emerging refugee regime.* Research Paper No. 205, UNHCR. www.unhcr.org.

Raijman, R., & Kemp, A. (2016). The institutionalization of labor migration in Israel. *Arbor, 192*(777), a289. http://dx.doi.org/10.3989/arbor.2016.777n1005

Raijman, R., & Kushnirovich, N. (2012). *Labor migration recruitment practices in Israel*. Final report for the Emek Hefer Ruppin Academic Center.

Rodriguez, R. M. (2002). Migrant heroes: Nationalism, citizenship and the politics of Filipino migrant labor. *Citizenship Studies*, 6(3), 341–356. https://doi.org/10.1080/1362102022000011658

Romero, M. (1992). *Maid in the U.S.A*. Routledge.

Rosenhek, Z. (2003). The political dynamics of a segmented labour market: Palestinian citizens, Palestinians from the Occupied Territories and migrant workers in Israel. *Acta Sociologica*, 46(3), 231–249.

Rosenhek, Z. (2006). Incorporating migrant workers into the Israeli labour market?. Cooperation project on the social integration of immigrants, migration, and the movement of persons. Robert Schuman Centre for Advanced Studies.

Ruth, S. (2003, Oct 15). Immigration police nab foreign workers who did not go home. *Ha'aretz*. https://www.haaretz.com/2003-10-15/ty-article/immigration-police-nab-foreign-workers-who-did-not-go-home/0000017f-df0a-df7c-a5ff-df7a95320000

Sabar, G. (2010). Israel and the "Holy Land": The religio-political discourse of rights among African migrant labourers and African asylum seekers, 1990–2008. *African Diaspora*, 3(1), 43–76.

San Juan Jr., E. (2010). Overseas Filipino workers: The making of an Asian-pacific diaspora. *The Global South*, 3(2), 99–129. https://doi.org/10.2979/gso.2009.3.2.99

Sassen, S. (2000). Women's burden: Counter-geographies of globalization and the feminization of survival. *Journal of International Affairs*, 503–524. https://doi.org/10.1163/157181002761931378

Smart, J. E., Teodosio, V. A., & Jimenez, C. J. (1985). Filipino workers in the Middle East: Social profile and policy implications. *International Migration*, 23(1), 29–43. https://doi.org/10.1111/j.1468-2435.1985.tb00565.x

Solomon, M. S. (2009). State-led migration, democratic legitimacy, and deterritorialization: The Philippines' labour export model. *European Journal of East Asian Studies*, 8(2), 275–300. https://doi.org/10.1163/156805809X12553326569759

Sri Tharan, C. T. (2009). *Gender, migration and social change: The return of Filipino women migrant workers*. Ph.D. Thesis. University of Sussex.

Stiell, B., & England, K. (1997). Domestic distinctions: Constructing difference among paid domestic workers in Toronto. *Gender, Place and Culture*, 4(3), 339–359. https://doi.org/10.1080/09663699725387

Tabuga, A. D., & Cabaero, C. C. (2021). Toward an inclusive social insurance coverage in the philippines: Examining gender disparities. Research Paper Series No. 2021-06, Philippine Institute for Developmental Studies (PIDS).

Tyner, J. A. (1999). The global context of gendered labor migration from the Philippines to the United States. *American Behavioral Scientist*, 42(4), 671–689. https://doi.org/10.1177/00027649921954417

Tyner, J. A. (2000). Global cities and circuits of global labor: The case of Manila, Philippine. *Professional Geographer*, *52*(1), 61–74. https://doi.org/10.1111/0033-0124.00205

Tyner, J. A. (2004). Made in the Philippines: Gendered discourses and the making of migrants. Routledge Curzon.

United Nations. (2020). *Mainstreaming ageing in Israel*. May 2020. United Nations Geneva. https://unece.org/sites/default/files/2021-03/Israel_CN_EN.pdf

Willen, S. (2003). Perspectives on labour migration in Israel. *Revue europeenne des migrations internationals*, *19*(3), 243–262.

Xiang, B., & Lindquist, J. (2014). Migration infrastructure. *International Migration Review*, *48*(1), 122–148. https://doi.org/10.1111/imre.12141

Yeoh, B., & Huang, S. (2000). Home and away: Foreign domestic workers and negotiations of diasporic identity in Singapore. *Women's Studies International Forum*, *23*(4), 413–429. https://doi.org/10.1016/S0277-5395(00)00105-9

2. "Unsettled Settlers" in South Tel Aviv

Abstract: This chapter provides a broad picture of the multi-ethnic neighborhood of *Neve Sha'anan* where shared flats have sprouted up and describes how the Filipino society is formed, transforming the marginalized and stigmatized urban periphery into the dynamic center of a migrant economy and network formation. Working as live-in care workers, Filipino migrants need cheap accommodation on weekends to retreat from their work and enjoy freedom in familiar atmosphere. The combination of cheap housing and a thriving service sector that caters to their specific needs, as well as easy access, function as a magnet for migrant workers. This chapter also shows how the flat serves as a settlement location and gateway to Filipino society for the migrants, drawing their settlement experiences.

Keywords: *Neve Sha'anan* neighborhood, migrant settlement, spatial segregation, informal economy

In Tel Aviv there is a hidden place of *Neve Sha'anan* neighborhood that exists like an isolated island. The largest bus terminal in the country, simply called *Tachana Markazit* (Central Bus Station of Tel Aviv), is located at the entrance of the neighborhood. Although thousands of passengers come and go through this building, almost no one emerges to visit the neighborhood because this area is notorious as an urban slum. More distinctively, the neighborhood has different life rhythms. When *Shabbat* begins on Friday afternoon, the neighborhood begins to bustle with foreigners from the Philippines, China, Nepal, Thailand, India and African countries, while other parts of the city stop. On Sunday when a new week begins, on the contrary, the neighborhood abruptly turns into a quiet and empty place.

In this chapter I trace how the Filipino migrants turn the *Neve Sha'anan* neighborhood of Tel Aviv into the greatest migrant settlement in the country, addressing their social and spatial segregation in Israel. The first section explores how the *Neve Sha'anan* neighborhood has emerged as a migrant settlement, providing the historical context of the neighborhood and mapping out the urban setting of *Neve Sha'anan*. The second section provides a broad picture of the Filipino society in the ethnically diverse neighborhood where the shared flats sprouted out. And it also describes the ways in which the Filipino migrants develop an informal economy sector, which is activated only on weekends, drawing attention to a variety of activities that are practiced outside legal and formal frameworks.

Emergence of a Migrant Neighborhood

Historical Overview of Neve Sha'anan

Neve Sha'anan, along with *Shapira* and *Hatikva*, is a typical low-income residential neighborhood located in the southwest side of Tel Aviv (see Map 2). As the fastest growing city in Israel, Tel Aviv has undergone rapid change since its foundation in 1909 under Ottoman control of Palestine. Following the British conquest of Palestine in 1918, Tel Aviv was granted municipal status and rapidly expanded. On this process the dividing line between north and south has been drawn as a barrier between different national/ethnic and socioeconomic groups (Rotbard, 2015). Since the 1990s, the affluent, veteran Israeli, modern northern neighborhoods have often been juxtaposed with the poorer, highly segregated south, which is composed of migrant workers, asylum seekers, and aging low-income Israelis (Shachar & Felsenstein, 2002).

The neighborhood is bound by Tel Aviv Central Bus Station and *Shapira* neighborhood to the south, *Ha'aliya* Street to the west, *Levanda* Street to the east, and by the Old Central Bus Station (hereafter Old CBS) and Menachem Begin Street to the north. *Neve Sha'anan*, which literally means "tranquil oasis," was originally founded in 1921 by a group of Jewish socialists who shared a utopian ideology (Hatuka, 2010). At the beginning of the 1930s when middle-class Jewish immigrants from central Europe arrived in the city, the area started to attract light industry and was declared officially as an industrial zone (Fenster & Yacobi, 2005, p. 193).

In the 1940s, with the construction of Tel Aviv's first Central Bus Station (now known as the Old Central Bus Station), this area turned into a "transport center" for the country (Hatuka, 2010, p. 128). Throughout the 1950s and 1960s, Tel Aviv's first Central Bus Station continued serving as the largest transit area for public transportation in Israel and the center of commercial activities, offering various types of goods and entertainment. The most modern movie theater in Israel (*Hamerkaz* movie theater) opened on *Neve Shanan* Street in September 1956, while cheap shoe stores occupied the street in the following decade, reflecting the significance of this neighborhood as a commercial and social center.

However, when the Tel Aviv Central Business District (CBD) located in southern neighborhoods began to develop northwards, the southern neighborhoods soon became seen as peripheral to the rapidly expanding modern neighborhoods. Rental prices in the area also began to drop (Fenster & Yacobi, 2005, p. 193). In addition, the construction of the New Central Bus Station (hereafter CBS) adjacent to the existing CBS (Old CBS), which was planned in 1967 to resolve the problem of congestion and overcrowding in the Old CBS, further marginalized this area (Ben-Peshat & Sitton, 2011). The construction stopped in 1976 due to a national economic recession until it was renewed in 1983. During those seven years the unfinished building was left empty, and the CBS became a haven for drug addicts and criminals. Although the construction was finally completed in 1993, it aggravated the physical and economic deteriorations of its surrounding area.

This spatial change caused major social shifts in the character of the neighborhood in the early 1990s (Hatuka, 2010, p. 128). According to Menachem (2000), *Neve Sha'anan*'s deterioration was one of the main reasons residents left after a few years (p. 649). As lower-income neighborhoods with neglected infrastructure and environmental hazards, *Neve Sha'anan* and *Shapira* served new Russian immigrants as points of entry to the Tel Aviv labor market from 1989 to 1994. However, most of them moved to better areas after they improved their economic status, looking on these areas as a stepping-stone in upward social mobility and progression in the housing market (Shachar & Felsenstein, 2002, p. 50).

The "vacant" space was soon filled by the migrant workers who have arrived in Israel since the early 1990s. According to city estimates, within three years after the labor immigration began in 1993, the estimated number of migrant workers in Israel exceeded 200,000, with about 60,000 of these living in Tel Aviv (Schnell & Yoav, 2001, p. 631). There is no accurate statistical data, but the real estate offices in *Neve Sha'anan* agree that currently migrant workers constitute 70% of the total residents in the area.[1] Since the mid-2000s, the influx of asylum seekers from various African countries into the neighborhood has reinforced its urban character as an "exotic" and heterogeneous space. Despite their temporariness and vulnerability, the sojourners from around the globe have found their home in the periphery of the global city, carving economic and social niches for themselves.

This is not only due to the advantages of cheap housing and easy access, but also due to the greater employment opportunities and the basic rights

---

1   This information is based on the interview conducted in 2011 with the staffs from real estate offices in *Neve Sha'anan* neighborhood.

Figure 4. A view of Tel Aviv City from an apartment rooftop in *Neve Sh'anan*

such as education and health provided by the Tel Aviv municipality and NGOs. The establishments of MESILA in 1999 and Bialik school in 2001, which absorbed the largest number of migrant workers' children, are representative examples. Garden Library, founded in 2009 in Levinsky Park under the support of the Tel Aviv Municipality, loans books to refugees, migrant workers and their children. In addition, Tel Aviv-based NGOs such as *Kav LaOved*, The Hot Line for Migrant Workers (HMW), and Physicians for Human Rights-Israel filled the niches of responsibilities for migrant welfare which was ignored by the state-level guest-worker system.

A Sketch of the Urban Setting

The structural fabric of the *Neve Sha'anan* neighborhood consists of residential apartments, a pedestrian mall on *Neve Shanan* Street, the Central Bus Station, and Levinsky Park, which are the area's prominent landmarks. Many buildings in the *Neve Sha'anan* neighborhood are designated for mixed-use. While the upper floors of the buildings are typically used as residential units, the basement spaces of most buildings are rented primarily for retail shoe stores, which used to be the "specialization" of the area, even after most of the retail shoe stores were transferred to the shopping mall in the CBS in the 1990s upon its opening. In what follows, I provide a background sketch of the setting in which Filipino migrants open a weekly market and carry out their weekend routines.

Neve Shanan Street

Neve Shanan Street is regarded as the main road of the *Neve Sha'anan* neighborhood. In 1996, the street was designed as a pedestrian mall partly to ease the way of pedestrians walking between the New and Old CBS, and also to revive the street. However, the project ended in vain. As a main thoroughfare, *Neve Shanan* functions as a commercial center to fulfill the everyday needs of its foreign residents. The ethnic diversity of the area is most manifest on this street, with shop signs written in various foreign languages. The street is lined with a variety of commercial facilities such as grocery stores, laundries, ethnic restaurants, hair salons, bars, telephone card shops, butchers' shops, internet cafes, and real estate offices.

When I visited *Neve Sha'anan* in the earlier 2000s, particularly on *Shabbat* when the foreign residents of the neighborhood used to return to their apartments, the market was especially lively due to the flea market, which opened throughout the year on the sidewalks, providing cheap second-hand goods. However, when I visited *Neve Sha'anan* again in June 2015, there was no festive mood on weekends anymore because the flea market was closed. Although any form of business transaction without a permit is currently not allowed by the municipality, the street still remains as the center of the neighborhood.

Central Bus Station of Tel Aviv

The Central Bus Station of Tel Aviv, which is often called *tachana* by Filipino migrants, functions as a large shopping center as well as a transit point for almost all cross-country and urban bus lines. Comprised of bus terminals and a shopping mall, CBS has emerged as a social and commercial center. This is particularly true for Filipino workers because every Saturday night a temporary market especially for Filipino migrants is held in a designated corner on the ground floor, while most of the stores officially open again on Sunday morning.

Here Filipino sellers rent a small space in front of the retail stores to hawk Philippine foods and products, making the space of unregistered businesses the most bustling area in the building. Most of the retail stores on the line provide a wide range of services for Filipino migrants from money remittance to international phone cards, as well as Philippine foods and products informally shipped from the Philippines. Since the flea market on *Neve Shanan* Street had closed, shops inside the CBS have become the most important public space for Filipinos as a social and economic center. Recently, Israel's Ministry of the Transport and Tel Aviv-Yafo Municipality have announced that the CBS will close in 2026 for relocation.

Figure 5. Levinsky Park on a Saturday afternoon (2011). Photo by author

Levinsky Park
Levinsky Park, which is across Levinsky Street from the CBS, is the only public park in the *Neve Sha'anan* neighborhood. In 2005, the Tel Aviv municipality built the park between the Old and the New CBS with the purpose of renovating the deteriorated urban environment, and as a means to deal with the problem of drug addicts congregating in the area (Yuval, 2005). However, since its foundation this park has been occupied by migrant workers and later asylum seekers who were visible 24 hours a day, either sleeping on the field or in tents at night or sitting on the grass waiting to be picked up for work during the daytime.

Throughout the year, festivals and events among the migrant communities are held in the park during the weekends. According to my informants, in the past the migrant workers had barbeques or socialized in small groups in the park every weekend. However, increasing numbers of African groups dominated the park (see Figure 5). At present, the space for foreign residents' social gathering is reduced. Instead, children's fenced playgrounds and social facilities such as a children's library and public kindergarten are located in the park. Nonetheless, Levinsky Park still remains home to homeless asylum seekers and refugees.

Strangers in an Urban Slum

At first glance, *Neve Sha'anan* is an urban slum, which is often associated with filthiness, drugs, violence, crime and the sex industry. The marginality of the neighborhood is inscribed first in the facts of its physical dilapidation and isolation from other parts of the city. The neighborhood is adjacent to the modern and European "White City" inscribed by UNESCO as a World Heritage Site. However, the boundary is rather distinctive. The features of the low level of urban services and deterioration are evident in worn-out apartment buildings on the verge of collapse, the ruins of the Old CBS and the brothels in its vicinity, as well as the frequent appearance of rats in the streets. Some Filipinos argue that the Municipality has never taken any measures against rats because the neighborhood was an abandoned area.

The lack of security is another factor that stigmatizes the neighborhood as a "dangerous urban slum." Due to the deteriorated urban environment and the security concerns, *Neve Sha'anan* is often described by local citizens as an undesirable place to visit. Actually, it is rare to see Israelis walking around the neighborhood, except for a small number of veteran local residents and retail shop owners working during weekdays. With the massive influx of foreign populations in the neighborhood over the decades, however, the area that once carried the stigma of a deteriorated residential neighborhood with insufficient infrastructure and the threat of terrorism was further isolated, being "characterized as a signifier of social degradation as well" (Fenster & Yacobi, 2005, p. 193).

Some researchers (Alexander, 2003; Kemp & Raijman, 2004) note that from the early 1990s to 1996 the strong presence of migrant workers in *Neve Sha'anan* posed a threat, or rather they were perceived by city authorities as a threat to the city, and thus *Neve Sha'anan* became the object of city planners' rehabilitation with a goal to expel migrant workers. Despite the municipality's efforts, migrant enclaves thrived in the southern neighborhood. Kemp and Raijman (2004, p. 39) point out that by the late 1990s, the recognition period, the city planners reframed the migrant issue as "urban renewal" by considering ethnic pluralism in their project, since they recognized that the presence of migrant workers was not a temporary phenomenon.

However, the strong presence of undocumented migrants and their children in the area was still perceived as threatening to the state's Jewish character. This led the state to enact a deportation policy in 2002, officially deploying immigration police to arrest and deport the "illegal" residents. The state carries out a mass deportation policy that allows the arrest and expulsion of undocumented migrants at any time by simple administrative decree. Over the decades, *Neve Sha'anan* has been construed as a hide-out for "criminals," typically those undocumented who violate the immigration law, "contradicting the state's interest in relation to its demographic agenda and sovereignty" (Yacobi, 2008, p. 1) and are supposed to be directly sent to detention facilities to be deported.

A complex web of social, cultural, political and economic forces serves to keep the foreign residents in *Neve Sha'anan*, stigmatized as a source of pollution and illegality. The social prejudice over the inferiority of its foreign residents with symbolic degradation associated with their poverty and ethnic origins as non-Jewish reinforced the stigmatization of *Neve Sha'anan* as a dangerous urban slum. A public concern arose that the rise of the crime rate in the area was closely related to the collective presence of the Africans.

The media also reported that there was a significant rise in migrant crimes in Tel Aviv in 2012, relying on the police figures, while the local NGO argues that there is no accurate way to reasonably determine what the actual crime rate is in *Neve Sha'anan* (see McDonnel, 2013, p. 18). The mix of fear and anxiety toward the aliens was manifested by protests against African and migrant workers at the community level. For example, nationalist protesters from the adjacent *Hatikva* neighborhood demonstrated against the presence of the foreigners in the area, calling for the ousting of African asylum seekers and foreign workers from Israel. They claim that Africans are responsible for the rise in crime and argue, "This is not Africa. Blacks out."

A group of Rabbis also released a letter, warning the local society not to rent apartments to the "illegal migrants" and foreign workers, claiming that it violates Jewish law (Dona, 2010), and petitioned the Tel Aviv Municipality to this effect. Subsequently, the letter was rejected by the Ministry of Interior. Eventually, the increase in racist and ethnic hostility toward the foreign residents escalated to the level of physical violence. The term "cancer" is frequently used in the local society to describe the status of the Others in Israel, particularly Africans. Although Miri Regev, an Israeli politician, apologized for calling African migrants "a cancer," the Israel Democracy Institute Peace Index for May 2012 reports that 52% of Jewish Israelis agree that African migrants are indeed "a cancer in the body" of the nation (Toi, 2012). Although anti-urban discourse among the Israeli residents most often gets expressed as fear of crime and violence, the issue at root is social divisions and the urban "Other," as marked by class, race, and ethnicity.

It is also noteworthy that the tension and competition arise not only between the migrants and the local residents. Despite the co-presence of the migrants with different countries of origin in the bounded neighborhood, the Africans are singled out as the object of stigmatization even by the Filipino migrants. Those who have lived in *Neve Sha'anan* for about a decade pined for the "good old days" when Africans were rarely present in the neighborhood. Richard, a 42-year-old Filipino man, has vivid memories of *Neve Sha'anan* of the mid-1990s. To his recollection, there were more Filipinos in the neighborhood before the massive arrival of Africans and the enforcement of mass deportation in 2002. He emphasizes, "*Neve Sha'anan* was not like this before. It was *sheket* (quiet). *Ein balagan* (No trouble)." In addition, undocumented migrants have argued that their survival was being threatened by Immigration Police due to the public attention over the neighborhood.

Stigma is not an attribute of the individual who bears the difference but rather resides in interactions between the person with the noted difference and others who evaluate that difference in negative terms (Goffman, 1963). Filipino migrants' hostility towards their African neighbors is created at the everyday level, particularly in connection with spatial occupation. According to Grace, for example, all the non-African residents in a building were ousted from the building. The reason she explained was that Africans had offered the landlord a higher price to rent the building to open a bar and an internet café. The news quickly spread in the neighborhood and the Africans' actions were criticized as immoral by Filipino migrants.

Filipino migrants' narratives of Levinsky Park are another example of the local strife. The park, which is now occupied by Africans, has become a place of "nostalgia" for Filipinos. After its establishment in 2005, Filipinos used to gather in the park for barbecues and weekend picnics. However, as Gary, a Filipino man, argues, by 2008 Filipinos had already lost the park to the "Africans" and had to find an alternative social gathering place on the beach. This situation is evident in the changing pattern of facility use in the park. The basketball court for instance, which had been tacitly shared by Filipinos and Africans at differently scheduled times, has been gradually "monopolized" by Africans. On Sundays I often witnessed that Gary went out for a basketball game but turned back to the flat as he failed to compete for use of basketball court.

Living in a multi-ethnic neighborhood requires a coming to terms with the existence of fear of the strange Other. Distinctively, Filipino migrants' negative perceptions about African migrants as "suspicious criminals" function to construct those Africans and the parts of *Neve Sha'anan* they inhabit as "dangerous." Filipino migrants' narration over the fear of crimes tends to legitimate a racist discourse of exclusion against African neighbors. My informants, most of whom were females, displayed an excessive sense of fear of crimes since there were several reports of sexual assault or rape cases by African migrants in *Neve Sha'anan*, targeting migrant women.

For example, in the summer of 2010 I found my flatmates in a state of agitation. Against the backdrop of rising racial prejudice and hatred toward Africans in the local society, the rumor circulated amongst the Filipino community that five Filipino women had been the victims of rape, robbery, or murder. For this reason, especially at night the flatmates went out in group and walked the other way when finding themselves approaching an African area.

Under these circumstances, those Filipino women who had sexual relations with African men became the target of criticism and were socially ostracized. As I noted already, the overseas labor market in Israel is highly gender-differentiated across the job sectors, and the majority of Filipino migrants are women, while the majority of Chinese, Thai, and African migrants are men. The Filipino society witnessed that Filipino women dated or married male workers from other countries, including Israeli men. Although interracial marriages are socially acceptable in the Philippines, according to my informants, a stigma is strongly attached to the Filipino women who date or marry African men in *Neve Sha'anan*.

I recognized that a woman's flatmates negatively responded to her dating an African man, attaching a social dishonor to the Filipino women who have relationships with African men, whereas they did not criticize relationships with Thai men. The case of Mary, who dated an African man after dating a man from Thailand, provides an interesting example. When I visited her flat and inquired about each flatmate in Banessa's flat, Nancy and Jasmine embarrassedly told me that Mary, one of the flatmates, had gone out with her new boyfriend, "Black." Especially Nancy argued that "most of us, Filipinas, we don't like black men. If your boyfriend is a black man, unless he is Michael Jordan, they will degrade you."

As seen above, the nexus among territorial stigma, insecurity, and racial prejudice toward strangers is highly distinctive among the foreign residents. The stigma of certain people can be transferred to a place they occupy; alternately, people can be stigmatized for their free choice of, or especially for their involuntary residence in an area (Krase, 1979, p. 252). *Neve Sha'anan*, which once carried the stigma of being a deteriorated and chaotic residential neighborhood, has been constructed as a distinctive place with the settlement of working-class foreigners and unauthorized residents.

Mapping out Filipino Society

While *Neve Sha'anan* is home to different nationalities, constituting an ethnically mixed and culturally heterogeneous neighborhood, Filipino migrants establish their own space and exhibit a high degree of temporal concentration by spending their day-off in the neighborhood. In this sub-section, I explore how Filipino migrants carve out their own society, transforming the marginalized and stigmatized urban periphery into the dynamic center of a migrant economy and network formation. Firstly, I provide a broad picture of the Filipino migrants' particular routine based on the flat and then describe how the migrants are channeled into *Neve Sha'anan*, drawing on their settlement experiences. Finally, I briefly sketch the urban dynamics during the time period of my study and present the self-sufficient economic sector that evolves among the Filipino migrants in the neighborhood only on weekends.

Flat on Weekends

When it comes to the routine of Filipino migrants, the spatial-temporal disjuncture between "flat on weekends" and "workplace on weekdays" is brought to the fore. Some scholars use Goffman's metaphor of the stage (Goffman, 1971) to describe how differently domestic migrant workers behave when they are on and off work. In her research of Filipino domestic workers in Taiwan, for example, Lan (2003) argues that Sunday activities constitute a "backstage" for the domestic workers, describing that they reclaim their identities by controlling their dress codes, behavior, and activities. During weekdays in the house of their employers, the migrants identify themselves differently and act like a maid. In contrast, on the weekend they perform an offstage identity beyond the direct observation of their employers (Constable, 1997; Lan, 2003; Yeoh & Huang, 1998).

On weekends, the flat in *Neve Sha'anan* provides an important backstage function for Filipino migrants in Israel. When I asked my flatmates about the purpose of renting a flat outside their workplace, they explained their motivations in relation to their work conditions which are inherent in the live-in status. When I asked Levy why he rented a flat, he asked back, "Where should I go on my day off? If you don't have somewhere to go during the weekend, it is more painful." He claimed that he got depressed with his work together with a bed-ridden old man the entire week, so he needed to go out of the house even if for few hours for refreshment. Levy emphasized that "I feel I am just [out] from a jail. Saturday is a gold day for us. It doesn't come every day. It allows Filipino care workers to enjoy their privacy and life."

The story of Ella illustrates how significant it is for live-in workers to take their weekly day-off because there are some employers who need care around-the-clock or do not allow their care workers to go out on weekends. Ella had worked as a live-in care worker for the first two years without taking her weekly rest. When she continuously claimed her rights for weekly rest, finally her employer dismissed her. Through a recruitment agency she was able to find a legal job as a live-out care worker for a handicapped child. Because it was a part-time work with lower wage, however, Ella had to work as a part-time house cleaner in the house of her employer's friend in the afternoon. Nevertheless, Ella says that she desperately needed one day of rest every weekend and had to find a live-out work.

Taking a brief look at the ways in which Filipino migrants spend their day-off on weekends may provide clues to understandings of the significance of the flat as a key site in their weekend life, which is linked to the "backstage" of the migrant life in Israel. Most of the migrants returned to the neighborhood every weekend, away from their employers' houses, and carried out their own activities based on their flat. The majority of the flatmates worked in North Tel Aviv, Ramat Gan, and Jerusalem, etc., which are located within half an hour's drive away by *Monit Sherut*, while some worked far away from Tel Aviv, namely in Ashkelon and Eilat.

For instance, Wilma in Liza's flat, a single Filipino woman in her 30s, takes her day-off on Saturday afternoons which lasts until Sunday evening around 6 p.m. On Saturday when the family of her employer arrive at her employer's house in Netanya, a small city located north of Tel Aviv, Wilma leaves the house with a suitcase that she packed the night before and heads toward *Neve Sha'anan*. Upon arrival she unpacks her suitcase and goes straight to *Neve Sha'anan* street market. During my stay in the flat, every Saturday afternoon I would go out together with Wilma. While staying in the market, Wilma does many things; she visits an internet café where she buys telephone cards and meets hometown friends there. Waiting for Jennifer, Wilma goes around looking at second-hand clothing in the flea market.

Meanwhile, Jennifer, another flatmate, calls Wilma to join her in the market. When Jennifer joins Wilma around 4 p.m., they go to a grocery to buy meat and vegetables for dinner and go back to the flat. Around 5 p.m. they start to cook and eat dinner with other flatmates. After the dinner, sometimes they go to a flat where they usually remit money to their family in the Philippines or to a hair salon where a Chinese woman had cut their hair. Around 9 o'clock, which is known as the "time to go to *takana*," Jennifer and Wilma fix their make-up and go to CBS where the temporary market for Filipino migrants opens on the ground floor. As the market provides a variety of stuff and food only on Saturday nights, the ground floor transforms into the busiest and most cramped space in the neighborhood, where they have more chances to run into their acquaintances, during the short opening time.

During their stay in the confined quarter inside the CBS, Jennifer and Wilma often meet acquaintances and chat for short time, mostly about their working conditions and flat. The majority of the peddlers and customers inside were Filipinos, and only Tagalog and other dialects were spoken there. On Saturday in the CBS one might feel as if they stand inside an indoor market of a village in the Philippines. Then they come back to the flat around 11 p.m., while other flatmates are already drinking beer and watching a Filipino movie in the salon. Sometimes they visit other flats to join birthday parties instead.

After watching the movie, they start singing with a karaoke machine until 2 or 3 a.m. During this time, flatmates share everyday experiences with each other. The issues of their talk are diverse but mainly about their work conditions and relationship with their employers. The next day many of the flatmates get up late in the morning, while some flatmates leave in the early morning for their part-time work or go back to their work. The remaining flatmates, including Wilma and Jennifer, take off the rest of the morning until they go back to their work around 4 p.m. In between times, on Sunday morning Wilma usually talks with her family in the Philippines via internet phone call or packs a cargo box with a variety of items, which is also an important part of her day-off activities.

The everyday life of Filipino migrants is patterned in a different temporal and spatial order given their work conditions as live-in care workers, and their particular routine gives a different form to the migrants' experiences. As described in Wilma's case, the migrants' weekend routines show a stark contrast with their weekday routines in their employer's house, provoking a carnivalesque atmosphere. Despite the predominant gaze of *Neve Sha'anan* as a dark and deviant place, it is recognized that the flat becomes "a backstage area" in which those "homeless" migrants form a vibrant and familiar place, serving as the key site for their weekend lives. In this way, the flat is redefined as a temporal home place in opposition to the outside world, particularly their employers' houses.

Settlement Paths: Transplanted into Flats

As several scholars have emphasized, migrants' social networks have a great influence on their choice of settlement location (Logan et al., 2002; Massey, 1985; Wilson & Martin, 1982). For instance, Massey (1985) argues that an "individual migrant within a stream increases the propensity for others to migrate in that same channel, thus creating high levels of migration to a specific location." New migrants are attracted to peripheral urban spaces where prices may be low and other residents of similar status reside. An influx into one such location facilitates the formation of a distinctive migrant settlement. In a similar vein, the majority of my informants reported that upon arrival they were directly channeled into the flats in *Neve Sha'anan*, which were inhabited exclusively by the more veteran Filipino migrants.

Considering that the migrant care workers come to Israel through a recruitment agency which is located in their hometown or big city near it, it can be expected that the new comers might be gathered in a flat based on their place of origin or at least a small group of new comers who share place of origin join a flat that accommodates migrants from different places. Significantly, indeed, migrant networks engaged in a recruitment process made a great impact on migrants' choice of settlement location.

Filipino migrants enter Israel as live-in care workers with the work visa, which is already issued to a specific employer, and do not need to arrange a housing accommodation out of their workplace. Nevertheless, I found that usually the migrants' agents or family members determined weekend housing accommodations upon their arrival, even before their arrival. Although it is not obligatory, the task of arranging accommodation for newly arrived migrants is included in the nearly full circle of services that agents provide in the recruitment process. Particularly, those who lack social ties in Israel entirely rely on their agents for weekend accommodation arrangements. The majority of my informants explained that upon arrival they rented a flat in *Neve Sha'anan* because their agents or their family members in Israel instructed them to stay there.

In practice, there was tendency for an agent to manage a shared flat as a *ba'al habait*. For example, Mike and Emma, who came to Israel through the same agency in Manila and underwent the job training course together, explained that they were informed about a flat by a returned migrant who gave a lecture during the course. Upon arrival in Israel, Mike and Emma directly went to the flat of their agent, Mark, and continued to reside there. Like many other agents, Mark works as an agent while working as a care worker in Israel, and manages a shared flat in *Neve Sha'anan*. Most of the flatmates in Mark's flat, including Angela, underwent recruitment processes to Israel through Mark. Although Mark did not push Angela to reside in his flat, Angela rented a bed in Mark's flat upon entry. She thought that Mark was a reliable person because he was a cousin of her close friend and helped her enter Israel as a care worker.

The case of Laura specifically illustrates how agents play a major role in arranging the initial settlement of new migrants who have no family members in Israel. Laura paid USD 6,500 for her brokerage fee and came to Israel in 2010 as a care worker. Laura stayed only one month in the first flat her agent arranged for her. She moved to another flat when she got accustomed to the new environment and established new network. Laura said that she had no choice but to rent the flat through her agent at first but wanted to find better apartment.

> My agent gave me the address of her workplace. When I arrived at the airport, I tried to go to my agent by taxi [at] her employer's house. The second day I went to my agency office, and they gave me the address of my job. Before I go to my employer's house, I first went to my agent's flat [in *Neve Sha'anan*] and stayed there a few days. I think I rented my agent's flat for one month. And then I rented another flat. A neighbor in my work introduced me to her flat.

However, the decision of initial location is not always made voluntarily. Regardless of their network ties in Israel, many informants borrowed money from their agents and had to rent the flat that their agents arranged for them, in most cases living together with the agents. As a money lender, the agents requested "debtors" to stay in their flat. Then the migrants rented the flat over the period of their repayment, which ranged from one to two years. My informants believed that their agents were concerned to lose contact with their debtors and that they might run away without repayment although the agents already secured the required documents from the migrants against default in the recruitment stage.

As already described, Grace borrowed USD 5,000 from her agent for her brokerage fee to migrate to Israel as a care worker but had to pay the money back monthly including the interest. Grace says, "My agent gave me the flat and all of them [other residents] were Filipinos from *Batangas*. The flat was too crowded. We were like sardines." Although the flat was shared by other Filipino women who were recruited from her hometown, given that the agent usually recruited care workers through her own personal networks based on their home town, Grace confessed that she always wanted to flee from the flat which was in an unfavorable locale and uncomfortable for her. Despite the unsatisfying living conditions, Grace had to stay in the flat for three years until she almost settled her debt.

As indicated in the case of Grace, new migrants are forced to live in the flat their agent allocates if they have debt. To illustrate another case, Lisa, who came to Israel in 1997, was able to pay half of her brokerage fee, USD 2,500, with the money collected from her children who worked abroad. But she borrowed USD 2,500 from her agent for the rest of her brokerage fee, a total sum of USD 5,000. When she arrived in Israel in 1997, she met her agent at Ben-Gurion Airport, and they came together to the flat in *Neve Sha'anan* where a group of Filipino migrants lived. Over the period of repayment, according to Lisa, she was forced to stay in the flat whether she liked to stay there or not. She paid back around USD 500 to her agent every month at a high interest rate over a year. After she paid back all her debts, she eventually left the flat.

> My first flat was located near Carmel market. I stayed there more than one year. [We had] many problems in the flat. After I paid all my debt back [brokerage fee], I left the flat. If I cannot pay all, I cannot leave the flat because my agent doesn't allow. My agent was working in Jerusalem and came to the flat only once a month to meet us. Other flatmates also borrowed money from her. After I finished paying all, I found another employer in Tel Aviv. Then I left the flat. I told her I will move together with some of the flatmates. I went to another agency to change employer. We had too many in the flat, twelve. Sleeping like sardines. In the flat, some ladies brought their boyfriends. As I paid my fee back, I had the right to leave the flat.

Joy's account also supports the practice of forced renting among newly arrived migrants. She explains, "If you have a debt, you stay in agents' flat because you have to pay every month your debt to the agent. But I am okay because my sister paid for me at one time. So I went to my sister's flat." Now, the case of Joy, contrary to the experience of Grace and Lisa who were obligated to stay in a specific place, illustrates the role of family networking in providing the newly arrived migrants a housing accommodation and useful information. As Joy owed no money to her agent, she was free to choose a flat. According to Joy, she didn't feel lonely in her first flat because all the flatmates were from her hometown and helped her adjust in the new environment.

Jasmine also shared her story that she received a range of support from her two sisters in addition to the financial support. When Jasmine arrived in Israel in 2010, she directly came to Banessa's flat where her sisters lived with other Filipino women from her place of origin, *Bisayas*. "You know, when I came here, I was sick. I stopped working almost one month. Maybe it was homesick. I regretted [that I left the Philippines for work abroad]. That I have sisters here was much better because they took care of me. All the flatmates here, they took care of me also in the flat. It's very difficult if you don't have anyone. I feel it. If I didn't have a flat, it's very hard." As seen in the case of Joy and Jasmin, many informants emphasize the importance of the shared flat, which provides them a variety of aids, mitigating the loneliness in the unfamiliar society.

Although migrants are channeled into the *Neve Sha'anan* through their network in the settlement phase, they keep renting a flat within the neighborhood during their stay in Israel. As such, co-renting a flat is observed as a common practice among Filipino migrants. Significantly, the migrants rent a flat not merely because they need a cheap accommodation for their day-off and emotional or social aids from the existing Filipino community. As I present in the following sub-section, the development of informal services that meet the distinctive need of Filipino migrants plays an important role in attracting those migrants into *Neve Sha'anan* every weekend, enabling those live-in care workers who are dispersed throughout the country during weekdays to have regular interactions and create communities of belonging amongst themselves even temporarily.

An Informal Economy and Black Market Jobs

When *Shabbat* begins on Friday afternoon, the quiet atmosphere in the *Neve Sha'anan* neighborhood changes as people return from their work in various locations, either nearby or far away. On weekends, the streets begin to bustle with people shopping or selling, sending money home, sending boxes, or standing and talking in groups of friends. Especially the aroma of roasted pork marks the full-fledged return of the Filipino migrants who have been away from their flat. Migrant care workers' particular routine creates a distinctive form of sociality, enabling them to stay "in their place."

The festive mood gradually builds from Friday afternoons and rises to a climax on Saturday night when the majority of live-in care workers take their day off. On the contrary, on Sunday when most foreign residents go back to their work, the quiet atmosphere returns, transforming *Neve Sha'anan* into a more typical neighborhood. In practice, the weekend lives of Filipino migrants cannot be fully understood without taking into account their unregistered enterprises and the informal business activities in the neighborhood.

Weekly Market in Neve Sha'anan

Every weekend the neighborhood is tinged with various counter-hegemonic stances. Filipino migrants practice illicit or subversive activities in the neighborhood, which are not supposed to occur in this or other parts of the city. While living in the host society far away from their home, the migrants create a niche for "building home" that serves their own needs, transforming the marginalized urban area into a vibrant space every weekend. Apart from the benefits of affordable housing and easy access, proximity to this infrastructure draws migrants to *Neve Sha'anan*. Many of my informants preferred to rent a flat in *Neve Sha'anan* in which all services are provided within close walking distances. As Liza explains, "I don't want to move because it's too far. I can get whatever I want here. And all my friends are here."

On any given weekend, all kinds of business and activities take place in *Neve Sha'anan*. As illustrated in the previous section, the *Neve Sha'anan* pedestrian market and the ground floor of CBS form the primary sites where such commercial activities occur on weekends. There are facilities such as "*sari sari* stores" (a retailing operation in the Philippines) in fixed places. The *sari sari* stores in *Neve Sha'anan* provide various stuffs brought from the Philippines only for Filipinos. As most of these products are brought through informal routes and hidden from taxation, the exchange activities of these products are carried out illicitly.

There are several shops which are run by Israeli men together with their Filipino wives inside the CBS. Most of those *sari sari* stores sell a variety of daily supplies, ranging from Israeli products to the frozen fish shipped from the Philippines. May, who entered Israel as a care worker in the late 1990s and eventually received a fiancé visa because of her Israeli husband to be, was one of those Filipino women who contributed to attracting Filipino workers to the CBS on Saturday night. She installed a large size television in front of her store and kept Filipino broadcast turn on.

The entrance of the store was all the time crowded with Filipino migrants who waited for their friends or just watched Tagalog news. On Saturday night, some Filipino care workers who become weekend street vendors rent an empty space in front of May's store in order to spread out their products to sell. As May brought those Philippine products through informal route, she had to quickly conceal those illicit products whenever she noticed that the police came near. The vendors pay 200 NIS to May every weekend and sell home-made Filipino food and vegetables.

The Filipino store, which is located near the entrance of *Neve Sha'anan*, is also notable. The store serves as a social center for Filipino migrants, which provides the opportunity to send cash remittances to the Philippines and offers a locker service. Locker service is useful for the migrants who come to the neighborhood only on weekends for a few hours and have no time during the week to arrange special meetings or receive stuff ordered from a peddler online. On weekends, for example, Joy often visited this store to pick up the stuff she ordered from an online shopping mall, which was operated by Filipino care workers based on SNS. On Friday or Saturday night Joy went to the store to pick up her purchases. She must pay a small amount in usage fee to the store. For instance, the seller leaves her stuff such as clothing and shoes shipped from the Philippines in a locker after paying fees and Joy, her patron, comes to pick it up after paying fees as well.

Street vendors appear also on the street in *Neve Sha'anan* every weekend. Some Filipino care workers become vendors on weekends and open a stand in a fixed location, hawking home-made food and snacks such as roasted pork, rice cakes, *chicharron* (fried pork rinds) and *halo halo* (a popular Filipino drink) to other Filipinos. Such economic activities among Filipino migrants on the street take place within the informal sector, which is unregulated by law. The street market has long functioned as a central part of the construction of *Neve Sha'anan* creating a distinctive place. However, Tel Aviv municipality prohibited any business activities in the open pedestrian market, and the number of vendors has finally declined. When I visited the neighborhood in 2015, the street was almost empty and the atmosphere was not the same, even on weekends.

Flat-Based Businesses
It is noteworthy that these business activities were typically constituted by informal networks and largely confined to the flat. Firstly, flat-based businesses in which patrons go to visit a specific location for transactions are distinctive. On weekends, some flats turn into hair salons, dental clinics, remittance booths, clothing shops and nurseries. As the service providers work as live-in care workers in most cases, they practice the businesses only during the weekends, when the majority of Filipino migrants converge on the area for their day-off. Information about the businesses and their specific locations usually spread through personal networks by word of mouth and the transactions are fulfilled within flats. Accordingly, I might not have been aware of such businesses without following my informants to those sites during my fieldwork.

For instance, Angela regularly goes to a flat where Joan, a live-in care worker, runs a remittance business. One day when Angela received a call from her mother that she needed extra money for living expenses, she went to Joan's flat with me on a Friday night. When we entered the flat, there were already several Filipino women waiting to remit money. Angela went straight to the desk in the salon to write the amount on the order book and paid USD 220 (including commission). Then Joan sent a message to her brother in the Philippines transferring the transaction details. The next morning, Joan's brother in the Philippines transmitted the requested amount to the bank account of Angela's mother. According to Angela, this is the cheapest and fastest way to remit cash to her family in the Philippines. In actuality, this is the only way to remit money to the Philippines on *Shabbat* when all the businesses are suspended.

Sending cargo boxes to the Philippines is another important service together with cash remittance. Several researchers define the Filipino migrants' practice of sending cargo boxes to relatives as the "materiality of trans-local relations" (McKay, 2006; Rafael, 1997; Szanton Blanc, 1996). On weekends in *Neve Sha'anan*, it is hard to miss the sight of Filipinos packing diverse sorts of goods into these cargo boxes and sending them to their families in the Philippines.

In practice, packing and sending is one of the important practices that take place in the flat on weekends. The flat is the only place where migrants can put their boxes and the only place from which they can send them. Angela sends a cargo box to her family in the Philippines four times a year on average. She places a big size cargo box on the corner of the salon and fills it up with sugar, soaps, champagne, chocolates, kitchen items, clothing and so on. Angela tags recipients' names on each item and explains, "The box is an expression of gratitude. I prepare more expensive gifts for those who helped me to finish my college."

When the Filipino migrants finish filling a box with various kinds of stuff over a few weeks or months, they call the deliverers to set the pick-up date. Then the deliverer visits the apartment to pick up the box at the appointed time and date and transfers it to the storage until it is shipped. When she completes filling the box, she calls Peter and he comes to the flat to pick up the box, charging USD 80 for the service. According to Peter, an employee for a box delivery company, there are six cargo delivery service companies—five in Tel Aviv, which limits the range of delivery within *Neve Sha'anan*, and one in Haifa.

Although these companies are owned by Israeli citizens, the delivery services are carried out by Filipino men. Peter began working as a deliverer in 2009 when he lost his visa abruptly. He bought a second-hand white van for the delivery business and tried to secure fixed customers from among the Filipino care workers who wanted to send boxes to the Philippines on regular basis. According to Peter, his cargo delivery service picks up approximately 300 boxes on average each weekend and 3 to 15 boxes during the weekdays.[2]

---

2   A container accommodates around 150 boxes. First of all, the deliverer buys empty boxes at the price of USD 4 with a 10 NIS tip to the box seller who helps the deliverer to transport the empty boxes and receives the filled boxes from Filipino customers with USD 60 or USD 70 as the delivery fee. In sum, the deliverer takes USD 15 per box for his profit, and he can earn as much

The nursery is also an interesting example of a flat-based business. The nurseries provide a service especially for mothers who work without a work permit. According to Rose, who runs a nursery in her flat, there are several apartments where mothers run a nursery for the infants and children of illegal migrants. Rose started to run a nursery in her flat when she gave birth to her son and became "illegal." As there were many women who faced a similar situation, Rose realized that she could make money with the day-care business. She takes care of infants and preschool children of other Filipino migrants, enabling them to work outside during the daytime, and charges USD 200 per head every month or 50 NIS per day.

Door-to-door services are also provided based on the flat. Sending cash (*padala nang pera*) or gifts (*padala nang regalo*) to the Philippines by someone is an important informal money transfer system. The alternative remittance system called *padala* (send) is significant for the migrant workers who are restricted in Israeli banking service. When a Filipino care worker is going to the Philippines for vacation or a newcomer is coming to Israel, his or her friends ask the person to hand-carry the gifts or cash to their own family in the Philippines, paying 10% as a commission.

Padala is practiced usually among those with the same place-of-origin. If the migrants want to send *padala*, they should come to *Neve Sha'anan* on weekends to contact a person who will be traveling. For instance, May always sends money to the Philippines through *padala*, not though other remittance services, because in *Neve Sha'anan* there are many Filipinos who came from her hometown, which gives her many opportunities to use the service.

Another example of door-to-door services is the peddler. Like Meggie, some Filipino migrants run businesses for extra income by selling various products from flat to flat during their day off. These products are mostly brought from the Philippines through informal channels. For example, Sarah sells underwear and jeans which she receives from the Philippines via other Filipino migrants who visit the Philippines for vacation or from newly arrived migrants after paying them a commission. Angela also worked as a peddler to earn extra income. She usually sold telephone cards, or cosmetics and clothing shipped from the Philippines.

In addition, there is a money lender, who is considered to be one of the most profitable businesses among Filipino migrants. Not all the Filipinos

---

as the orders he gets produce in fees. The deliverers have business partners in the Philippines, who deliver the shipped boxes to recipients. Those who receive the boxes pay commission to the Filipino partners such that they may earn around USD 3,000 for a container.

can manage such a business because it demands significant capital, both economic and social. For instance, Angela started lending money to other Filipino migrants after she earned USD 8,000. For the migrants who have difficulties accessing a bank loan in Israel, money-lending provides an important source of funds. Angela explains that "money-lending is profitable because Filipino migrants always need money."

She takes out a loan payable within a six-month grace period and the interest rate is between 7.5 and 8%. She limits her customer to those within the network of her acquaintances and requests them to attach to the agreement a copy of their passport and documents on their employment. In order to lend money or get her money back, she visits the flat of her delinquents and writes a detailed account of the payments on her note.

Overall, the spatial concentration of Filipino migrants on weekends is related to the feelings of being "out of place" in the host society. Weekend flats and activities are seen as compensation for their marginalized and excluded status. By spending their day-off in *Neve Sha'anan*, Filipino migrants' time and space are detached from everyday routines, allowing them transformative experiences. Significantly, the variety of service-oriented businesses in *Neve Sha'anan* enable migrants to maintain transnational links to their homeland in addition to providing for their distinctive needs by serving them the cheap, useful, and familiar products and services in the unfamiliar environment. Through both visible and invisible activities, Filipino migrants form a virtual territory within their distinct urban landscape on weekends, creating a Filipino *ethnoscape* in the detached marginal urban space (Appaduari, 1996).

Part-Time Work
In this sub-section I describe the informal part-time work of migrants, which is mostly illicit. The informal sectors are composed of all economically relevant activities that avoid state regulation and are unprotected by the state (Quassoli, 1999, p. 213). During my stay in Jane's flat, I had little chance to interview Angela, who is a live-out care worker, because she usually came back to the flat late at night and was on such a tight schedule. Upon leaving her legal employer at 5 p.m., she rushed into the next block from her workplace and cleaned another house for two hours before cleaning yet a third house. On Thursday afternoons she cleaned the house of her employer's daughter who lived upstairs. Even on weekends, she never missed the chance to earn extra money.

The informal activities of Filipino migrants must be understood within the total pattern of the overseas labor market in Israel, which is of particular relevance to the paid care workers working in the domestic sphere. Under the binding system, migrant care workers in Israel are not admitted to take part in the labor market generally, but work only for a single employer in their care sector (Mundlak, 2008, p. 7). However, many of the migrants are actually engaged in the informal sector as described above, and their involvement is not limited to self-employment businesses that meet the needs of migrants themselves, but extends to meet the needs of the local market.

Because the migrants lack access to the resources available within the boundaries of formal institutions, part-time work emerges as an important source of income for them. The presence of an underground economy among Filipino migrants is marked by two job categories: working as a "part-time house cleaner" and as a "reliever." Notably, both job categories contribute to filling a gap in occupational niches in the local labor market. The abundant chances for finding cleaning work in Tel Aviv, the most affluent city in the country, allow Filipino care workers to decide to overstay and remain in Tel Aviv even without a work permit putting them at risk for deportation.

Firstly, part-time house cleaning is one source of income for undocumented migrants. For instance, Richard and Linda, who came to Israel as care workers in 2000 and 1999 respectively, married in Israel and became undocumented when Linda gave birth to a baby. Since then, Richard and Linda have been earning a livelihood by working together as house cleaners. They attempted to find jobs through their Filipino friends who work as care workers and who could match them with their employers or the family of the employers.

Richard and Linda have several employers and work every day six hours for each house on average to earn 300 NIS for a day. According to Richard, he considers the payment, working hours, distance, and other variables when he gets job offers. For the last decade, the couple has survived in Tel Aviv without legal status as part-time house cleaners. In 2015 when their children were granted permanent residency, the couple began performing the cleaning jobs legally.

Part-time house cleaning is an important source of extra income also for care workers with work permits like Angela. Particularly, live-out care workers who work within clearly defined working hours are able to take advantage of jobs through the black market. Many informants reported that they have frequent job offers through their legal employer or even through strangers they meet on the street. Angela also started her cleaning job when her employer's daughter gave her a job offer. After that, the neighbors of her employers also asked Angela to clean their houses. Because live-out care workers daily commute between their flat in *Neve Sha'anan* and an employer's house they are free to take on additional labor once their legal work is complete. This was the reason that Angela changed her work pattern from live-in to live-out.

Reliever work is also an important way to earn extra money. As already mentioned above, the employment of a reliever is popularly practiced among migrants. This informal job niche was created by live-in care workers who tightly constrain their time off. If these migrant employees wish to take some time away from their jobs, they usually employ a part-time reliever who will replace them during their absence. According to my informants, the term "reliever" indicates the person who "relieves the burden or pain of the long-lasting work of other care workers by temporarily replacing them." When the care workers need a reliever to take some off-hours, they ask other Filipinos in a colloquial way, "Can you relieve me one night?"

Every Friday night, for instance, Angela works as a reliever to take care of an old woman from six on Friday evening to noon next day for 300 NIS. She worked as a reliever for other Filipino care workers who were not given day-off on *Shabbat* because their employer who was bedridden or had severe dementia needed care. Once Angela suggested me to take the job, saying, "It is easy job. You earn money overnight. It's a waste not to take it." According to Angela, migrant workers' time in the host country is limited, so they must make the most of a job opportunity. Angela claims that by taking up part-time work, she was able to save money and start her sideline business as a money lender, even though the major part of her salary was remitted to her family in the Philippines.

Every Thursday after her work, for 100 NIS Joyce also would go to Petah Tikva to relieve her friend who regularly joins a church service on Thursday evening for three hours. Linda also sometimes relives her friends who are live-in care workers when they need to go out for shopping or for arranging other private things. In this case, according to Linda, she cannot say "no" when she is asked to relieve them. The existence of a reliever becomes more important in a case in which the care worker has accumulated vacation time over several years and is due a one-month vacation for which she seeks a reliever.[3]

This puts reliever work in great demand and produces a relatively long-term replacement job niche. In such cases the migrant worker usually "hires" an undocumented migrant as her reliever. If a worker fails to find a reliever,

---

3   According to the rule, migrant care workers are annually given 12 days for vacations and up to 21 days for the tenth year. The migrants usually accumulate their vacation to make it more than one month for traveling to the Philippines (*Kav LaOved* website).

they might not be able to take their vacation. Most of my informants agree that it is very hard to find a reliever when they are in need. Angela states that finding a reliever at the very moment is "like getting blood from a stone." Workers pay extra money to meet the higher salary of their relievers. According to Grace, as of 2011 relievers receive USD 1,000 per month while a legal workers' wage is between USD 800 and 900. The difference is paid by the worker who hires a reliever.

Bibliography

Alexander, M. (2003). *Host-stranger relations in Rome, Tel Aviv, Paris and Amsterdam: A comparison of local policies toward labour migrants*. Doctoral Thesis, University of Amsterdam, The Netherlands.

Ben-Peshat, M., & Sitton, S. (2011). Glocalized New Age spirituality: A mental map of the new Central Bus Station in Tel Aviv, deciphered through its visual codes and based on ethno-visual research. *Journal of Visual Literacy, 30*(2), 64–90. https://doi.org/10.1080/23796529.2011.11674690

Constable, N. (1997). *Maid to order in Hong Kong: Stories of Filipina workers*. Cornell University Press.

Dona, W. (2010, July 8). Tel Aviv rabbis: Renting apartments to foreign workers violates Jewish law. *Ha'aretz*. https://www.haaretz.com/2010-07-08/ty-article/tel-aviv-rabbis-renting-apartments-to-foreign-workers-violates-jewish-law/0000017f-db9d-d856-a37f-ffddf2e80000

Fenster, T., & Yacobi, H. (2005). Whose city is it? On urban planning and local knowledge in globalizing Tel Aviv-Jaffa. *Planning Theory & Practice, 6*(2), 191–211. https://doi.org/10.1080/14649350500137051

Goffman, E. (1963). *Stigma: Notes on the management of spoiled identity*. Prentice-Hall.

Goffman, E. (1971). *The presentation of self in everyday life*. Anchor Books.

Hatuka, T. (2010). *Violent acts and urban space in contemporary Tel Aviv*. University of Texas Press.

Krase, J. (1979). *Stigmatized places, stigmatized people*: Crown Heights and Prospect-Lefferts Garddens.

Lan, P. (2003). Negotiating social boundaries and private zones: The micropolitics of employing migrant domestic workers. *Social Problems, 50*(4), 525–549. https://doi.org/10.1525/sp.2003.50.4.525

Logan, J. R., Zhang, W., & Alba, R. D. (2002). Immigrant enclaves and ethnic communities in New York and Los Angeles. *American Sociological Review, 67*(2), 299–322. https://doi.org/10.2307/3088897

Massey, D. S. (1985). Ethnic residential segregation: A theoretical synthesis and empirical review. *Sociology and Social Research, 69*, 315–350.

Massey, D. S. (1994). *Space, place and gender.* University of Minnesota Press.

McDonnell, L. (2013). *The Balagan: Issues of crime and state interaction in South Tel Aviv.* African Refugee Development Center (ARDC), August 2013.

McKay, D. (2006). Translocal circulation: Place and subjectivity in an extended Filipino community. *The Asia Pacific Journal of Anthropology, 7*(3), 265–278. https://doi.org/10.1080/14442210600979357

Menachem, G. (2000). Jews, Arabs, Russians and foreigners in an Israeli city: Ethnic divisions and the restructuring economy of Tel Aviv, 1983–96. *International Journal of Urban and Regional Research, 24*(3), 634–652. https://doi.org/10.1111/1468-2427.00269

Mundlak, G. (2008). Circular migration in Israel: Law's role in circularity and the ambiguities of the CM Strategy. *CARIM Analytic and Synthetic Notes* 2008/32. European University Institute.

Quassoli, F. (1999). Migrants in the Italian underground economy. *International Journal of Urban and Regional Research, 23*(2), 212–231. https://doi.org/10.1111/1468-2427.00192

Rafael, V. (1997). Your grief is our gossip: Overseas Filipinos and other spectral presences. *Public Culture, 9*(2), 267–291. https://doi.org/10.1215/08992363-9-2-267

Rotbard, S. (2015). *White city, Black city: Architecture and war in Tel Aviv and Jaffa.* Pluto Press.

Schnell, I., & Yoav, B. (2001). The sociospatial isolation of agents in everyday life spaces as an aspect of segregation. *Annals of the Association of American Geographers, 91*(4), 622–636. https://doi.org/10.1111/0004-5608.00262

Shachar, A., & Felsenstein, D. (2002). Globalization processes and their impact on the structure of the metropolitan Tel Aviv area. In D. Felsenstein, E. W. Schamp, & A. Shachar (Eds.). *The emerging nodes in the global economy: Frankfrut and Tel Aviv Compared.* Springer.

Szanton Blanc, C. (1996). Balikbayan: A Filipino extension of the national imaginary and of state boundaries. *Philippine Sociological Review, 44*(1–4), 178–193.

Toi, S. (2012, June 7). 52% of Israeli Jews agree: African migrants are "a cancer." *The Times of Israel.* https://www.timesofisrael.com/most-israeli-jews-agree-africans-are-a-cancer/

Wilson, K. L., & Martin, W. A. (1982). Ethnic enclaves: A comparison of the Cuban and black economies in Miami. *The American Journal of Sociology, 88*(1), 135–160.

Yacobi, H. (2008). *Irregular migration to Israel: The sociopolitical perspective.* Cooperation project on the social integration of immigrants, migration, and the movement of persons (CARIM).

Yeoh, B., & Huang, S. (1998). Negotiating public space: Strategies and styles of migrant female domestic workers in Singapore. *Urban Studies*, *35*(3), 583–602. https://doi.org/10.1080/0042098984925

Yuval, A. (2005, June 6). Tel Aviv launches green plan to combat inner city drug-addict colonies. *Ha'aretz*. http://www.haaretz.com/print-edition/news/tel-aviv-launches-green-plan-to-combat-inner-city-drug-addict-colonies-1.160502

3. Flat as a Nodal Site in the Mobile Circuit

Abstract: In this chapter I address the dynamics of the flat as a distinct migrant space, which is made up of mobile migrants and yet has a permanent structure as a settlement with multiple advantages. In pursuit of common causes as care workers, the migrants attempt to form a cohesive community with an ideal of equality and homogeneity. However, migrants reposition themselves in a given social context and constantly negotiate the differences and identities of competing discourses within the flat. The practice of transfer is seen as the most important strategy by the migrants for dealing with these internal differences and conflicts in shifting situations. Thus, the disparate but mutually related themes of place attachment and disruption are necessarily integrated to confine the role of the flat to that of a key point of departure and arrival, serving as a nodal site in migrant mobility.

Keywords: organization of flat, shared accommodation, place attachment, differences, transfer, mobility

In this chapter I explore the construction of a shared flat and demonstrate how the flat with a permanent structure of settlement serves as a nodal site in the migrants' mobile circuit. I first highlight the organization of the flat as a shared accommodation, illuminating the emergence of new social forms that are in effect only within the flat. Then I take into account the interrelations between different social forms and the hierarchical order within the flat and show how the practice of transfer is a major mechanism through which dynamics of the flat are driven, both by creating and disrupting the social ties of migrants. Finally, I elucidate the construction of the flat that involves seemingly contradictory spatial processes of fixity and fluidity and emphasize the significance of the flat as a permanent settlement for the Filipino migrants.

Lim, Anna. *Filipino Care Workers in Israel: Migration, Trans-local Livelihoods and Space.* Amsterdam: Amsterdam University Press, 2025.
DOI: 10.5117/9789463720403_CH03

Organizing the Flat as a Shared Accommodation

In this section, I describe how the flat is established and organized as a shared accommodation, the ground for community formation among Filipino migrants, signaling its otherness within the majority society. Significantly, co-renting a flat inevitably involves a wide range of cooperative activities among the flatmates who share the space and facilities and split the cost of the monthly bills. It is thus worth noting the organization and management of the flat as a shared space.

Structure of the Flat
There is no reliable data, but according to several informants, Filipino migrants have rented apartments in *Neve Sha'anan* and its vicinity since the early 1990s. According to Richard, when he entered Israel with a tourist visa in 1995 and overstayed for three years, he joined the flat in the neighborhood, where his aunt and other relatives were residing. Most of whom arrived in Israel during the late 1980s and early 1990s, just before the Israeli government recruited migrant workers on a large scale. According to the interview with informants who arrived in Israel in the 1990s, the current form of shared flat has gradually developed in the neighborhood since then.

The flat where I stayed for my fieldwork was usually shared by a number of migrants, ranging from 10 up to 20 or more. In fact, co-renting a flat is a cheap option for the migrants who need the space only on weekends and have little financial resources. While the majority part of the city was under an urban renewal project, the Southern neighborhoods of Tel Aviv were exceptional. Urban renewal ignored this portion of the city even though the apartment buildings in *Neve Sha'anan* were old and in danger of collapsing. Despite the poor condition of the neighborhood structures, migrants decided to rent flats in this neighborhood because it was the only place the migrant workers are accepted as tenants.

Significantly, the communal living space establishes a unique social structure that embodies specific roles and statuses of the migrants, which are defined by the migrants themselves and acted upon. Although there is a tendency for each flat to have a dominant sub-ethnic group and the regional origins play a significant role in determining the company of close friends amongst flatmates, the flat is not necessarily constituted by a particular sub-ethnic group. In order to collect a sufficient number of co-residents to appease the economic burden of renting the flat, ethnic boundaries may be ignored within limits, particularly national limits. Each flat where I conducted my fieldwork was comprised of Filipino migrants with different backgrounds in terms of their place of origin, dialect, gender, age, religion, work pattern, and legal status.

The flat further diversifies the already heterogeneous group of flatmates by dividing them into new social categories. The flat is composed of a tenant, called *ba'al habait*, who made a contract with the landlord and the rest of the other flatmates, the sub-tenants who rent a "bed" in the flat from the tenant. The term *ba'al habait* is used by the migrant care workers usually when they refer to their "Israeli employers," with whom they establish an unequal relationship in their work. In the flat, however, the migrants reuse the term to refer to the Filipinos who make contract with an Israeli landlord for rent and perceive that they occupy the highest position within the flat as a landlord themselves. The *ba'al habait* not only acts as a landlord by subletting beds to individual flatmates, but also performs diverse tasks to manage the household matters.

The residents in the flat are classified into two groups: "live-in" and "live-out." The flat is originally established as a place for one's day-off, serving as temporary housing on weekends to meet the distinctive needs of the migrants, most of whom are live-in care workers. Live-in care workers who return to the flat only on their day-off are labeled "live-in" in the flat notwithstanding the fact that they are absent from the flat during the week. In the same way, live-out care workers who daily commute between flat and workplace are still called "live-out" even though they regularly stay in the flat. In their taxonomy, therefore, I was categorized as "live-out" due to my dwelling pattern that was identified with that of live-out care workers, even though I was not working as a care worker.

While the flat is commonly structured around divisions between *ba'al habait* and tenants and live-in or live-out, it is comprised of more diverse categorical groups. It is worthwhile to note, however, that while the existing categories of gender and place of origin are fixed, the categories of live-in/live-out and *ba'al habait*, and legal/illegal are constructed in constant negotiations. Thus, these features of identities are embedded in social roles and are transitory and unstable, even though composition of each flat is not static and the residents are floating. I describe the four flats where I stayed for my fieldwork to give an idea of their residents and basic living arrangement.

Firstly, Jane's flat is located on Levinsky Street, just in front of the CBS. This was the first flat I moved to for my fieldwork through the help of Angela, a member of the flat. It had 20 flatmates, of which 16 were live-in and four were live-out. The majority of the flatmates were married women in their 40s and 50s from *Pangasinan*, while some were from Manila and provinces such as *Illocos* or *Batangas*. Three of the flatmates were undocumented during the period of my stay in the flat. There were two couples who shared a bed in a separated space. The living room was separated into two rooms by wood panels, one for the couple and the rest for communal space. Another couple occupied an isolated space built on the veranda. As this flat was full of beds, accommodating more than 20 persons, there were no empty spaces in each room.

Secondly, Banessa's flat is one block away from Jane's flat, located in a quieter area inside the neighborhood. I moved into Banessa's flat following Angela and Malou who transferred to this flat from Jane's flat. It accommodated 10 persons, including two *ba'al habait*, Banessa and Analyn who shared the flat's deposit and guarantee cost. Analyn occupied one room in the two-room apartment with her Egyptian partner and acted as a *ba'al habait* together with Banessa. Although Analyn was a formal tenant who made contract with the landlord, Banessa also paid half of the deposit and guarantee. Banessa managed another room where two persons were live-out and eight persons were live-in. All the flatmates were from *Bisayas* except three, Angela, Malou, and Mary, the cousin of Malou, from *Pangasinan*. Most of the flatmates were single women, either married or unmarried, in their late 30s and early 40s and were all documented workers.

Thirdly, Liza's flat is located at the center of the neighborhood, which is very close to the flea market. I moved into the flat through the help of Angela again, where Joy, one of my main informants, lived. The flat was composed of four live-out and nine live-in flatmates. In the flat, Liza was the actual *ba'al habait*, but John, her partner, also acted like a *ba'al habait*. Eight persons, the majority of the flatmates, were from *Illocos* and four persons were from *Baguio*.[1] The majority of the flatmates were in their late 30s and 40s and married. It is also distinctive that more than half of the flatmates established couple relations within the flat. There were four couples including Liza and John, and Ella and Gary. There were two undocumented migrants in the flat during the period of my fieldwork. In addition, Richard should also be introduced as a close neighbor who lived upstairs with his wife and two sons. Finally, Grace's flat is located downstairs of Liza's flat in the same apartment building. It was shared by two live-out and nine live-in persons, while there was one live-out *ba'al habait*, Grace. In the two-room apartment, Grace occupied a room with her daughter, while the other nine live-in flatmates shared the other room. As other flatmates

---

1   I included Joy into the category of Baguio, although she was originally from Pangasinan because she moved to Baguio where her husband was born and lived.

in another room were live-in care workers, they came back to the flat only on weekends, and I occupied the room alone during the weekdays. The majority of the flatmates, including Grace, were married women in their 40s and 50s from *Batangas*. In the flat, Grace and Aileen, mother of her partner, Tom, were the only undocumented persons. When her daughter reached school age in 2015, Grace left the flat and rented a small one-room apartment near *Bialik-Rogosin* school in *Shapira* neighborhood.

The Economy of Shared Housing

The shared flat reveals a "communal" space distinct from other residential houses, with many of the characteristics of the Filipino homeland. What are commonly found in the flat are piles of plastic chairs, karaoke machines with a big screen TV and microphones in the salon, and paper notices including expense accounts for common necessities. Kitchens have dozens of spoons, forks, and dishes, indicating that a large number of people live in the flat. A domestic altar carrying icons of the Virgin Mary and Child Christ is usually in the salon. However, what most attracted my eyes in the flat were the bunk beds that filled the shabby rooms, reminding me of a dormitory, the piles of suitcases, and the big boxes, all of which are material traces signaling the "temporariness" of migrant workers (Figures 6 and 7).

One important consequence of the redrawing of boundaries between inside and outside in the flat is the alternation of public-private meanings due to the migrants' collective use of the flat. The Filipino migrants, who need a place for their days-off only on weekends at a low price, co-rent a flat with other migrants and begin to manage living in a community. Considering that a group of migrants share the space and weekend life, the flat does not serve as a private space but rather is a communal space. A number of migrants share the space and the facilities, while evenly dividing the bills for food, electricity, and water. In this way, the flat is not merely a residential place but exhibits a distinct spatial representation with a distinct temporality for day-off usage.

The space in the flat is designed to maximize the capacity for beds. What is rented to individual migrants is a bed, although the bed is often not rented to only one person but can be rented to two people who have different days-off. When the migrants look for a flat, they usually ask, "Do you have a bed in your flat?" Jane's flat for instance, had two rooms, a big salon, two verandas and a kitchen. The room where I slept was packed with four beds which had folded cots, while another room had two bunk beds and a sofa, which was also used as a bed. Part of the verandas and the corner of the salon were also made into small room compartments, in

Figure 6. Beds in Jane's flat. Photo by author

Figure 7. Carriers in the room of Grace's flat. Photo by author

which double beds were placed respectively to be rented to couples who needed a more private space.

Commonly, each flat requires a certain number of people who are bound by mutual support to share the rent and bills in order to reduce the cost. According to my informants, the maximum price that each of them is willing to pay for rent is around 200 NIS (approximately USD 60). As I describe in the next chapter, the price is one criterion for deciding to join or leave a flat. Such an interdependent relationship among flatmates is particularly notable between *ba'al habait* and sub-tenants. The sub-tenants rely on the *ba'al habait* who "owns" the contract of the rental to secure a space for their days off. Although *ba'al habait* alone makes the contract with the landlord after paying a deposit and guarantee and acts as the landlord, the *ba'al habait* still needs the economic support of the sub-tenants who intend to sustain the contract by sharing the monthly rent.

The management of a flat can be illustrated with specific examples from my fieldwork. For instance, in Jane's flat, the rent was 2,800 NIS as of 2010 and was also raised to 3,500 NIS in late 2011. Upon moving into the flat, I paid 200 NIS in advance to the *ba'al habait* and was given keys for doors, a bed, and a small space for my things. As of June 2010, 21 persons lived in the flat and each tenant paid less than 150 NIS. The rent per head was 90 NIS, but numbers 12 and 13 were couples who paid more to occupy the compartment rooms (400 NIS for a compartment room). In addition, bills were split by head, and *pondo* (maintenance) was calculated by summing the flat expenses. As seen in Figure 8, numbers 6, 8, and 16 (me) paid double for the bills because they were live-out members. According to my informants, this is the rule commonly accepted in the flat wherein Filipino migrants co-rent.

Looking now at another example, in Liza's flat which was shared by 12 persons as of 2010, there were two rooms and a salon with a kitchen. As of August 2010, the rent was 2,800 NIS, which was raised to 3,500 NIS in late 2011. As indicated in Figure 9, while the rent was equally split among flatmates, the bills—including *arnona* (a municipal tax) charged bi-monthly, electricity, and water—were paid differently according to the residents' live-in and live-out status: live-out paid double because they were counted as two persons. There were twelve tenants in the flat, and each tenant paid 235 NIS for rent, except one person, number 9, who paid 215 NIS for rent but did not pay bills because she was absent for her vacation on weekends. Numbers 2 and 6 who paid double were live-out.

As depicted above, the flat constitutes a communal living space, not merely a residential place, and the flatmates who share the space are bound into a web of exchange relationships by splitting the rent and expenses

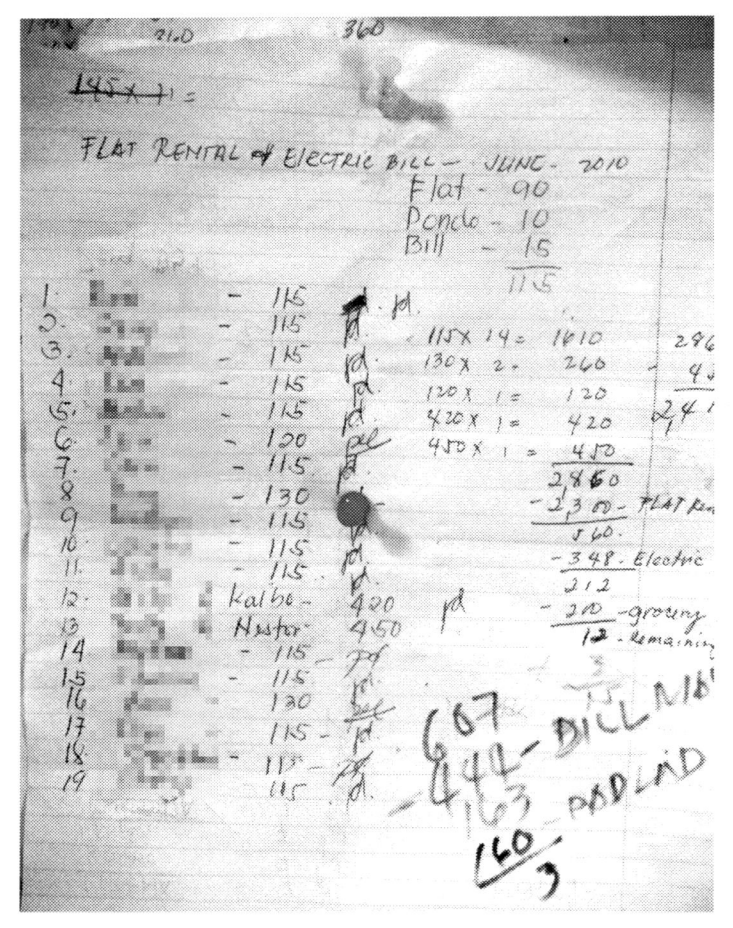

Figure 8. Payment in detail for June 2010 in Jane's flat. Photo by author

hereby sustaining the flat. To be part of a community involves "paying dues" as a supportive member. It gives the flatmates a sense of belonging and membership through responsibility to raise money for rent. Significantly, the flat provides a platform for constructing a community with a unique social structure among the migrants with different backgrounds. The social categories, which are formed within the particular context of the shared accommodation, may influence the ways in which the migrants appropriate the flat as a distinct social space.

Significantly, co-renting a flat inevitably involves a wide range of cooperative activities among the flatmates who share the space and facilities as well as cooperation in splitting the cost of the monthly bills. When I started my fieldwork in Jane's flat, my name was written "Koreana" on the

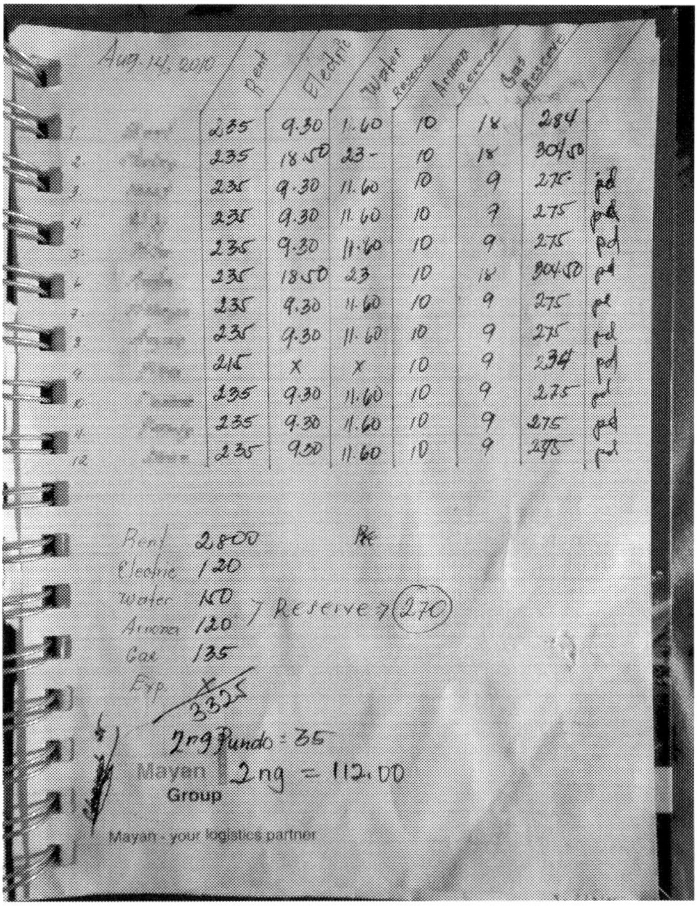

Figure 9. Payment in detail for August 2010 in Liza's flat. Photo by author

list. However, it was changed into "Anna" only after I established intimate relationships with the flatmates after six months of my stay in the flat. It is thus important to note that a sense of belonging is not only achieved by paying rent. Co-renting a flat is a cheap option for the migrants and being involved in the web of exchange relationships provides a good starting point for building a community.

Dynamic Construction of the Flat

As Rodman (1992) contends, "A single physical landscape can be multi-local in the sense that it shapes and expresses polysemic meanings of place for different users. This is more accurately a multi-vocal dimension of place, but multi-locality conveys the idea that a single place may be experienced quite differently" (p. 647). Filipino migrants in Israel share their job identity as care workers as well as an ethnic/national identity as a Filipino. Within the flat, however, migrants with different backgrounds gather together, and existing distinctions may become blurred or clearer. The old order or categories of the migrants no longer "hold together" but are deconstructed. Instead, a new order replaces them.

In this section, I describe the inter-relations between different social forms and the hierarchical order within the flat and also explore how the flat produces different perceptions and meanings for a holiday place among the migrants. I draw on those cases of Banessa's and Liza's flats and investigate how each is formed and rebuilt, while highlighting the driving force of migrant mobility within the neighborhood. I first explore how the flat creates new social forms and relations and further investigate the inter-relations between different social forms and the hierarchical order, delineating the hybrid form of the flat that embraces incompatible realities. Finally, I argue that plurality, conflict and fluidity are the main ingredients in the process of making the flat a distinct social space.

Banessa's Flat
The six founding flatmates of Banessa's flat, including Analyn, came to Israel in 2008. They were "training mates" arriving through the same agency in *Bisayas* province. When they arrived in Israel, they moved together into the flat that their agency arranged for them. According to Analyn, the [Filipino] *ba'al habait* handled two flats, upstairs and downstairs. In the beginning they lived upstairs but moved downstairs because the *ba'al habait* wanted to unite the two flats as many sub-tenants outflowed. Analyn claimed that the six flatmates from *Bisayas*, including herself, repeatedly experienced discord with other flatmates and had no choice but to rent a flat for themselves.

> All the Bisayans [we] who stayed upstairs joined the downstairs. There were more than 40 people and we paid only 100 NIS. But all the tenants in downstairs, they didn't like Bisayan. I don't know the reason why they don't like us. I don't know how many times we transferred. Then one of my friends suggested me to take a flat. So we started to live together, only Bisayans.

In this situation, Analyn and Banessa, who had available cash at that time, made a contract with the local landlord by paying the deposit and the advance in 2009. In this way, Analyn and Banessa began their role as a *ba'al habait* in their own flat. Analyn occupied one room in the two-room apartment with Sam, her partner from Egypt, and acted as a *ba'al habait* together with Banessa. In actuality, it was Sam who paid half of the deposit and advance for their room. Another room was shared by other flatmates including Banessa. Although Analyn stayed in a separated room with her partner, and Banessa was a formal tenant who made a contract with the landlord, Analyn engaged in the communal activities, acting as a *ba'al habait* with Banessa.

I moved into Banessa's flat following Angela and Malou who transferred to this flat from Jane's flat in 2010 July. At that time, it accommodated 10 persons; two persons were live-out and eight persons were live-in. All the flatmates were from *Bisayas* except three, Angela, Malou, and Mary, the cousin of Malou from *Pangasinan*. Mary moved into this flat a few months before Angela and Malou moved in. Jasmin, one of the existing flatmates, was one of her "workmates." Most of the flatmates in the flat were single women, either married or unmarried, in their late 30s and early 40s and were all documented workers.

In March 2011, however, the *ba'al habait* decided not to renew the contract, and all the flatmates left the flat. There were some interrelated conflicts between live-in and live-out over the bills and also the cultural differences between Sam and the Filipino flatmates. During my stay in the flat, I observed that Sam left the flat and came back Saturday night or Sunday morning. According to Sam, he had a tough time every weekend when all the Filipino flatmates returned and cooked with pork meat, which is prohibited as *haram* to Muslims. He asked them not to eat pork at least during Ramadan. However, Filipino flatmates ignored the request and enjoyed their meals. When I asked the Filipino flatmates why they ate pork meat during Ramadan, they firmly answered, "What can we do? We have to eat. I come to this flat to eat pork!"

After a series of disputes over the issue, Analyn and Sam decided to leave the flat and find a one-room apartment for themselves. In that situation Banessa and other flatmates had to give Sam half of the deposit and guarantee, and they sought to recruit more flatmates who would take Analyn's room but failed. Finally, they also decided not to renew the contract. They tried to transfer together but found that it was not easy to move in group including two live-out members. Eventually, all the flatmates were separated. The Bisaya group moved into another flat together, while Angela alone moved back to Mark's flat. As Angela has wanted to join her hometown friends, she just moved into Mark's flat which needed one more sub-tenant at that time. I moved into Liza's flat through the help of Angela.

Liza's Flat

The contract for the current flat started in 2006. Before moving into the flat, Liza and John lived in the same flat as sub-tenants. John's wife lived there until 2005 when she returned to the Philippines. As Liza and John were in a secretive relationship, they wanted to find another flat where no one knew them. Finally, they planned to rent a flat and so recruited flatmates, contacting their friends. When they recruited four more persons, Liza began to look for a flat to make a contract. Just in time, a friend of John was looking for someone who renewed the contract for his flat because his wife and son were deported by the Immigration Police, and he also had to leave the country. Then Liza gave him the money he had paid to the Israeli landlord for deposit and guarantee, and she became the formal tenant.

Since then, Liza and her flatmates struggled to recruit more flatmates through their personal networks to lower the cost that each paid every month. Liza recalled that, in the beginning, each paid almost 500 NIS and sometimes 700 NIS when someone moved out. When I asked Liza why she did not join other flats, she firmly answered, "We don't want other apartment. If you go to another flat, it's very hard to adjust again. It's better to take another flat. So we decided to take this flat."

Among the migrants, those initial members who share the burden are called "pioneers." Liza found more flatmates, and some of the flatmates brought their friends with them. This was the way Jennifer came to join Liza's flat in 2010. Cora, sister-in-law of Jennifer, first moved into Liza's flat with her Turkish partner, and after a few months she asked Jennifer to join the flat.

In 2011 when I moved into Liza's flat, the majority of the flatmates, eight persons, were from *Illocos* and four persons were from *Baguio*,[2] while a third of the flatmates were live-out. Liza and John were live-outs from *Illocos*. In this flat, social divisions were mainly associated with place of origin. This is most clear during the dinner gathering on weekends, which becomes a visible marker of solidarity or boundaries. In many flats, eating dinner meals is the most important and regular event among the flatmates. In Liza's flat, however, dinner gatherings on weekends usually occurred separately in two groups, one from *Illocos* and one from *Baguio*. Joy, originally from *Pangasinan*, joined the *Baguio* group because her husband is from *Baguio*. I was invited to the weekend dinner by each group, and I decided to join those groups alternately.

---

2   I included Joy into the category of Baguio, although she was originally from Pangasinan, because she moved to Baguio where her husband was born and lived.

The majority of the flatmates in Banessa's flat were from *Bisaya*, thus conflicts between different regional groups were not relevant. In case of Liza's flat, however, the flatmates were divided into two groups in terms of place of origin, and the boundary between those two groups was clearly drawn. Tensions grew in Liza's flat when both the identities of live-in and live-out and ethnic/regional identities collided. As seen above, the construction and engagement of people in these ethnic categories constituted an effort by Filipinos to generate social relations where there were none, but the efforts were fraught. These categories operate to enable the creation of social ties in accordance with principles of similarity and difference. In what follows, I provide more detailed descriptions of the differences and conflicts among the flatmates, which become the driving force of moving out.

Contesting Home Ownerships and Regulations

For the Filipino migrant workers, the flat functions as a home far away from Home. The majority of the migrant care givers work on a live-in basis and as temporary workers; thus, they are not expected to own their home outside their workplace. Nevertheless, the migrants transform the rented flat into a home place not only through home cooking, but also through pseudo-family relationships, developing a sense of belonging and place attachment. Although the informants called their shared flat a "flat," they emphasized that their flat is the only place they consider home in Israel, a place that enables the migrants to feel at home and satisfy their desire for intimacy.

Being a *ba'al habait* not only sets symbolic boundaries from other flatmates, but also potentially produces inequality, reinforcing the social distinctions among flatmates. Bourdieu (1989, p. 375) conceptualizes resources as capital when they function as a "social relation of power" by becoming objects of struggle as valued resources. Following this concept, the economic resources that *ba'al habait* holds, with which s/he makes a contract for a flat, convert into cultural and social capitals that can be transformed into irreducible forms of power in the flat. The hierarchical relationship between employer and employee in the workplace is replaced by the relationship of *ba'al habait* and other flatmates, with its strict emphasis on obedience to authority and control.

At first glance, the hierarchical order between the *ba'al habait* and other flatmates is manifest in the occupation of personal space within the flat. To illustrate, Banessa's flat has two rooms. One room is occupied by Analyn and her partner, Sam, and another room is occupied by Banessa and other Filipino flatmates. On Fridays the room of Banessa is packed with several beds and mattresses spread on the floor leaving no space. There are three single beds, two camp beds, a double-size mattress and a sofa in the veranda. While most of the flatmates slept on the mattress and occupied the bed randomly each time on weekends, the bed in the best condition was exclusively occupied by Banessa and all the flatmates tended to consider it as hers. Most of the furniture in the flat was owned by the *ba'al habait* and some part of closet and drawers were distributed to each flatmate for their individual use.

Ba'al habait not only acts as a landlord but performs a role as a leader who manages and maintains the flat community. In actuality, the decisive role of *ba'al habait* in practicing diverse events and rituals related with the flat also reflects the privilege of *ba'al habait* over other flatmates. For instance, my flatmates tended to practice diverse home rituals for house blessings and for getting rid of ghosts according to their religious beliefs. Many of them explained that they participated in such rituals "because the *ba'al habait* wants [them to]." In Liza's flat, when some flatmates left the flat after they claimed they saw ghosts in the room, the *ba'al habait* invited a Filipino shaman living in *Neve Sha'anan*, who was called *manghuhula*, to cast out the ghost. In addition, it was the *ba'al habait* who regularly set and managed the domestic altar in the flat. Every weekend when the *ba'al habait* returned to the flat, they lit the candle, changed the flowers and foods on the altar.

However, the most important dimension of the hierarchical order in the flat is a membership regulation by the *ba'al habait*. It was December 2009, when I tried to rent a flat for my fieldwork, that I first recognized the position of a leader called *ba'al habait*. Commenting on my permission to join the flat, Angela mentioned that "I persuaded *ba'al habait* to accept you in our flat." My informants firmly admitted that *ba'al habait* had the most influence over the process of determining residence either in admitting or evicting someone, while other flatmates had to respect the *ba'al habait*'s decision.

The experience of Angela also specifically illustrates how the *ba'al habait* exerts power in the domain of membership regulation. Whenever Angela was looking for a new flat, for instance, she was first interviewed by the *ba'al habait* who asked several questions about her such as age, job status, religion, and place of origin. When she applied to Banessa's flat, the *ba'al habait* asked her if she drank alcohol because both Analyn and Sam, a Muslim man, hated the smell of alcohol. Angela was accepted only after she assured the *ba'al habait* that she would not drink inside the flat.

According to my informants, at the same time, being a *ba'al habait* carries responsibilities for contacting the landlord to pay rent, equipping facilities necessary for living and purchasing gas and most importantly for recruiting new flatmates to maintain a proper number of flatmates. In the case that the *ba'al habait* fails to fulfill these responsibilities, she would be the subject of criticism. Even though Analyn and Banessa paid the same amount of money for deposit and guarantee, Analyn admits that Banessa is *ba'al habait* of the flat because she is the eldest. However, Banessa was judged by other flatmates as unfit to assume the responsibility of the *ba'al habait* because she failed to effectively carry out those tasks. Analyn claims that Banessa lacks the qualifications to deal with the position, saying, "She doesn't know how to do it."

According to my informants, the *ba'al habait* is often perceived as an individual who saved a lot of money during their long-term stay in Israel, since they can afford to pay the relatively high cost of a guarantee and deposit for making a contract to rent an apartment. Mary claimed that the *ba'al habait* is highly regarded "because they paid a lot of money in the beginning with only five flatmates including an advance, deposit, guarantee and so on. They have right." While the amount of payment to initiate the rent is more than USD 2,000, it is not easy to decide to spend lots of money to rent a flat and take the burden to manage it, especially for those temporary migrant workers whose contract termination is unpredictable.

In practice, most of the informants admit that the *ba'al habait* has the right of decision-making in the household matters and has control over membership. Nonetheless, they do not agree that the *ba'al habait* should control their privacy and personal freedom by exerting an exclusive ownership of the space. It is noteworthy that the conflicts between *ba'al habait* and other flatmates often arise mainly due to the incompatible notions of flat ownership. In short, sub-tenants tend to have a sense of a "collective ownership," whereas the *ba'al habait* tends to have a sense of "exclusive ownership." The disjuncture is well captured in the words "our flat" and "my flat," which are often used by the flatmates and *ba'al habait* respectively.

According to Gary, his *ba'al habait* of the past flats strictly prohibited the flatmates from smoking or drinking inside the flat. He said that "there was even a case that the *ba'al habait* did not allow them to invite their friends. There was lots of nonsense. He always told us, 'Don't do that, don't do this.' They control our privacy." Like Gary, many of the informants argue that the flat is "our house" since there is a degree of interdependency and shared working to sustain the flat because the flat can be sustained only when several flatmates share the rent and expenses, although it is the *ba'al habait* who initiates the contract.

Marginal Status of Live-Out

In general, live-out work is seen as an unusual job given that migrant care workers in Israel are expected to work as live-in care workers to decrease a family's burden. This marginalized status of live-out care workers in the local labor market is strikingly continuous in the flat. The categories of "live-in" and "live-out" are created and effective only within the flat where Filipino migrants co-reside. Within the flat, which is constituted mostly by live-in flatmates, live-out flatmates are regarded as marginal, interpreting the exceptional dwelling pattern as non-normative or even deviant.

Several informants negatively assessed the life pattern of the live-out care workers because live-out care workers unnecessarily had to spend money by living out of their employer's house. For instance, Lisa, a live-in care worker, said that she could not understand that some migrants chose to work as live-out care workers and unnecessarily spent money for food, emphasizing her own idea of the ideal migrant workers who tighten their belts during their stay in Israel for their family back in the Philippines. She said, "They came here to earn money, but they cook and cook every day. It's enough to eat pork once a week. How will they save money if they enjoy life here? They should go back to the Philippines someday."

Live-out flatmates are regarded as marginal also in terms of moral discourse. For example, Sandy emphasized the advantages of live-in working condition, compared to the live-out work. She firmly argued, "Live-in care workers are safe from sexual temptation." In her perception, to stay in the employer's house during the week reduces the chance for the migrants to be engaged in affairs. On the contrary, she believes that live-out care workers are more likely to establish an extramarital relationship, avoiding the watchful eyes of their employers and Filipino community.

Some informants also believe that those who seek to cohabit with their partners or to be engaged in part-time work mainly change their work status to a live-out. Although this is not the only reason they decide to work as live-out care workers, couples are encouraged to work as live-out care workers, and many of them do. Accordingly, a minority with a different residential pattern live-out flatmates are lower on the hierarchical reckoning in the flat. The privilege of the live-in flatmates may be enacted in the myriad taken-for-granted actions of everyday life, reaffirming the binary distinction between live-in and live-out. When I moved into Jane's flat, Angela defined me as a "live-out" even though I was not working as a live-out care worker. She provided me with a general introduction about the flat and the responsibilities of live-out flatmates. For instance, every Friday morning live-out flatmates cleaned the floor before going to their work and also on Sunday morning when all the live-in flatmates left the flat. Angela explained that "We [live-outs] are the maids in the flat." According to Angela, she feels obligated to clean the flat to reciprocate the unbalanced exchange of rent and bills between live-in and live-out flatmates.

However, the live-out care workers believe that they enjoy better working conditions than live-in care workers because their daily working hours are more clearly defined. Scheduled time for work protects their freedom and privacy. On the contrary, live-in care workers have limited freedom of movement, living and working in the employers' houses. For this reason, some of the Filipino live-in care workers change their status to live-out to secure the time for sideline businesses, part-time work, or more privacy and freedom. The status of "live-out" provides the migrant workers time to earn extra money in underground opportunities.

Place for "Rest" or "Recreation"

The different expectations from residents and different ways of using a flat represent a further example of fragmentation and heterogeneity. Individual migrants experience the space quite differently, either as a place for rest or as a place for recreation. Despite the fact that flatmates share the perception of the flat as a space for a day-off, involving a transformative experience that allows them to retreat from their work and pressure as caring laborers for others, they experience the space quite differently and have very different perceptions of "what the flat means." The notion of a day-off covers many possible views. Significantly, some of the tensions among flatmates are generated by different patterns of space use, which derive from different desires for their day-off place. As Levy emphasized in his comments noted in Chapter 4, the only way for dealing with his emotional burden was getting out of the workplace and enjoying freedom even for a short time. By contrast, some flatmates who do not join in pleasure seeking activities on weekends complain about the noise. They put more weight on rest rather than recreation when they talk about the function of the flat for a day-off, even though they admit that the weekend is the only time that live-in care workers can enjoy their freedom and autonomy.

Liza's flat provides an interesting case that illustrates how these incompatible views collide with each other, leading to conflicts among flatmates. In Liza's flat, I observed that some flatmates spent most of their off-hours seeking entertainment, by recreating after-dinner gatherings. Playing a variety of card games for money, including *tong-its* ("a three-player rummy type of game from the Philippines"), drinking and singing with karaoke machines were typical examples. In particular, playing cards through the night is the most popular recreational activity in Liza's flat. During my stay in the flat, I had to give up sleeping on Saturday nights when the majority of flatmates returned to join these activities. For those who participate in such activities, Saturday night is the only time that flatmates can join together and practice group activities for entertainment.

To get a good rest on one's day-off, however, is important for some flatmates. Many of my informants reported that they ordinarily experienced disruption in their sleep at midnight because of their employers who often wake them up during the night. Mary, a 50-year-old woman in Liza's flat, works as a live-in care worker in Jerusalem and visits the flat every other week. However, she has never participated in the drinking parties. After dinner, she entered into the room to sit on her bed and surf the Internet. From an outsiders' view, she seemed to just kill time on her off-day, but Mary argued that "I am happy enough for taking time to myself."

In Banessa's flat where I stayed with Angela, on the contrary, many of the activities were concerned with relaxation. Most of the flatmates took to resting on their own beds after sharing the dinner meals. Besides, drinking in the flat was prohibited by the *ba'al habait* because, Sam, the partner of Analyn, was a Muslim who didn't drink alcohol. In addition, the majority of flatmates were unmarried women in their late 40s and Catholic. In this situation, Angela, who was in her 30s and outgoing, often told me that she wanted to leave the flat because she felt bored with the flatmates. When all the flatmates had to relocate in 2011, Angela found that she could not move together with them because their new flatmates did not want to accept a live-out as a flatmate. In this situation, she decided to separate from them and finally moved into Mark's flat where she lived upon arrival in Israel. Fortunately, at that time, Mark was just looking for a flatmate as one of the existing members had moved out.

At the same time, I also had to move out. Although my flatmates and Angela both wanted to bring me to their new flat, there was only one vacancy in each flat. Instead, Angela helped me to move into Liza's flat. Angela considered the lifestyles of the potential flatmates in the flat because the flatmates in Mark's flat were similar in age to her and went out to discotheques or held a drinking bout every weekend. When I asked Angela why then she moved into Banessa's flat, she answered that she desperately needed a flat when she was driven from Jane's flat and had no choice but to move into a flat available at the moment.

Sani, who moved into Grace's flat, represents the case for seeking for rest. He argued that he needed a rest after the live-in work during weekdays. In the previous flat, he was not able to sleep at all due to the noise from the hilarious partying and the lack of privacy. Sani said, "They always invite people. Okay they can enjoy in the living room but they come inside the sleeping room to get their stuff because their luggage is there. But they don't knock on the door. And they are eating and singing until 3 in the morning." Sani further stated that "I want to sleep at night, at least on my off-day. I couldn't stay like this. Even if I have to pay more, I want to take rest once a week. Only once a week. I want to be in a quiet home." Significantly, the different lifestyles on weekends facilitate the outflows of the flatmates who seek for a flat that fits with their desire for an ideal place on day-off.

As indicated above, the formation of flat membership involves not only forging and sustaining networks but producing differences. In pursuit of common causes as Filipinos and care workers, the migrants, who may have nothing else in common otherwise, gather in the flat every weekend and form a cohesive community with an ideal of integration, equality, and homogeneity. However, the flat frustrates the realization of *communitas* (St. John, 2001) and rather becomes the source of internal differences and intersections of conflicting interpretations and ideas. Although the flat is a confined space with a clear boundary, movement of migrants within *Neve Sha'anan* and between flats is remarkable.

Settlement of Transient Permanence

Migrants are firmly attached to the flat they live in and retain strong connections and loyalties to the flat-based community. In the course of my fieldwork, however, I recognized that many of the migrants internalized mobility as part of their migrant lives and even while they desire to settle in a single flat. Ana paradoxically claimed that "It [transfer] is normal. That's our life in Israel is moving on and on. I am already tired of moving always. I want to settle." In my study, migrants' transfers are not just about getting from one flat to another or not a mere consequence of conflicts, but about producing and reproducing the notion of flat in a complex relationship. Both place attachment and mobility are crucial for constituting the flat as a distinctive social space, through which migrants come to experience their flat.

In this section, I elucidate the construction of the flat that involves seemingly contradictory spatial processes of fixity and fluidity and attempt to show how the tension between those concepts constitutes the flat as a space of "transient permanence." It first explores how the coexistence of incompatible differences becomes the key driving force of migrants' mobility and then examines the ways in which the Filipino migrants realize their movement between enclosed spaces, transforming the flat into a transitional space where transit takes place. I trace the trajectory of the flat-based networks through mobility and demonstrate how the flat remains an eternal space of settlement, serving as a nodal site in the migrants' mobile circuit.

"Transfer" in Search of an Ideal Flat

During their stay in Israel, Filipino care workers constantly move in search of a better place for themselves. They decide to move for various reasons in shifting situations, distinctively as a strategy to cope with the problems which derive from the communal life in the flat, such as conflicts with other flatmates and high expenses. Different expectations from flat residents and different ways of using a flat engender conflicts, disrupting the ideal of an equal and homogeneous space in spite of the shared perception of the flat as a place for a day-off. Different notions of the flat, either as place for rest or as a place for recreation, and different lifestyles on weekend, also facilitate the outflows of the flatmates who seek a flat that fits to their desire for an ideal place on their day-off.

To illustrate movement from the perspective of an individual flatmate, Angela transferred six times in five years. When Angela entered Israel, she moved into her agent's flat, but after half a year she left because she suffered from the noise in the flat which accommodated a Filipino woman with her baby. When she moved into another flat, she converted her work status into live-out but the *ba'al habait* didn't want live-out members in her flat. For this reason, she was forced to move out again. Instead, she rented a one-room apartment with some live-out care workers.

When the landlord charged them a high price without showing them the bills, however, all the flatmates decided not to renew their contract. Then all the flatmates decided to scatter, and Angela moved into Jane's flat where Joy, her aunt, belonged. But after seven months, Angela left that flat due to the conflicts with Jane, the *ba'al habait*, who assigned an overcharged bill to the live-out flatmates. Finally, Angela left that flat and moved into Banessa's flat. However, she moved back again to her agent's flat due to the reason described in the case of Banessa's flat.

Liza's flat illustrates the role of boundaries of place of origin and residential pattern that overlap in flat living. Live-in flatmates often complained about the expensive bills to their live-out counterparts and claimed that the existing rule of payment was unfavorable for the live-in flatmates given that the number of live-outs reached nearly half the flatmates. Jennifer, a live-in member from *Baguio*, suggested that live-in and live-out equally split the bills. In return, the live-out flatmates contradicted what live-in flatmates suggested. When I asked Angela her thought about this issue, Angela explained that she agreed with Jennifer because there are more live-out than live-in members in the flat. In the end, it was the live-in flatmates who left the flat because the *ba'al habait* was a live-out.

After the Baguio group, except Joy, moved out, the remaining flatmates suffered financially because seven were not enough to split the monthly cost at a proper price. Joy also moved out when she found a flat to move into. As Joy was working as a reliever without a permit and came back to the flat once a month, she didn't want to pay more than 200 NIS. After Joy moved out, Ella and Gary, who shared a live-out status and their place of origin with Liza, decided to transfer. Even though Ella and Gary had a close relationship with Liza and John, they could not afford the monthly expenses. The flatmates left one after the other and the flat risked being closed down. After a tough time, Liza and John successfully found new flatmates and maintained the flat.

Notably, the place of origin tends to be important criteria for selecting a flat or flatmates who share the place of origin and language. As indicated also in the case of Banessa's flat, the migrants have a greater affinity toward their regional group since they can bond together apparently through the same dialects and foods from home. When the flatmates in Liza's flat were looking for flatmates after the Baguio group moved out, Joy called her friends to ask if they or their friends were looking for a flat. One of her workmates called back to Joy and checked the age, gender, work conditions, and place of origin of the other flatmates. However, when she heard that the majority of the flatmates came from *Illocos*, she stopped asking about the flat since she, from *Bisaya*, said she didn't like *Illocano* folks, and then Joy also moved out.

Back to the stories of other flatmates, Jennifer alone joined another flat where the flatmates shared Igorot identity, while Joy and others moved into different flats in the neighborhood. When I visited Jennifer in her new flat, she said, "I just got a flat from some friends from *Baguio*. You know, every Saturday I went to the Levinsky Park to join the *Igorot* meeting. It is not so important to live with someone from the same province, but I feel comfortable with them." What Jennifer stated tells us the implications of the regional orientation in choosing a flat to move in.

Each flat or sub-tenants have their own criteria for selecting a flatmate, such as ages, gender, legal status, place of origin, religions, dwelling patterns of live-in or live-out, sexual orientations, and lifestyles. The tendency of migrants to associate with others who share the same religious orientation and lifestyle is also noteworthy. I noticed that practical churchgoers who belong to Catholic churches or evangelical churches are more likely to share a flat. When Liza was trying to recruit more flatmates, 10 persons came to see the flat after finding the advertisements on the street and interviewed with Liza. However, they decided not to move into Liza's flat after they heard more about the existing flatmates. According to Liza, they were faithful Christians who belonged to a born-again church and five of them desperately opposed moving into Liza's flat because they found that the majority of the flatmates in Liza's flat were secular and even involved in extramarital relationships.

On the contrary, all the flatmates in James's flat belonged to the Church of Christ and shared the norms and lifestyles in the community life. In practice, the church meeting became a major source of information on a flat. Irene, who was a flatmate in Liza's flat, had trouble with the flatmates who did not share her religious and moral views. The flatmates in Liza's flat, especially Liza, often complained that Irene was absent in the flat on her day-off because she spent several hours in the church. She had chances to interact with church mates on weekends because she spent most of her day-off in the church and obtained information from them. Finally, she was able to move into the James' flat where many of her church mates lived.

Significantly, the system of inclusion-exclusion is an important instrument with which the flat is produced and reproduced as a distinct social space. In a sense, the flat is "a space of inclusion" for the marginalized and excluded migrants who seek to escape exclusion and stigma attached to them in the host society. At the same time, it is "a space of exclusion," by explicitly excluding the unwanted. In this way, the flat creates effects of difference and contrast but as a perfected imaginary form of the dominant society. The inclusion-exclusion system of flat mirrors the inclusion-exclusion system of the host society that allows the foreigners to enter its territory only under specific conditions that require them to work in a specific job section and return to their own countries after contract.

Migrants reposition themselves in a given social context of a flat and constantly negotiate the differences and identities through competing discourses. Distinctively, the interrelations between *ba'al habiat* and other flatmates, live-in and live-out flatmates and the disparate concepts of holiday show how the flat produces multiple or confronting realities within a single site. The acquisitions of power and status established in the flat are culturally generative and exercised in the experience of everyday lives during migrants' stays in Israel.

In this light, the flat encompasses different, often contradicting, identities and meanings in a single site. In considering the co-existence of incompatible differences, the flat appears as a space of disorder. However, the disturbing qualities or the new spatial juxtaposition between differences dynamically reconstruct the flat as a distinct social space, and contrast with these flows from the ideological and institutional orders of the host society. The co-existence of incompatible notions in a single flat enhances the feature of flat as a heterogeneous and contested space, disrupting the ideal of an equal and homogeneous space. In the following sub-section, I turn to explore how the boundary of flat is continually changing with its destruction and rebuilding and demonstrate that the flat serves as a nodal site in the migrants' mobile circuit.

Moving Through Network
In my study, transfer involves not only place disruption but also the disconnection of the "strong ties," which are developed based on a specific flat among flatmates. The notion of flat in my study thus cannot be fully understood without reference to the transformation of network alliances followed by migrants' transfers, as network formation among migrants cannot be understood without reference to the flat. Significantly, movement between flats through one's personal networks tends to affect the dynamic composition of the flat community because such friendship networks may facilitate onward mobility, being involved in bringing people to a specific flat, and this tends to lead to the evolving of a social clique. Therefore, the spatial boundary of the flat is not strictly fixed but remains in constant negotiation and tension with the ideal of a truly communal space.

Understanding migrants' acts of transfer entails exploring the channels through which migrants transfer. There seem to be at least three main routes for migrants to find a flat from informal real estate agents, advertisements, and personal networks. Firstly, there are some local agents who manage the flats in *Neve Sha'anan* for landlords. According to Matan, who manages three apartments, there are five agents in the neighborhood who work in partnership with either real estate offices or with individual landlords. Next, the advertisements, posted on the walls in the streets, are a more direct way to find a flat or flatmates among Filipino migrants. However, finding a room or flatmates through random advertisement is not a preferred method but the last way due to the uncertainty entailed. Finally, the most popular and important way to find a flat is the personal network.

An incident that occurred in Banessa's flat provides insight into the significance of trust in accepting "an utter stranger" as one's flatmate. When I moved into Banessa's flat, Jenny, who was supposed to return to the Philippines, stayed in the flat until her flight. Not long after her departure, all the flatmates realized that their valuables and cash were missing. Soon they gathered in the salon and concluded that they erred in accepting Jenny as she had become knowns to them through random advertisement. Analyn said, "I regret I brought her from the street. At that time, we had no choice. We needed someone in our flat urgently." It was within this context that Analyn asked other flatmates to search for new flatmates only within their own networks.

For the migrants, trust matters because of the risk they often encounter. The role of perceived trustworthiness within networks is crucial for linking two unfamiliar actors. For example, when I tried to find a flat in *Neve Sha'anan* for my fieldwork, I called Angela to ask if I could move into Jane's flat where Angela was living at the time. Some flatmates didn't agree to accept me because I was neither a Filipino nor a care worker. Moreover, they were concerned about my "live-out status" as they had already three live-out flatmates in the flat. Jane, the *ba'al habait*, confessed that she finally accepted me because Angela guaranteed me. For the same reason, however, I had to leave the flat when Angela left the flat. Jane said, "I accepted you because Angela brought you. She already left us. Now you don't need to stay here. I don't know who you are. How can I trust you?"

Although strong ties are characterized by high levels of trust, weak ties are most instrumental in linking migrants within the enclosed and tightly clustered space of the flat. These ties provide the migrants both with more opportunities to access other circles or networks for information, and social trust for lowering the uncertainty (Granovetter, 1983, p. 202). According to Putnam (2000), weak ties generate some level of trust, namely thin trust, which is less personal, based on indirect social relations, creating "bridging (inclusive) social capital" that is formed across diverse social groups. Strong ties generate thick trust through intensive daily contact between people in small face-to-face communities, creating bonding (exclusive) social capital that cements only homogenous groups.

The migrants develop loose but wide social networks that typify the sort of weak ties that Granovetter (1983) suggests. The network categories can be complex, consisting of at least two different kinds of ties between two actors. For instance, a hometown friend is also a workmate. The practices of mobility are inextricably bound up with the capital of social networks. The newly arrived migrants are channeled into a flat through their pre-existing ties such as family or their agents. As the majority of the migrants borrow money for brokerage fees from their agent, the migrants are expected to move into a flat arranged by their agents and stay until their agents paid off. Over time, however, they find opportunities to develop different social ties, largely based on their flat and workplace, through which they can gain access to other flats.

Upon arrival migrants form network ties very quickly, and these networks play a central role in sustaining and supporting their movement from flat to flat. The importance of personal networks in linking individual migrants with a flat is inherent in the character of a fortified space that is designated to protect its residents against hostile environment outside. As I describe in Chapter 5, migrants seek to build a shelter through spatial strategies by mutually protecting each other's security and privacy through the tactic of silence as well as physical barriers. Under these circumstances, the migrants prefer to recruit their flatmates within the scope of their networks, seeking to find others who invoke a feeling of trust based on ties of similarity, rather than bringing utter strangers into their private space. Significantly, those who are directly or indirectly linked to many contacts are more likely to find a flat because they function as an intermediary that guarantees applicants' reliability and accountability (Granovetter, 1995, p. 53–54).

The experiences of Angela suggest some of the ways in which migrants combine "bridging" capital with "bonding" capital to access a flat and enter into the enclosed space to become an "insider." When Angela was looking for a flat, she contacted most of her acquaintances to ask for information. In a short time, she received calls from several of her friends and relatives. Every weekend, she visited those flats which were offered by them and interviewed with the *ba'al habaits*. Finally, Angela moved into a flat through Joy, her aunt. Joy connected Angela with Annie, one of her workmates. According to Annie, she helped Angela even though she didn't know Angela in person because Angela was a niece of her close friend. In essence, one needs to be at least "a friend [or relative] of a friend [or relative]."

Flat as a Nodal Site in Migrant Mobility

Transfer involves not only place disruption but also the disconnection of the "strong ties" which developed among flatmates. As a network of flatmates forms and disbands quickly, it seems to be adaptive and relatively transient. Although the flat is a space of exclusivity, which regulates outsiders' access, it is simultaneously an open space because migrants are able to negotiate the boundaries entering and leaving the flat. Once migrants get permission to join a flat, they enjoy privilege as insiders within the fortified space where their privacy and security are protected. On the contrary, they become outsiders when they get out of the flat or return to the Philippines.

The creation of an enclosure contains, in Simmel's words, the "possibility at any moment of stepping out of this limitation into freedom" (Simmel,

1994, p. 10). Although attachments to the community of a flat left behind inevitably fades, the migrants attempt to be quickly attached to a new flat where they move in, forming cohesive ties with new flatmates. While living in Banessa's flat, Angela established intimate relationships with other flamates and a strong sense of belonging based on place attachment. When she moved out of the flat, however, Angela and other flatmates did not contact each other anymore and did not catch up on each other's lives. Although the old flat was only one block away from her new flat, Angela never visited it.

The situation was the same when Ella and Gary transferred. Although they had close relationships with Liza and John, who shared a live-out status and their place of origin, they quickly disconnected their ties with Liza's flat when they moved out. Instead, they started joining the weekend dinner and *paluwagan* with new flatmates in working to integrate themselves within their new flat. Many informants reported that their flatmates treated them coldly and even expressed their anxiety when the flatmates became aware of the informant's plans to leave. Joy shared her experience, saying, "When I lived in Jane's flat, Jane was so kind to me. But she was so angry with me because I left the flat. Now we are enemies." Joy experienced this situation also in Liza's flat. When she told Liza about her plan to move, Liza first tried to persuade her to stay. However, she finally criticized Joy.

Such responses can be understood in the context that someone's leaving may threaten the continuation of the flat community, potentially facilitating a series of the flatmates' outflows due to increasing expenses as membership declines. Migrants constantly look for a flat to settle in and congenially disrupt ties with old flatmates once they transfer because of their strong desires for communitas. Day-offs are rare and involve limited time and space. According to Angela, she was not motivated to travel to other flats during her short day-off, except for some special occasions like birthday parties and business transactions. She felt obligated to participate in the communal activities in the flat where she presently belonged, especially during the prime time of weekends. It is an agreed norm that flatmates share the dinner meals and spend time together on weekends.

The transformative trajectory of the flat-based networks through mobility reveals that the flat is constructed as a space of "transient permanence," which is made up of mobile migrants yet has a permanent structure as a space of rootedness. The phenomenon of migrants' mobility makes us reconsider the significance of the flat, challenging the "sedentary" paradigm of place. In my study, therefore, migrants' transfer is not just about getting from one flat to another or not a mere consequence of conflict, but is about producing and reproducing the notion of flat or community with a complex set of relationships.

More importantly, the ideal flat is permanent or constant with a unique structure and conditions designed to meet the distinctive needs of Filipino migrants. Flats in *Neve Sha'anan* commonly offer readily available facilities and pre-existing networks of flatmates that allow migrants to continue their unique lifestyles on their days-off. For example, when Joy moved into a flat upon arrival, she didn't need to buy kitchen appliances and bedding because the flat had everything. Whenever she transferred, since then, she brought only her carrier. In addition, she was able to enjoy community life based on an attachment to a place, even though the specific place and the flatmates were not the same.

Secondly, migrants need to rent a flat and form a clique in order to adapt to their uncertain and precarious migrant life. As I describe in Chapter 6, the migrants seek to gather together, creating an intimate space far away from their Home, and shield themselves against a hostile environment through the territorial strategy based on the flat. The physical attachment to flat serves as a precondition for the development of a shelter where the migrants find security and privacy. In order to build and sustain a shelter space, flatmates need to rely on mutual help and trust. Under these circumstances, it is a crucial strategy for the migrants to attach themselves to a particular flat and become part of the community, within which they can build friendship and secure their own privacy and security.

Even though migrants use a specific flat temporarily and the entire experience in Israel is "not oriented toward the eternal," the flat itself as a physical space provides a permanent structure with multiple advantages, in which individual migrants can enter and have chances to get out when they wish to move or return to the Philippines. Despite the migrants' temporary status, the flat as a "structure" lasts not only despite the continuous flux of migrants, but mainly as its result. The nomadism of the migrants can be appreciated in the given structure of the flat, which has evolved over time with the influx of Filipino migrants, providing the advantages of affordable price, readily available facilities, pre-existing support networks, and an unlimited contract. Within this, the migrants with temporary status and limited financial resources maintain the continuity of their lifestyles on their days-off.

The boundary of flat is continually changing with the destruction and rebuilding of its membership. The same flat is used by different migrants and the next comers during different times. In this light, the flat is constructed as a fluid space, in a constant state of flux and change, since the residents' attachment to the flat is transitional and in-determinant (Isin & Rygiel, 2007). At the same time, a flat gradually develops certain social forms, while always serving as a reception zone for the migrants who are either newly arrived from the Philippines or move in from another flat. Although the flat is a transient place, an uncertain step in the journey for most of the migrants, in this regard, the disparate but mutually related themes of place attachment and disruption are necessarily integrated to confine the role of flat to that of a key point of departure and arrival, serving as a nodal site in a mobile circuit.

In the next chapter, I explore how the Filipino migrants with diverse social and ethnic backgrounds seek to build a cohesive community based on the flat and sustain it by scrutinizing the interlocking relationships between reciprocal exchanges and network building among flatmates.

Bibliography

Bourdieu, P. (1989). Social space and symbolic power. *Sociological Theory, 7*(1), 14–25. https://doi.org/10.2307/202060

Granovetter, M. (1983). The strength of weak ties: A network theory revisited. *Sociological Theory, 1*, 201–233. https://doi.org/10.2307/202051

Granovetter, M. (1995). *Getting a job: A study of careers and contacts*. University of Chicago Press.

Isin, E. F., & Rygiel, K. (2007). Of other global cities: Frontiers, zones, camps. In H. Wimmen (Ed.), *Cities and globalization: Challenges for citizenship*. Saqi Books.

Lagman, M. S. (2011). *Home-cooked food, basketball leagues, phone calls and cargo boxes as reflections of transnational intimacy and identity among Baltimore-based Filipinos*. International Conference on International Relations and Development (ICIRD), Bangkok, Thailand, May 2011.

Law, L. (2001). Home cooking: Filipina migrant workers and geographies of the senses in Hong Kong. *Ecumene, 8*(3), 264–283. https://doi.org/10.1177/096746080100800302

Putnam, R. D. (2000). *Bowling alone*. Simon and Schuster.

Rodman, M. C. (1992). Empowering place: Multilocality and multivocality. *American Anthropologist, 94*(3), 640–656. https://doi.org/10.1525/aa.1992.94.3.02a00060

Simmel, G. (1994). Bridge and door. *Theory, Culture and Society, 11*(1), 5–10. https://doi.org/10.1177/026327694011001002

St. John, G. (2001). Alternative cultural heterotopia and the liminoid body: Beyond Turner at ConFest. *The Australian Journal of Anthropology, 12*(1), 47–66. https://doi.org/10.1111/j.1835-9310.2001.tb00062.x

4. Networking Through Weekend Rituals

Abstract: This chapter inquires how the Filipino migrants with diverse social and ethnic backgrounds reconstruct collective identity and imagine a cohesive community based on the flat. In the absence of their existing network of support and welfare system in Israel, the migrants develop support networks based on the place attachment, instilling a sense of inside-ness that differentiates flatmates from non-flatmates. Significantly, regular meetings, especially dinner gatherings, birthday parties, and *paluwagan* ("rotate saving association") function as a mechanism to unite individual migrants into a social unit, delineating the flat as a self-defined community and creating distinctive social order beyond the economic advantage. The ongoing process of exchanges and interaction among the flatmates forms a core support network through which they can get social and emotional aid.

Keywords: weekend gathering, flat-based community, support network, pseudo-family relationships

Over the course of my fieldwork, I have stayed in the neighborhood of *Neve Sha'anan*, but not only for my research. As a "migrant" student I had to struggle to settle in the country, and my two-year stay in the flat helped me deal with my homesickness. By sharing rental costs and becoming a flatmate, I came to feel at home and had a sense of belonging. Whenever I moved into a flat, the *ba'al habait* asked me to leave a contact number for one of my friends or family, saying that "we have to know because you are in this flat." They explained that they would try to contact the number if anything happened to me. As time went by, I became aware that the sense of belonging and place-attachment are formed not just by renting a bed and sharing the bills among the members. Although I was not a Filipino, at least in the flat I was accepted as an insider among the flatmates.

In the previous chapter, I delved into the dynamics of flat construction and showed how the flat becomes the source of internal differences and the intersection of conflicting interpretations and ideas. I also described that the migrants endlessly move between flats, seeking for a better place for them, and showed how the boundary of flat is continually changing with its destruction and rebuilding. Significantly, the flat provides a permanent "structure" with multiple advantages, which lasts not only despite the continuous flux of migrants who either move into it or out, but mainly as its result. In this chapter, I turn to explore the ways in which Filipino migrants with different backgrounds and identities struggle to build a homogenous community based on their flat and transform the flat into a community space through their lived experiences and practices.

I investigate how the migrants make the flat a space of belonging through transformative or "un-normative" practices in organizing their migrant lives, with the ideal of an equal and homogeneous space. For this exploration, I focus on the weekly events of dinner meals, birthday parties and rotating saving associations, which are differentiated from the migrants' ordinary activities in their workplaces. I trace the ways in which the migrants establish networks and solidarity, transforming a flat into a community space with a distinctive social order in the local society. By scrutinizing the interlocking relationships between reciprocal exchanges and network building, I demonstrate how the flat provides a site and medium for the highly condensed symbolic representation of social relations among the migrants with different backgrounds, not merely offering an accommodation for the weekly days-off.

Mealtime Socialization: Dinner on Day-off

The analysis of the dinner ritual in this sub-section is concerned with the ways in which migrants imagine a cohesive community, precisely delineating the flat as a social group. The regular dinner gathering on weekends provides flatmates opportunities to establish and sustain intimate relationships, which grounds the development of a sense of community bringing together migrants from different backgrounds. I first highlight the significance of consuming Filipino foods, which are restricted in the employers' house but allowed in the flat, and investigate how the flat provides a key site for solidarity, enabling the migrants to experience autonomy by claiming Filipino food.

Implications of Consuming Filipino Food
Food is a recurring theme in studies on migrants and their communities and it is presented as important in maintaining connections to their home and

signifying ethnic identity among diasporic community members (Sutton, 2000). The significance of food among the Filipino migrants has also been highlighted by some researchers (Lagman, 2011; Law, 2001). These researchers commonly underscore the centrality of Filipino food for evoking a sense of home and reconnecting with other Filipino migrants in the host countries.

For example, Law (2001) shows how Filipino domestic workers in Hong Kong transform public places into a home space through the consumption of Filipino food. According to Law, such everyday experiences can become a performative politics of ethnic identity, beyond the formation of a place where the migrants feel at home (Law, p. 280). In his research on the Filipino migrants in Baltimore, Lagman (2011) also demonstrates how Filipino food has become a means to generate a sense of camaraderie among Filipino neighbors in apartment complexes. He insists that "of all the characteristics and identities of overseas Filipinos that can be observed in their homes, none is more pronounced in its ability to help people remember, imagine and reconnect with home than with the preparation and consumption of Filipino food" (p. 5).

Beyond providing the taste of home, however, the significance of consuming Filipino food is salient for live-in care workers who often face restrictions of food choice at their employers' homes. During my visit to the workplaces of my informants, I recognized that many of them were not able to eat meals at consistent times. They often missed their own meal because they had to prepare special meals for their employers who were required to eat only soft food at an expected meal time. For instance, when I visited Joy in her workplace, I observed that she usually ate simple foods like biscuit or bread. For dinner, instead, she cooked *pansit,* a Filipino style dish, in her free time when her employer was sleeping or resting at night.

According to Joy, live-in care workers who care for elderly people are likely to miss the right time for meals because they have to prepare meal for their employer first and perform activities of daily living including house cleaning, bathing, dressing, toileting and ironing. In addition, Joy claimed that the food in Israel did not suit her taste, although some informants argued that they had a more difficult time in Singapore or in Taiwan because their employers gave them "only chicken noodles." Because the live-in care workers spend the whole week in their employers' houses, they are driven by their desire for Filipino food on weekends. Under the circumstances, consuming Filipino food is a significant part of their weekend activities for the migrant care workers who usually eat alone in their employers' house.

Throughout my fieldwork, food often emerged as an issue among my informants especially during dinner time on weekends. Many of them were not allowed to bring pork into their employers' homes where kosher food is prepared. Pork, however, is a major Filipino cuisine. Some informants confessed that they did cook pork in the kitchen of their employer if their patient had Alzheimer's disease. Jean, a live-in care worker in Banessa's flat, shared her experience that one time she ventured to cook pork in her employer's kitchen. By accident, her employer tasted the pork and asked what it was. Jean said, "I just answered her, 'This is a Philippine food. I didn't tell her it is pork. If she knows, she will get angry with me.'"

John in Liza's flat also shared his experience. Craving for Filipino food John sometimes packed the left-over of the weekend dinner in the flat and brought the food to his workplace in Jerusalem. According to John, his employer is *'dati'* (religious) and keeps the dietary law of kosher very strictly, thus prohibiting John from bringing non-kosher food into the house. John said that he hid the food in his backpack and ate it secretly without his employer knowing. Sometimes he came to the flat at night on a weekday only to take Filipino foods that Liza, his partner, prepared for him. Several informants claimed that the most distinctive cultural differences they deal with in their workplace are associated with food, especially the requirements of kosher eating that prohibits pork meat.

Sally's experience provides an extreme case, showing that live-in care workers have difficulty with "eating" in their employers' house. Sally, who has been living together with her employer, claimed that her employer did not give her enough food during her stay there. According to the government rule, the employer is allowed to deduct up to 10% of the minimum salary (not mandatory) if the care worker gets food from the employer and doesn't buy everything alone. However, Sally claimed that her employer provided her with some snacks, chicken wings and rice and cooked only on Fridays, her off-day. In this situation, Sally had to spend extra money for her food. When the daughter of her employer came to visit her mother, Sally complained about the situation. She was subsequently let go.

Under these circumstances, the flat serves as the only place where migrants are allowed to consume Filipino food in their own way, constructing a space of autonomy in contrast particularly with the workplace where the migrants have limited freedom. Within the flat on weekends, the migrants have freedom to enjoy their autonomy through the elements of resistance and transgression in the sense that they eat whatever they want, specifically pork, which is widely prohibited in Israel society. Sally explains, "We eat with hands only in the flat because my employer will think we are barbarian if they see us eating like this." Their persistence of eating Filipino food with their hands (*Kamaya*n) can be a way of "feeling at home," enhancing their sense of control in their own space. In this way, the flat obtains its meaning as "a space of autonomy," in contrast with the workplace where the migrants have limited autonomy in regard to food choice and privacy during weekdays.

Sharing Meals as a Community Ritual
In many flats weekend events involve eating together at the same time. Eating dinner meals in the flat is the most important and regular event among the migrants on weekends. Accommodations are made in flats where residents do not all have the same days-off and some flatmates even come to their flat only to join the communal dinner and quickly return to their work. But the typical and desired custom is for flatmates to share their dinner meal. In this context, a substantial portion of days-off is dedicated to preparing and sharing meals in the flat, allowing migrants to build regularized personal relationships. Recurrently participating in the cooperative activities of preparing and sharing the meals, flatmates establish and sustain relationships. This was the most important way for me to establish rapport with flatmates whenever I moved into a flat during my fieldwork.

Let's look at the case of Banessa's flat. The majority of flatmates in Banessa's flat returned to the flat every Friday for their weekly day-off and endeavored to prepare and eat together on that day. On Friday afternoon, the neighborhood of *Neve Sha'anan* begins to be full of cooking smells flowing out of each apartment and from outdoor barbecues. The festive mood continues until Saturday afternoon. On Fridays, those who arrived earlier went to *Neve Sha'anan* market to buy the ingredients for dinner and put a notice of the detailed expenditure on the refrigerator. Once the shopping was done, cooking started at around 6 p.m. and dinner began between 9 and 10 p.m. when all the flatmates had arrived.

Although Banessa and Analyn mostly cook in the flat as they were considered good cooks, flatmates usually cook voluntarily on rotation. Sharing meals among flatmates include also the activities of deciding on the menu and cooking together. Considering that day-off dinners were the only opportunity to enjoy home-made Philippine dishes for live-in care workers, it was not strange to see that they prepared an elaborate dinner on weekends even if it was time-consuming and labor-intensive. Thus deciding on the menu was not a trifling issue.

In Banessa's flat, the flatmates decided on the menu for the communal dinner through online chatting while they were doing their work. Various kinds of Filipino dishes were cooked for weekend dinners. Just to list some of the menus: *Humba* (a stew of pork), *Lechon kawali* (pan-roasted pork), *Sinigang* (a stew of pork with sour and savory flavor), *Bicol Express* (a spicy stew of pork), *pancit* (a dish of noodles) and more. Flatmates pooled money and were drawn together to participate in the practices of purchasing ingredients, cooking, eating and washing the dishes. On each week, eight flatmates pooled around 25 NIS (7 USD) on average for shared dinner.

In actuality, taking the time for preparing and eating dinner meals with other flatmates involved being physically close to others from whom they were separated during the weekdays, providing an opportunity for communication. While the volunteer led the preparation, others sat together around the table to help the volunteer by preparing vegetables and meats, during which flatmates caught up news and shared gossip. All the flatmates scheduled the food preparation for the whole afternoon. As such, the mealtime is shared physically among flatmates who come together after being apart throughout the week. A communicative event bounded in time and space is created, allowing intense contact among flatmates.

Significantly, the weekly event of sharing dinner meals in the flat functions as a mechanism to bind heterogeneous migrants into a social group and create an imagined community based on place attachment, through which they identify themselves as part of the community and have a sense of obligation to share the weekend dinner meals with their flatmates. Each flatmate has their own background in terms of age, gender, religion, place of origin, education, marital status, and so on, but they gather as a group based on the flat, restructuring their networks. It is important to note that the flat is not always made up with members with similar concern or place of origin, but this is sustained by those who have more interest in renting a flat at a cheap cost rather than establishing a homogenous community itself.

Nonetheless, it is observed that place of origin becomes a basis for group formation among flatmates. As already noted, Filipinos have a greater affinity toward their regional or ethno-linguistic group more than to their own country (Aguilar, 2003; Espiritu, 2003; Law, 2001). In her research of Filipino domestic workers in Hong Kong, for example, Law (2001) observes that regional networks are strong in Hong Kong, partly for reasons of language, but also because of networks of families and friends. Law describes that on Sundays each ethno-linguistic group bonds together to share Filipino food: "Cebuanos congregate around City Hall, Nueva Vizcayans in the northeastern part of Statue Square and Illocanos near the statue of Sir Thomas Jackson" (2001, p. 274). The case of Filipinos in *Neve Sha'anan* is somewhat similar although the flat is a smaller place to congregate and while groups based on ethno-linguistic ties are strong, others are also included.

The case of Banessa's flat is illustrative of the integrating mechanism of the flat itself. When Angela, Malou, and I moved into Banessa's flat together from Jane's flat, Angela and Malou did not feel at home there because they were all strangers to the existing flatmates. The only exception was Mary, a cousin of Malou's, who helped us move into the flat. Furthermore, there were distinct social divisions along the lines of place of origin, language, age, as well as work pattern. While Angela, Malou and Mary were from *Pangasinan*, the existing flatmates were from the Bisayan Islands, working as live-in care workers. In addition, the Bisayan group was similar in their age, in their late 40s, and already had a strong bond as "training mates" who met each other in the training course provided by the recruiting agency in the Philippines.

In the beginning, Angela often complained to me about feeling excluded from other flatmates. There was a tendency for the majority of the flatmates to chat together in Bisayan language and to speak in Tagalog when they needed to communicate with Angela and Malou. Angela said that she understood them because she also felt more comfortable when she speaks Pangasinan even they all could have spoken together in *Takalog*, the official Filipino language. In addition, the flatmates tended to cook Visayan food, while the flatmates from Pangasinan preferred their own local food. With that reason, Angela and Malou frequently skipped the communal dinner in the flat. Instead, Malou brought Angela and sometimes me to another flat for dinner on Friday nights, where a hometown friend of Malou's lived.

Consequently, our absence in Banessa's flat deprived us of opportunities to develop relationships with the flatmates because Friday night was the only time when all the flatmates converged to establish intimate relationships with each other. Although we found this flat through Mary, Mary could not help us mingle more easily with the existing flatmates since she came to the flat only once a month on Mondays. Our Friday "excursions" to another flat lasted until Malou moved out. After contacting a number of acquaintances, Malou finally moved into the flat where the majority of flatmates was from *Pangasinan*. After Malou left, Angela and I needed to strengthen our ties with our Bisayan flatmates because we had to stay in the flat on Fridays as long as we shared the flat with them.

As seen above, it is through the dinner gathering that new flatmates come to be integrated into the existing community. Through dinner-related activities, Angela and I successfully initiated relationships with our flatmates. Above all, Angela voluntarily broke into the circle of dinner-related activities. She told other flatmates that she would cook *lezon baboy* and fried chicken for the coming Friday meal. Although Angela told me that she decided to cook the dinner for the coming Friday because she didn't want to eat the

Bisayan-style food, her active participation in the dinner activities helped her to mingle with other flatmates.[1]

Eating Together as a Shared Identity

The act of eating together in a private residence allows the live-in care workers to form a sense of belonging and feel at home far away from Home. Flatmates differentiate themselves from others through the boundaries, generating feelings of similarity and group membership among the insiders. That is, the ideal of togetherness is represented by the dinner gathering, which becomes an important marker of identity and boundaries, creating pathways of inclusion and exclusion in the migrant society. The flat becomes the primary unit for shared eating and community formation among the migrants.

It is also noteworthy that the practice of sharing dinner meals becomes a visible marker of internal solidarity. The continual practice of such social relations and the act of sharing weave a social fabric in which personal encounters, ways of life, and beliefs combine to give the migrants a sense of togetherness. Through recurrent participation, there arise boundaries that distinguish the people who belong from those who do not. The role of boundaries is particularly relevant to a community formation. Migrants confirm their sense of community while organizing bodily experiences of sharing meals. Weekend mealtime is a cultural site for the socialization of flatmates into competent and appropriate members of the community. The act of sharing dinner meals invokes ideals of togetherness and offers migrants a way to enter into established networks.

The boundaries become distinctive particularly in the absence of someone during dinner time in the flat. During my stay in Liza's flat, for instance, I was invited by some of my informants to several birthday parties and occasional dinners in their flats on weekends, thus sometimes I was not able to participate in the dinner gathering in my own flat. Then John, one of the two *ba'al habait*, asked me, "Where are you going now? You don't like this flat? It is only one time on Saturday. Everyone gathers only today. Why are you going out?" Similarly, when Jennifer, one of the flatmates, was sometimes absent on Saturday night as she went to the regional meeting for *Igorots* in Levinsky Park, her absence emerged as a problematic issue,

---

1   Eating habits are not homogenous throughout all of the Philippine Island, having specific cooking styles and ingredients in each region. For example, northern Luzon is characterized by its use of fish and shrimp sauces as well as its ocean fish, while the Bisayan Islands offer an abundance of seafood and raw fish marinated in vinegar (Doria, 2008, p. 7).

especially for the *ba'al habait*.² John's expression of the flatmates' obligatory presence in the flat on weekends gives a sense of the migrants' perception of what a shared flat must be like.

As indicated in the case of Jennifer, in practice, a frequent absence of someone in the shared dinner tends to be interpreted as a sign of his or her leaving the flat. For instance, Joy expressed her disappointment when Carol, a flatmate, frequently skipped the dinner gathering on Saturday. "Before, we shared together. But from someday she didn't. I don't know where she ate but she always said she ate and suddenly disappeared. Maybe she is looking for another flat." Indeed, Carol was planning to leave the flat soon and moved into the house of her friend's employer where she intended to stay for two months until her flight back to the Philippines. When I asked Carol why she moved to another flat only for two months, she explained that she just wanted to stay in a safer place.

A story that I heard from Sandy in Grace's flat also supports the centrality of the act of eating together in maintaining a sense of community. According to Sandy, Lisa, one of her flatmates, had conflicts with Grace two years ago around the issue of sharing dinner meals. On Saturday when Lisa came to the flat from her work, she often cooked food in the kitchen to bring it to another flat where her close friends lived. Her behavior provoked criticism from other flatmates, especially from Grace. In Sandy's opinion, Lisa's use of the utilities was not the only problem. Rather, the issue was that Lisa ate the food with other people, not with flatmates. Eventually, Lisa left Grace's flat to join her close friends.

As indicated above, it is certain that Filipino foods and commensality create and sustain a sense of belonging among Filipino migrants. During the mealtime on weekends, Filipino food appears to be a direct link among migrants, enabling them to reconnect with a sense of a Filipino community in a new environment and evoke a sense of Home. Through the practices of sharing expenses, cooking and eating together, and singing karaoke, the shared dinner gathering serves as a key point of social contact, far beyond simply providing a taste of Home and the autonomy of food choice. By the intense contact that occurs in limited time and space, in their flat on weekends, the migrants produce regularized social relationships as "flatmates" and maintain high degrees of social interaction.

2   Jennifer was a member of the "Association of Igorot Migrant Workers in Israel" (AIMWI). The word Igorot, which means "mountain people," indicates the ethnic groups who inhabit Abra, Apayao, Banquet, Kalinga, Ifugao as well as Baguio City.

Sharing meals include various activities for spending time together as well. Such activities range from watching Filipino TV programs to playing games in the flat, but singing karaoke is most distinctive. In Janes' flat where more than 20 flatmates belonged, once most of the flatmates finished their dinner, they gathered around a karaoke machine, singing both English and Tagalog pop songs. When I visited flats in *Neve Sha'anan* on weekends I found that most of the flats had a karaoke machine, seemingly bringing them "Home."

They emphasized that "Filipinos are naturally good singers and love singing." Their pride seemed to be heightened when Rose, a Filipino care worker, advanced and finally won in a season of *X-Factor Israel*, an Israeli reality show which is equivalent of *American Idol*. Since then Rose has been singing in the hall of CBS on Philippine national holidays such as Labor Day and Independence Day events. Filipino migrants enjoyed singing karaoke and releasing their emotions.

Birthday Celebrations: The Banquet and Exchange of Gifts

While the dinner gathering on weekends is a regularly practiced communal event in the flat, the migrants hold a special feast in their flat on occasions such as farewells, birthdays, Christmas, and wedding anniversary parties. Particularly, birthday parties are a good reason to hold a special feast. I observed that most of my informants celebrated their birthday by offering a banquet in spite of the economic burden it entailed.

Maya, a flatmate in Liza's flat, remarks, "This [parties] is the life of Filipino here in Israel. In the flat we make a big party for someone's birthday because we have only Saturday, and it's a good chance to enjoy." As Ella also stressed, "the significance of a birthday is special because it is only one day in the year and the only way of giving thanks to God." While participating in mass in a Catholic church in Jerusalem on Saturday morning is an individual rite, birthday parties that occur in the flat become a communal event.

However, birthday parties provide not only "a good chance to enjoy," but also useful insights for understanding the flat. This sub-section focuses on the birthday parties that take place in the flat in replacement of regular dinner gathering on weekends and explores the ongoing process of exchanges of invitations, gifts, and labor. Through this examination, I demonstrate how the flat facilitates the formation of a core support network that is comprised of flatmates. I also elaborate on how the recurrent and often purposeful interaction during the party articulates the degree of closeness in relationships between givers and recipients, manifesting a distinct social order and values.

Inviting and Being Invited

Someone who has a birthday gives a feast in the flat, inviting guests to the party. Invitations are usually delivered by online messages, SMS, and phone calls, or indirectly passed on to selected guests. There are no special invitations among flatmates, but the host merely announces the party date to the flatmates in advance. It is interesting to note that the flatmates of the host invite their friends as if it were their own birthday party. I realized this pattern during Liza's birthday party when other flatmates were surprised that I didn't invite my friends. Joy informed me that the flatmates of the host were tacitly allowed to invite their friends "because you are from this flat." We can draw an inference from Joy's statement that "flatmates" of the host connotes a special status, as illustrated bellow.[3]

Inviting and being invited involves etiquette, which is based on commonsense knowledge among the Filipino migrants. According to several informants, it is customary that the invited guests bring their own friends to the party. Under these circumstances I joined a number of birthday parties in different flats. Angela often brought me to the birthday parties of her acquaintances. Many of them do not know each other but might become acquaintances through the party, while some have chance to renew or develop their existing relationships. Angela sometimes visited more than two parties in different flats on one day with a short stay at each. This was the way that she developed new relationships and maintained them. This was particularly important for her as a seller and moneylender who needs a wide circle of personal networks.

However, someone invited to a party from outside the flat should only bring one or two guests at most, whereas the flatmates may invite three or four. On Liza's birthday, for instance, Angela came to the party although she was not directly invited by Liza. Angela knew the people in the flat through her aunt Joy and also because she conducted some business with some of them, to whom she loaned money. However, Liza was upset because Angela brought too many people to the party. Joy also criticized Angela's behavior

---

3 As Embree (1939, p. 401) notes, one of the best ways to observe the way in which the kin and local group substitutes arise is to examine the way in which an immigrant group reorganizes itself in the host society. By fictive kin, I mean a relationship, based not on blood or marriage but rather on close friendship ties, that replicates many of the rights and obligations usually associated with family ties (Ebaugh & Curry, 2000, p. 189).

when she came to the party even though she was not invited, without any contributions or gifts, and with too many companions.

In actuality, birthday parties can be viewed as an immediate reciprocal act made by the host to the guests, and an invitation can be used to shape and reflect social integration or social distance. By inviting guests to the party, the host and guests indirectly express their will to continue or strengthen their relationships, and the guests are obligated to invite the host to their own birthday parties in the future. During the fieldwork whenever birthday parties were held in Liza's flat, however, I never saw neighbors, Filipino migrants living in the same building. I asked Liza and John why they didn't invite the neighbors next door. They answered that they invited them but that the neighbors rejected the invitation. Liza and John ascribed their rejection to the social differences in religion and place of origin.

> I: Why didn't you invite our neighbor (living next door)? You invited only Richard's family (living upstairs).
> Liza: We invited [them] but they didn't like coming. They have different religion called *Igleshia* (Church of Christ). They are different. They are not from Illocos. That's why.
> I: Where are they from?
> John: Maybe they are from "highland" [laugh]. They don't like to come when we invite them. Richard family came from Illocos.

After some time, I had a chance to visit the neighboring flat and asked why they didn't accept the invitations from our flat. According to James, a live-out in the flat, he was afraid of being pressed to drink alcohol at the party. Most of his flatmates are faithful Christians, who belong to the *Iglesia Ni Cristo*.[4] James and his flatmates spend their entire days off involved with church service and prayer gatherings, abstaining from drinking alcohol and smoking cigarettes. The weekend lives of the neighbors, "who are from highland" as John put it, showed a sharp contrast to the "Dionysian" lives in John's flat on weekends. The different lifestyles originating from religious differences as well as a different place of origin disturbed both groups and prevented interaction despite their physical proximity and similarity as working-class Filipino migrants in the foreign country.

---

4 *Iglesia Ni Cristo* describes itself as an independent Christian religion and the largest religious organization that originated in the Philippines, being regarded as posing a threat to Roman Catholic in the country. It was founded in Manila in 1913 and was officially registered as a formal religious corporation.

Significantly, the private networks of the party host are reflected in the guest list, which generally includes a wide range of networks such as flatmates, close friends, relatives and new acquaintances, as far as resources permit. Liza invited only Richard's family in the apartment building, in which three other flats were occupied by Filipino migrants. As described so far, Filipino migrants usually spend their day-off with their flatmates, practicing a variety of communal activities including communal dinners, while their contact with other acquaintances becomes reduced. Therefore, it can be said that birthday parties provide a good chance to eat together and maintain social networks. Besides, the party provides a good chance to establish new relationships. Only when invited, can one visit the other flat and meet or socialize with the residents.

Due to the economic burden, however, some informants said that they celebrated their birthday only with their "flat company" or do not celebrate at all. This is the case for Joy. Sometimes she prepared some special foods and shared with flatmates on her birthday but did not throw a party. Even she stopped to celebrate her birthday in her flat after she became undocumented. Considering that birthday parties are festive occasions frequently organized in migrant society, to accept all the invitations means high expenses. For this reason, my informants do not accept all the invitations they receive because of the burden of gifts, even though they are invited to several birthday parties on weekends. This is true also for the party host. In what follows, I further delve into the ongoing process of the exchange of gifts and labor, illuminating the operation of pseudo-family relationships and the degree of closeness among the flatmates.

Building Community Through Reciprocity

Birthday parties function as a mechanism to establish a transactional relationship between individuals through a sequence of reciprocal gift exchanges (Barth, 1966). The giver and receiver are bound by a moral obligation to give, receive and reply. As Mauss (1990) emphasized, to repay is the most important obligation in the circuit of gift-giving. When there is someone's birthday party in the flat, migrants exchange gifts. Interestingly, the flatmates and close friends of the host usually bring home-made Filipino dishes or cash as a gift, which indicates that the gift giver intends to share the burden of the host. The food that the host receives as a gift is also consumed immediately during the party, being put on the table. This is understandable given the economic burden for the host.

According to Ella, Gary's partner, in Liza's flat, Gary spent roughly 1,500 NIS (USD 400) for the feast on his birthday. Considering that the care workers' wage is around USD 1,000 per month and the majority of their salary is sent back to their families in the Philippines, it seems that throwing a party is indeed a heavy burden. On his and Ella's birthday, they buy meats, vegetables, and several boxes of beers and bottles of coca cola, and then their flatmates help them cook or cook foods for them.

The value of a gift partially reflects the weight of the relationship (Shurmer, 1971). In the context of my research, the sort of food which was reciprocally exchanged reflected the closeness between giver and recipient. The foods which are not simple to cook tend to be considered as more valuable gifts, and these items can be tangible expressions of a close social relationship. Notably, a head of a pig for *lechon*, which is roasted in oven for several hours, is an essential gift for a party among close friends. According to Ella, it would be disappointing if they don't have the roasted head of pig in the party.

In the interview with Joy about her birthday party, Joy proudly reported what gifts she had received from her friends: "In my birthday party last year, Richard, living upstairs, gave me one *lechon*. He roasted it and gave me. The pig's head is very, very big. And Angela, she bought me *Ninakdakan* (grilled pig head). Liza? Only salad. Wilma also [gave me] salad. Ella and Gary gave me *pancit* (noodles). And one of my close friends gave me *papaitan* (animal innards stew)."

During my stay in Liza's flat, I observed that, as the eldest member and *ba'al habait* of the flat, John's birthday party was held on the largest scale, even though he always had financial problems. The feast was prepared on the roof top of the building since the flat was not big enough to accommodate a large number of guests. Many of the guests visited the flat in a small group and left after eating food. Their stay ranged from half an hour to a couple of hours. Some of them gave a box of beers or cash to the host as a gift, while others gave material gifts such as cosmetics or a special brand T-shirt. In John's birthday party, Richard gave John *lechon* after roasting it all day long, as he did for Joy on her birthday. Richard had a very close relationship with John as much as Joy. Ella, who had a close relationship with John and Liza, also provided some cuisine, which was cooked several hours.

For Ella's birthday party, John and Liza, who were called "*abba*" (father) and "*imam*" (mother) respectively by Ella, spent almost two days cooking *lechon* and other cuisines, while Gary and Ella cooked the same menus for gifts in their birthday parties in turn. However, other flatmates "donated" a small amount of money for their gift. They participated in the whole process of the party, providing their labor. Having difficulty in deciding on a gift, it was suggested by Wilma and Jennifer that I contribute money for a box of beer. According to Gary and Ella, they also donated a small amount of money when they first moved into the flat, but the medium of gift exchange changed as they grew extremely close to Liza and John. That is, intimacy influences the budgetary expenditure on gifts and the time involved in cooking Filipino cuisines in this case.

Another form of gift exchanged is labor. In addition to a gift, most of the flatmates helped the host prepare the feast and accept the guests. Significantly, the role of flatmates as a support group is explicit. In most cases the host needs to mobilize labor through personal networks, mostly flatmates, because throwing a party is a time-consuming and labor-intensive job. In the matrix of the migrants' personal networks, flatmates are a core group for mutual support, becoming central to the expression of shared identities and commensality, through which the boundaries that distinguish between insiders and outsiders are drawn. Due to the lack of kin networks in the host country, migrants must rely on their support group for cooking and serving a large number of guests and the flatmates of the host constitute a helping group which may be "fictive kin." The custom that flatmates are allowed to invite their acquaintances to the party might be understood in this context.

Flatmates are not forced to participate in the process of feast preparation but are morally obliged to provide labor. There is a regular form of action and help given at parties, bringing flatmates together in common labor. Remarkably, the jobs of preparing ingredients, cooking, serving the guests, and clearing the table are in most cases taken by the host's flatmates who work as an efficient team. During my stay in Liza's flat, for example, I was always responsible for roasting barbeque with Wilma and Tom on the apartment roof, while most other flatmates worked in the kitchen putting pieces of pork on the skewers and cooking various dishes. Others cleaned the flat, carried the food to the apartment roof, or decorated the party place. These forms of help are usually returned when each flatmate's birthday party is thrown in the flat in the future.

The principle of reciprocity plays an important role in the system of gift exchange, and these exchange relations are sustained by fulfillment of the obligation to reciprocate a gift and labor. An interesting case is Carolyn, a flatmate from *Illocos* in Liza's flat. Carolyn did not come to the flat wherein Gary's birthday was held although it was her day off. According to Joy, Carolyn had a bad relationship with her flatmates in the beginning when she moved in due to her "selfish" character, which was manifest on her birthday. When Carolyn threw her birthday party in the flat, the flatmates neither helped her nor gave gifts. Therefore, she thought she was also not obligated to give gifts to them on their birthdays or labor in their parties. Nevertheless, Carolyn's behavior became a target of suspicion among flatmates because she failed to fulfill the social norm of *pakikisama*, the ability to get along with and enjoy others (Santos, 1997).

As demonstrated above, the feast in the flat serves in some ways to define the type of social networks and exchange relations that emerge within the flat and sustain it as a community, which is akin to a fictive family network. As a ritual event that regularly occurs in the flat on weekends, furthermore, birthday parties involve moral obligations to reciprocate between givers and receivers. A host provides a generous quantity of food and drink to guests while the guests contribute gifts in a consecutive circuit in the parties of each other. The exchanges of invitations, gifts, and labor serve as tangible markers of the degree of perceived closeness in relationships between givers and recipients and become "tie signs" (Goffman, 1971).

Paluwagan

As noted in the preceding sections, both the regular dinner and special events like birthday parties in the flat become a key source for creating a unique social structure, norms, and networks. I now turn to the *paluwagan*, a traditional Filipino system of a Rotating Saving and Credit Association (ROSCA). ROSCA have a number of variations in different countries but typically are defined as "an association formed upon a core of participants who agree to make regular contributions to a fund which is given to each contributor in rotation" (Light, 1996, p. 50; quoted from Biggart, 2001).[5] In this section, I illustrate how the *paluwagan* operates among the Filipino migrants given the absence of formal insurance and offers multiple functions to meet the distinctive needs of the migrants, describing the flat as a key site for the formation of an informal credit group based on the mutual trust.

Organizing a Self-Help Group Abroad

In the Philippines, according to Charito et al. (2012, p. 36), the practice of *paluwagan* is very popular among low-income people, particularly urban poor and workers who are employed in the same factory or reside in the same boarding house or street. The revolving system is known as a major source of financial and social capitals for the risk management, in which each member is encouraged to save money regularly.[6] According to my

---

5 The concept of ROSCA is known as *chit* in India, *kye* in Korea, *hui* in China, *arisan* in Indonesia, *Tanamoshi* in Japan, *cundina* in Mexico, *tontine* in Francophone Africa, and *partner* in Jamaica.
6 *Paluwagan* is a Tagalog term, which literally means "ease" or "loosen up" (Sandra, 2009, p. 57).

informants, *paluwagan* participation is higher abroad than in the Philippines, especially among women. As Liza remarks, "We do *paluwagan* only abroad. I have never joined *paluwagan* in the Philippines. In transnational context, *paluwagan* enables the migrant workers to save a fixed amount of money and form a mutual aid group since they are disconnected from support back in the Home country."

Coleman (1990, p. 306–307) clearly defines ethnic rotating savings and credit associations as exemplars of trust in informal financial exchange. Besley, Coate, and Loury (1993) note that "ROSCA uses pre-existing social connections between individuals to help circumvent problems of imperfect information and enforceability" (p. 805). Similarly, Handa and Kirton (1999, p. 177) point out that "crucial to the success of ROSCAs is the social collateral that ensures sustainability." In the absence of legal sanctions to assure enforcement of payment, the *paluwagan* participants' gains depend merely on the reliability of the other participants, becoming a guarantor to each other. For this reason, *paluwagan* tends to be small scale, face-to-face, and dependent upon social capital, formed by a relatively small group of individuals who live in the same area.

For the migrants who have difficulties accessing a bank loan in Israel, both money lending and *paluwagan* function as a distinct source of funds. However, most of my informants claim that they prefer to mobilize funds through *paluwagan* while using money lending only as a last resort because those who borrow money from Filipino money lenders in *Neve Sha'anan* are often situated in a prolonged condition of over-indebtedness due to high interest (8–10 %) and strict guarantor requirement. On the contrary, *paluwagan* groups are formed simply through mutual acquaintances and the funds are pooled from the participants. That is, *paluwagan* participants are held together based on a self-enforcing agreement to be sustainable, gaining access to big amounts. As such, money borrowing or lending and *paluwagan* were usually drawn as two main sources for capital by the migrants.

While *paluwagan* enables migrants to save in a more stable way, its purpose varies; it may pay for plane fare to the Philippines, a birthday celebration, or other personal needs in Israel. Many of the informants explained that they usually remitted cash to their family for relatively large expenses such as medical cost, tuition fees, or debt repayments. When Angela just arrived in Israel through Mark, an agent, she participated in the *paluwagan* in Mark's flat, which was organized by Mark. Angela wanted to pay her debt that she borrowed from Mark for her brokerage fee as soon as possible. She had to pay a high rate of interest every month until she settled her debt. By receiving a considerable sum of money at one point, she was able to reduce the repayment period.

After settling all the debt, she created a *paluwagan* also with her workmates, the Filipino care workers who were close to her workplace. When she received the *sahod*, she sent it to her family in the Philippines or to her bank account in the Philippines. Angela used the money saved through this informal saving scheme to build a house in her hometown. In actuality, the majority of the migrants have a goal to build a new house in their village in the Philippines. Angela proudly showed me the picture of her house under construction.

The way the *paluwagan* operates among the migrants can best be illustrated with the following example. Once someone organizes a *paluwagan*, the organizer becomes the first recipient, called *Issa* (number one), although the turn of rotation is thereafter determined by lottery. The organizer, usually the *ba'al habait*, is responsible for collecting money from each participant, called *sahod*, and for distributing it. In Banessa's flat, for example, Banessa organizes a *paluwagan* with nine flatmates. Every Friday Banessa collects 100NIS from each participant, usually their weekly pocket money, and gives the *sahod* (800NIS) to each recipient over two months. As the duration of the scheme varies depending on the number of participants and the given period of rotation, the cycle of contribution usually takes two months to complete. Once a full payout cycle is complete, the existing participants reorganize a *paluwagan*.

My research data reveal that *paluwagan* can be organized among the Filipino migrants in Israel based on various personal network ties such as church members, kin networks, hometown friends or fellow workers nearby their workplaces. However, it is organized mostly among flatmates, while some flatmates participate in more than one *paluwagan* beyond their flat. There are two inter-related conditions that make the flat a key site for *paluwagan* operation: their pre-existing social ties as trustful flatmates, which require regular reaffirmation through weekend gatherings, and the geographical proximity by which participants have a good knowledge of other participants and can monitor each other. According to Joy, "You must take only your friends even though it is a small amount. If you know all of them, it is not dangerous." When I mentioned the possibility of default, Liza also emphasized, "That's why we do *paluwagan* only in the flat."

Formation of a Support Group
Paluwagan is a useful method for the migrants to save money abroad, but the system is vulnerable to those who run away with the common fund. For

this reason, it is important to organize it among those who know and trust each other. The critical roles of geographical proximity and pre-existing relationships in operating *paluwagan* based on the flat are supported by my observations during my fieldwork. During my stay with Angela in Banessa's flat, Angela joined the *paluwagan* in the flat. After she moved into Mark's flat, however, she did not join the *paluwagan* in Banessa's flat. Instead, she started organizing one with her new flatmates in Mark's flat. Similarly, Ella, who was an active *paluwagan* member in Liza's flat for two years, stopped joining the *paluwagan* when she moved out. This observation sheds insight into the determinants of credit group formation among flatmates, in which geographic proximity to each other predicts trusting and trustworthy behavior.

At the same time, the criteria for membership is restricted. In general, *paluwagan* participants are carefully selected by its organizers on the basis of their reputation and reliability. Organizers also consider if the applicant has the ability to regularly pay their *sahod*. This was the reason why Joy was excluded from the *paluwagan*, even though she was a flatmate in Liza's flat. As Joy was an undocumented worker, she was not able to come to the flat to pay her rent during the week. In times of financial distress, besides, Joy could not make payments at the right time. As most of the flatmates knew that her monthly income was precarious, from her frequent overdue rental payments, Liza, the organizer, excluded Joy in the *paluwagan* membership afterwards. In a conversation about this issue, Angela clarified, "If you are legal, you can join even though you are new in the flat."

However, when a new flatmate wants to join the *paluwagan*, other participants strategically put the new participant at the end of the rotation cycle in order to lessen the risk of default. For instance, when I joined the *paluwagan* in Liza's flat for the first time, I was not invited to the meeting where each participant selected their number by a lottery draw. Instead, I was given the last number among seven participants. According to Liza, they gave me the last number because I was new in the flat. Although I was guaranteed by Angela and accepted into the flat, I was still not a trustful person because I was a foreigner, whose identity is hard to be proved. Only after I completed two sessions of *paluwagan* in the flat, I was able to select my number by a lottery draw and be invited to join a new session, which was operated with dollars, for a bigger amount.

In the case of *paluwagan* with dollars, however, the organizer has to recruit participants beyond their flat because the *sahod* is usually a big amount, thus the majority of the flatmates do not join due to the economic burden. Liza regularly organized a *paluwagan* among the flatmates and simultaneously, organized another one with dollars. In the flat, only Liza and Ella participated in the dollar *paluwagan*. Instead, Liza recruited more participants from her and Ella's personal networks. Angela, who can afford it, was also one of the seven members.

Each member paid USD 500 every month to receive USD 3,000 at one's own turn. Ella found a partner to share the *sahod* because she could not afford USD 500 every month. Ella said, "Usually I do *paluwagan* only in the flat. But this time I just joined because most of the members are friends of Liza. I don't know them, but I trust Liza." In the same conversation, Ella argued that "you must take only your friends even though it is a small amount."

To a large extent, *paluwagan* plays an important role as a mutual aid system with a risk management function rather than as a means of providing a lump sum of cash or of building networks. In case of a financial emergency, the money is transferred to the needier person based on the obligation of reciprocity. In Banessa's flat, for instance, Peggy got a call from her mother in the Philippines and heard that her father abruptly went into the hospital for cancer. As Peggy was asked by her mother to send money, she asked Banessa, the organizer, to withdraw her *sahod* ahead of schedule. Thus, Nerlose who was supposed to receive her *sahod* the coming Friday, switched her number with Peggy. According to Banessa, the person who is asked to switch the number in emergency situations is obliged to accept the request because he or she can also face difficult situations in the future.

It is also interesting to note that some enjoy organizing a lottery pool with their flatmates. This is another form of informal finance among the migrants, actually a variation of *paluwagan*. Together with *paluwgan*, organizing a lottery pool is also serving as a social function and a source of funding, although *paluwagan* relies more on mutual trust among the participants. During my stay in Liza's flat, some flatmates and their close friends who were from other flats organized a group to operate a lotto. Every weekend they put up different kinds of premiums such as footwear in fashion or electronic goods, and each participant paid around USD 30 every weekend to make around USD 500. On Saturday night the participants gather and settle the winner by lots. The flatmates operated their own lottery pool, and one of them certainly got it. I also joined this lottery several times, but I have never been selected.

As seen above, *paluwagan* is a multi-functional organization, serving as a source of funding, social connection, and a form of insurance. However, migrants do not organize it with strangers. While the informal saving scheme is widespread in many societies, it is formed only when strong communal ties exist. In the migrant society, which is characterized by uncertainty and temporariness, the flat provides a key site for the formation of such an informal credit group due to the advantages of spatial proximity and a certain degree of mutual trust among a pre-existing network of flatmates. The point to note is that the proximity in networks is closely linked with trust (Granovetter, 1983). Having a tie to a flat as a flatmate therefore enables the migrants with scant resources to obtain financial and social capital. In this respect, the flat can be viewed as a significant community space in their migrant lives through the provision of welfare assistance and mutual aid to the flatmates.

The shared flat provides the migrants with a holiday place away from their workplace on their days-off at a low cost and also with a place of autonomy where they can feel at home. More importantly, the flat serves as the first point of contact for assistance for the newly arrived migrants and as a support group during their stay in Israel. Establishing a support network is important in the migrants' lives, as has been similarly observed in other areas. In the absence of their network of support and welfare for the temporary migrants, the majority of the Filipino migrants in Israel depend on their flat, developing new fictive relationships with their flatmates based on place attachment. Significantly, regular meetings on weekends described above provide grounds for the highly condensed symbolic representation of social relations and unite individual migrants into a social unit.

Bibliography

Aguilar, F. V. (2003). Global migrations, old forms of labor, and new transborder class relations. *Southeast Asian Studies*, *41*(2), 137–161. https://doi.org/10.20495/tak.41.2_137

Barth, F. (1966). Models of social organization. Royal Anthropological Institute Occasional Paper, (23), London.

Besley, T., Coate, S., & Loury, G. (1993). The economics of rotating savings and credit associations. *The American Economic Review*, *83*(4), 792–810.

Biggart, N. W. (2001). Banking on each other: The situational logic of rotating savings and credit associations. *Advances in Qualitative Organization Research*, *3*(1), 129–152.

Coleman, J. S. (1990). *Foundations of social theory*. Harvard University Press.

Doria, R. (2008). Absence at the dinner table: Loss of eating habits through Filipino generations.

Ebaugh, H. R., & Curry, M. (2000). Fictive kin as social capital in new immigrant communities. *Sociological Perspectives*, *43*(2), 189–209. https://doi.org/10.2307/1389793

Embree, J. F. (1939). *Suye Mura: A Japanese Village*. University of Chicago Press.

Espiritu, Y. L. (2003). *Home bound: Filipino American lives across cultures, communities, and countries*. University of California Press.

Goffman, E. (1971). *The presentation of self in everyday life*. Anchor Books.

Granovetter, M. (1983). The strength of weak ties: A network theory revisited. *Sociological Theory, 1*, 201–233. https://doi.org/10.2307/202051

Handa, S., & Kirton C. (1999). The economics of rotating savings and credit associations: Evidence from the Jamaican "Partner." *Journal of Development Economics, 60*(1), 173–194. https://doi.org/10.1016/S0304-3878(99)00040-1

Jackson, V. (2011). Belonging against the national odds: Globalisation, political security and Philippine migrant workers in Israel. *Global Society, 25*(1), 49–71. https://doi.org/10.1080/13600826.2010.522982

Light, I. (1996). Self-help solution to fight urban poverty. *The American Enterprise, 7*(4), 50–52.

Mauss, M. (1990 [1925]). *The gift: The form and reason for exchange in archaic societies* (W. D. Halls, trans.). Routledge.

Sandra, Z. (2009). *Lifelines: The networks of Filipina domestic workers in Beirut*. Thesis for MSc in International Development Studies, Lebanon. University of Amsterdam, Netherlands.

Santos, R. A. (1997). Filipino American children. In G. Johnson-Powell, & J. Yamamoto (Eds.), *Transcultural child development: Psychological assessment and treatment*. John Wiley & Sons, Inc.

Shurmer, P. (1971). Gift game. *New Society, 18*(492), 1242–1244.

Sutton, D. E. (2000). Food and the senses. *Annual Review of Anthropology, 39*(1), 209–223. http://dx.doi.org/10.1146/annurev.anthro.012809.104957

Sutton, D. E. (2001). *Remembrance of repasts: An anthropology of food and memory*. Berg.

5. Seeking a Shelter Behind Gate

Abstract: This chapter explores how the Filipino migrants transform the flat into a safe shelter site, reinforcing boundaries between inside and outside. For Filipino migrants the flat provides the only site to safeguard their privacy where they can enjoy time away from never-ending work, the disciplinary gaze of their employers, Immigration Police and reporters, and the moral gaze of the Filipino society. The function of the flat as a shelter is salient especially for those who lack legal status and have extramarital relationships. The flat becomes a fortified space through two major exclusionary practices: access regulations and the mutual enforcement of anonymity. Significantly, dynamics in the flat are complicated as one's privacy and security are likely to be threatened by insiders even while internal solidarity is promoted.

Keywords: shelter, illegality, couple relationships, deportation, spatial strategies, space of autonomy

Drawing on the empirical data from my fieldwork, this chapter demonstrates how the flat provides an experience of spatial isolation and suspension of time for the Filipino migrants who seek security and autonomy. With particular attention to migrants' legal status and intimate relationships, I describe how the migrants attempt to build a shelter based on the flat, employing spatial strategies against threatening environments. The first two sections below describe how *Neve Sha'anan* constitutes a hostile environment for the migrants, in which migrants experience "illegality" and restricted autonomy. In the third section I explore migrant sexuality and intimate relationships in the context of Filipino migrants to Israel. In the final section I describe how the flat functions as the only safe place for the migrants who are in a constant state of fear and live under watchful eyes.

Lim, Anna. *Filipino Care Workers in Israel: Migration, Trans-local Livelihoods and Space.* Amsterdam: Amsterdam University Press, 2025.
DOI: 10.5117/9789463720403_CH05

Life in "Border Place"

When Filipino migrants enter the host country of Israel, they are classified into the categories of "legal" or "illegal" according to their visa status, which is defined by the labor sovereign. The category of "illegal" is considered "criminal" because such migrants are held to transgress the immigration law of the local migration regime, being outside the Israeli law and norms. Under these circumstances, those migrants who lack legal visa status are considered subjects of "exclusion," bearing the negative connotation of "disorder" in the host society. Deportation and detention, in particular, have become central technologies of immigration control (Bloch & Schuster, 2005, p. 492).

In what follows, I describe how the *Neve Sha'anan* neighborhood constitutes a hostile environment for the migrants, focusing on the experiences of the migrants under the threat of deportability. The *Neve Sha'anan* neighborhood has become the key area for surveillance and a deportation campaign, forming a "border space." Drawing on the lived experiences of migrants, I first explore how the Filipino migrant care workers become undocumented in relation to larger structural factors including restrictive laws and policies. I then describe the precarious life and experiences of illegality among the Filipino migrants in the neighborhood of *Neve Sha'anan*.

Becoming an "Illegal"

As already noted, the binding system is a major structural mechanism that pushes "legal" workers into "illegal" workers, paradoxically yielding the emergence of a large population of undocumented workers (Kemp, 2004; Willen, 2003, 2005, 2007).[1] In Israel the majority of workers entered the country as documented workers and overstayed their work visa or left their employer voluntarily or involuntarily. As of June 30, 2017, the number of migrant workers with permits stands at 104,199. Of the total, 85,932 were legal entrants who have a regulated status and 18,267 were legal entrants who overstayed (Nathan, 2017).

Amma's case illustrates how the migrant care workers were forced to step into a state of illegality under the highly restrictive binding system in the late 1990s. I was introduced to Amma by Kim, a Korean woman who

---

1 I will use the term "illegal" interchangeably with the term "undocumented" because my informants used the term in describing the undocumented migrant (De Genova, 2002). The "illegal" workers in Israel typically emerged through two channels: those who reached Israel on tourist visa and overstayed and those who arrived as legal workers but subsequently lost their legal status.

married an Israeli citizen living in Tel Aviv. When I first met her in 2010, Amma was working as a part-time cleaner for Kim's mother-in-law.

Story of Emma: "Finally I Got a Blue Card"
Amma came to Israel in 1999 and worked for an Orthodox religious family in Gush Katif, a Jewish settlement in the southern Gaza strip. This area had been the target of attacks by Palestinian militants during the Second *Intifada*. In 2000, Amma was seriously wounded by bombs. However, she had to leave the family for which she was working due to long-term hospitalization and as a result she became undocumented. Then she worked without a permit for a family in Tel Aviv but ran away to avoid her abusive employer who took her passport and mistreated her. She called her first employer to ask if she could work for them again, but the Ministry of the Interior rejected the request because Amma had already overstayed several years. After spending these years without a working visa, Amma finally married an Israeli man and eventually obtained permanent residency, a B/1 visa, which is often called a "fiancé visa" or a "friendship visa."[2]

In the late 1990s and early 2000s, the initial period of overseas employment, labor policies for migrant workers' welfare and protection for their labor rights were not yet settled. In this situation, Amma had no opportunity to be reemployed even though she left her first job involuntarily. However, I found that there were both push and pull factors for her to decide to overstay instead of returning to the Philippines. Like many other Filipino care workers, she had to pay USD 6,000 in a brokerage fee for her employment in Israel and she still had to pay that debt back. Besides, she had job opportunities for house cleaning in Tel Aviv and her relatives as support network in *Neve Sha'anan*.

In a private household, both workers and employers are likely to be placed in a vulnerable situation. While migrant care workers are often in abusive situations, the cases of abusing an elderly patient by a migrant worker has also been reported. As long as the workers are indentured to their employers, however, the workers' ability to struggle for decent working conditions and benefits is constrained. Ella explains that migrant care workers treat their employers more kind when their stay comes close to the maximum

---

2   In 2006 the Supreme Court in Israel ruled that a demand made by the Ministry of the Interior for an "illegal" foreigner to leave Israel as a condition to apply for a visa with an Israeli spouse was not just and canceled this requirement. From 2005 the Ministry of the Interior in Israel recognized the right of an Israeli to live with a foreigner without marriage and allowed foreign spouses working visas, thus the Filipino women didn't have to work as care workers (source: http://immigrationlaw.goop.co.il/Web/?PageType=0andItemID=43522).

contract period, because they are afraid that their employers will dismiss them if they are not satisfied with their care workers. As Ella remarks, "If you were [in Israel] already four years and three months and your employer died, that's the end of the world." The power of employers is encapsulated in the oft-heard phrase uttered by my informants that "he or she is my visa" when they refer to their employers.

The majority of undocumented migrants I met over the course of my fieldwork entered Israel after 2006 under the amended binding system. Although becoming an undocumented migrant cannot be understood strictly as an act of free choice, those who entered Israel around 2006 decided to become "illegal" in a more voluntary way than Amma did in the late 1990s. The case of Albert, a 48-year-old male care worker, reveals how a vulnerable migrant care worker decided to overstay to continue his work and support his family in the Philippines. He entered Israel as a care worker in 2000 and cared for an old man for 13 years. In 2013 when his first employer passed away, his employment contract was expired, and he had to leave the country.

According to the local law, Albert had to leave within two months. However, he could not book his air ticket back to the Philippines because the son of his employer refused to pay severance pay and his pension, which amounted to USD 17,000. Whenever Albert demanded the payment, the son of employer repeatedly said, "I will give you next time." In the end, he overstayed and became undocumented. Although flatmates encouraged him to ask NGO, Albert hesitated to do so, saying that "I don't want to fight with them because of money. My employer was my family." Albert was forced to become undocumented. At the same time, he also wanted to stay as long as possible in order to survive and support his family.

Another important reason that migrants become undocumented is related to the commercialized recruitment system. As I described in the latter part of Chapter 2, the privatization of the labor recruitment system under the state regulatory scheme has shaped the entry of migrant labor to the local labor market, through which the influx of Filipino care workers was perpetuated until 2021 when the new arrangement of government-to-government recruitment was implemented. Notably, paying an exorbitant brokerage fee as a condition for entry became an accepted practice in the Philippine–Israel labor migration system before 2021.

The development of the recruitment business has resulted in "indebted mobility" among Filipino migrants since they have had to borrow money at high interest rates from an agent or a moneylender in order to pay the cost of migration and the brokerage fee to enter Israel as a contract care worker. Under these circumstances, those who lost their work permit before paying off their debts have no choice but to overstay and work without a permit unless they leave Israel in debt. In practice, most of the informants argue that 51 months is not enough to earn and save money after paying off their debts. The story of Joy provides a good example.

Story of Joy: "I Just Hide and Work"
Joy, 55, came to Israel in 2006 where her elder sister was working as a care worker. She had two daughters and a son. As her husband had no work and her youngest son was a student, Joy decided to go abroad for work as a breadwinner. Her two daughters had also worked abroad but one of them was pregnant and her husband was also unemployed during her stay in Israel. Joy sent her entire salary back to her family in the Philippines while she lived on a weekly allowance her employer gave her and her additional part-time work. In October 2010 when her last employer, for whom she had worked for five years, passed away, Joy was in a position of having to quit work and return home. But Joy decided to overstay instead of going back home. Although Joy was supposed to leave Israel immediately, as she exceeded the minimum period of 51 months, she decided to "hide." According to Joy, five years was not enough to save money after repaying her brokerage fee. Moreover, she still had to earn money as the only breadwinner of her family and as her youngest son had not yet graduated from college. What enabled Joy to decide to overstay is the continuous demand for undocumented workers in the informal labor market. She worked as a long-term reliever for 7 years until she "decided" to go back to the Philippines in 2018.

The lives of undocumented migrants are precarious since they live in a closed and limited circle, planning their lives on a daily basis. Even though undocumented workers are in demand in the informal labor market and often receive a higher salary than legal workers, they rely entirely on their personal networks for job information, which puts them at a high risk for unemployment. According to Joy, to have lots of friends is a key for undocumented relievers to survive. Joy always assured me that she had a lot of friends to help her but said that she would go back to the Philippines if the unemployment situation lasted for two months. Despite her "illegal" status, she gets regular job offers from her Filipino friends.

In December 2017 when I went back to *Neve Sha'anan* for my fieldwork as a post-doctoral researcher, Joy was still in Tel Aviv, working as a reliever. At that time, I had a chance to follow her and observe her job interview in a local household. This was a job Joy did not take. During my stay with Joy in her workplace when she was working as a reliever, she received several calls from her friends offering her reliever jobs. She would consider the location, schedule, and salary of each offer before choosing her next employment. According to Joy, the elderly woman in need of care for the job for which I observed the interview was in such poor health that to work for her would be very challenging. Finally, Joy went back to the Philippines in 2018 when she thought she saved enough money to build her house in the Philippines.

When Filipina women become illegal workers due to giving birth, they face a different set of challenges. According to the Ministry of the Interior, if foreign women give birth in Israel, this results in the immediate revocation of their work permits. These women are given the option to send their baby abroad as a condition for retaining their work permit (Kav LaOved, 2010, p. 13). As the Israeli policy doesn't allow family reunification for migrant workers, married couples are not expected to come to Israel together, "nor are children born in Israel and to non-Israeli parents to receive any form of citizenship or residency rights" (Willen, 2003, 2005).

Despite the no-family policies, however, many of the migrant workers formed a family and gave birth to a baby. The majority of the mothers who seek help from a municipal aid center are Filipino women, who constitute the largest part of the migrant care sector (Kemp & Kfir, 2016, p. 381). Jenny, a Filipino care worker, became pregnant during her employment in Israel. Upon giving birth, she brought her new-born baby to her parents in the Philippines and came back alone to continue her work. In practice, however, I met several women who left their legal jobs due to giving birth, leaving their future to chance. Grace's story provides an insight into the complicated situation of a single mother without a work permit. As the majority of single mothers are responsible for child rearing, they work as part-time house cleaners and are more likely to be economically distressed and marginalized with a precarious and lower-paid job.

It was 2009, when I moved into Liza's flat, that I met Grace. At the entrance to the apartment, Grace approached me saying hello in Korean, recognizing me as a Korean. Before coming to Israel, Grace worked in South Korea as a factory worker for a year and ran away to become undocumented. After another year, finally, she was deported to the Philippines. Then Grace moved to Israel in 2008 as a contract care worker. However, Grace started living together with Joe, a married Filipino man, and became pregnant.

Story of Grace: Dilemma of Giving Birth
When she was nine months pregnant, she was not able to continue working and eventually left her legal job. Upon delivery, she had to choose between leaving Israel with her baby and sending the infant alone to the Philippines. Grace decided to stay with her newly born daughter in Tel Aviv as long

as possible, since she had no family in the Philippines. She believed that someday she would be granted a residential permit by virtue of her daughter who was born in Israel.[3] Since her delivery, Grace has been illegally working as a part-time house cleaner in Tel Aviv. During my stay in her flat, Grace and Joe separated because Joe had relationship with another Filipino woman. When Joe's new partner became pregnant, Joe left Grace, moving out of the flat. Grace did not receive any financial support from Joe because he was also undocumented and worked as a part-timer for a supermarket in *Neve Sha'anan*. After Joe left, Grace had to bring up Leni alone. Grace had to leave her 2-year-old daughter in the room which was locked from outside to go to work. But when her daughter turned three, she could leave her in Rose's flat every morning before going to her work and pick her up on her way back home. Rose's flat was one of several nurseries in *Neve Sha'anan* which cared for children of migrants older than age two.

Regardless of their birth in Israeli territory, the children of migrant workers are neither registered nor allowed to stay in the country. Some of them are registered to the country of their mother through the Embassy in Israel. According to a report (Friedlander, 2010, p. 140), most of the children (67%) are concentrated in Tel Aviv, 20% live in Haifa with the remainder resident in Jerusalem and Eilat. Some children who meet requirements under changing policies and regulations were granted permanent residency permits by the Ministry of the Interior, while the majority of the children were classified into "illegal residents." Estimates on the number of undocumented migrant children range from 1,500 to several thousands (Kemp & Kfir, 2016).

In August 2010, when a second "one-time arrangement" was announced, 701 families applied for legal status and 379 families received legal status. This was the case of Richard, who lives upstairs from Grace's flat. He received this opportunity for settlement by virtue of his children who met the requirements and finally got residence. When his eldest son, who was born in Israel and spoke Hebrew, reached 7 years old, he applied for legal status and became one of the beneficiaries. The remaining family members were also granted permanent residency.

Story of Richard's Family: "My Sons Are My Visa"
Richard, a 42-year-old Filipino man, entered Israel in 1995 with a tourist visa, where his mother was working as a domestic worker. His mother stayed

---

3   According to several informants, there was a time that many Filipino women got deliberately pregnant with the purpose of staying in Israel because it was known at that time that mothers with children were rarely arrested and sometimes given residence permits.

in Israel for 10 years between 1985 and 1995 and then headed for Spain to work. Richard lived in *Neve Sha'anan* for three years until he was arrested, working as a house cleaner without a work permit. Although he was finally deported, he re-entered Israel as a contract care worker in 2000, using the identity of his brother. At that time Richard married Jenny and formed a family. As Jenny gave birth to two sons, both parents lost their legal status and began working as part-time house cleaners. His aunt, nephew, and two sisters also came to Israel as care workers living together with him in the flat. He supported his two sons, sending them to *Bialik-Rogozin* School where they acquired Hebrew.

I came to know Richard when I moved into Liza's flat in 2011. Richard was living upstairs and frequently visited Liza's flat after work because he had a close relationship with John and Liza. But unlike Grace, Richard was not afraid of walking in the street with his sons. Richard seemed to believe that Immigration Police would not arrest children and their parents even if they were without documents. When I visited *Neve Sha'anan* in 2015 July, Richard and Jenny were in the Philippines for their first vacation in almost 20 years with their sons. Two years later when I visited *Neve Sha'anan* again for my fieldwork, I found that their two sons transferred to a local school, and Richard and Jenny were permitted to work; they worked as a cleaner not only for a household but for a building.

Living with Surveillance

> *Don't eat fish. So that they (Immigration Police) can't follow you.*
> *Pusa is a cat, and they love fish.* (February 16, 2012, interview with Joy)

A growing body of researchers are investigating the effects of "illegality" by focusing on the experiences of migrants. They recognize that "illegality" is not an essential condition of migrants but a condition produced and constructed by migration law and policies (Chavez, 2007; Coutin, 2000, 2005; De Genova, 2002, 2004). The laws and policies clearly draw the boundaries of legal and illegal to "further bureaucratic control of the migrants" (Chavez, 2007, p. 192). According to Willen (2007, p. 11), however, "illegality" is not only a form of juridical and political status but a sociopolitical condition and an element that generates particular modes of being-in-the-world.

Illegality entails a constant fear of deportation for those undocumented, thus making those migrants limit their presence to spaces in which they feel less threatened and can attempt invisibility to evade detection. Illegality changes the spatiality of the border by drawing it inward from the country's physical boundaries in ways that profoundly impact immigrants' daily lives (Hiemstra, 2010, p. 81). *Neve Sha'anan* has been known as a hide-out for undocumented migrants since the 1990s and thus has become a targeted site for the deportation campaign. With the launching of deportation campaign operations and the potential for 24-hour surveillance, *Neve Sha'anan* became a key area of surveillance where Immigration Police are most visible, forming part of an expansive patchwork of marginal "border space" (Isin & Rygiel, 2007).

Some literature notes that the "idea" of the border has undergone significant transformation due to globalization. Researchers are redefining the border through the lens of performativity and mobility rather than as a geographical boundary (Salter, 2007; Wonders, 2006). For example, Wonders (2006, p. 66) argues that many "border performances occur in locations that may be far from the actual geographical border and that day-to-day decisions by government agents, police officers, employers and others play a critical role in determining where, how, and on whose body a border will be performed."

Over the course of my fieldwork, Filipino migrants usually called Immigration Police *pusa*, which is a Tagalog term for cat; at times they are also referred to as *kalaban* (enemy), conjuring up the image of a cat that tries to catch a mouse, symbolizing the threat the police pose to the undocumented migrants. These nicknames are commonly used by Filipino migrants when they are aware of a police stakeout in the *Neve Sha'anan* neighborhood and warn their undocumented company against the police. According to Joy, when she walked with a group of Filipina friends, whoever first recognized the Immigration Police in plain clothes would say *pusa* to tell the others of the danger. My flatmates also often asked me to check whether there were *pusa* on my way home. They said these terms are a "sort of code that the Immigration Police don't understand."

Seen from this perspective, *Neve Sha'anan* forms a border space in which border performances occur every day. If you live in the neighborhood, you become "potential illegal migrants" even if you have a legal visa status. In the neighborhood, someone who does not carry his or her passport and fails to remember their ID number is doomed to be sent directly to detention facilities. Once a Chinese student at Tel Aviv University was arrested near the CBS for not keeping his passport with him and was kept at a detention facility for about five hours until another Chinese student and I broke into his room at the dormitory and found his passport.

In *Neve Sha'anan*, police enforcement functions to control the territory and its unwelcomed residents, further stigmatizing the neighborhood. Matan, a 60-year-old Israeli resident who worked as a middleman between real estate offices and migrants in the neighborhood, said, "You see? Now there are always problems. All of them are blacks [referring to African migrants in the district]. All the time police are here." Most of the informants I met over the course of fieldwork paradoxically claimed that Filipino migrants without legal visa status were a non-issue for the Immigration Police anymore "thanks to" their African neighbors who had become a greater concern for the state. Although implementation of deportation policies is changing over time according to circumstances, *Neve Sha'anan* has been known as a hide-out for the undocumented who "contradict the state's interest in relation to its demographic agenda and sovereignty" (Yacobi, 2008, p. 1).

The statement of Amma below illustrates how *Neve Sha'anan* was a main target site for the deportation campaign already in the late 1990s and the early 2000s. As described above, Amma arrived in Israel in 1999 with a valid visa, but became undocumented when she ran away from her second employer in 2001. She stayed on as an undocumented worker for 4 years until 2005, and then she married an Israeli man. She recalled those initial times when Filipino migrants began to arrive in Tel Aviv:

> At that time [in 1999] there were a lot of Filipinas here [in *Neve Sha'anan*]. At the time I came here, the deportation policy was not as strict as it is now. You did what you wanted, more part time jobs. You earned more money. But they [Immigration Police] started to take you if you didn't have a visa. I was one of them. All of my aunts and the family were caught when they lived in *Neve Sha'anan*. I was caught three times. Every time the Immigration Police asked me a lot of questions, I moved to another flat on Aliya Street. When I lived there, suddenly I heard a noise 3 o'clock in the morning. It was the Immigration Police. They gave me 15 days to leave Israel. Then I fixed again all my stuff and moved to the rooftop. I have a lot of experiences. Since then, I have never lived in *Tachana Markazit* (CBS). I lived in Frishman and Rothschild. We also lived near King George. It was more expensive. Do you know why we lived there? Because most of my flatmates had no visa. The downtown was safer. *Neve Sha'anan* was most dangerous.

In the mid-1990s, according to Amma, *Neve Sha'anan* already functioned as a focal site both for documented and undocumented migrants and became a place of surveillance. For this reason, Amma co-rented an apartment with other undocumented migrants outside the neighborhood, seeking a safer place, despite high expenses. Frishman and Rothschild Streets are located in the center of Tel Aviv, close to the beach, but in a 10–15-minute walk from *Neve Sha'anan*. She always said that she was lucky not being deported over the decade and finally married an Israeli citizen. After she married, Amma, with her husband, ran a famous Asian market inside the Central Bus Station of Tel Aviv, while working as a part-time cleaner for Israeli households, until 2015 when her husband and she migrated to the Philippines for settlement.

Nowadays, police surveillance of both public and private spheres in the neighborhood is ordinary: it is an everyday scene that passers-by are approached by the Immigration Police, who heavily patrol the *Neve Sha'anan* neighborhood. The co-presence of Border Police, Immigration Police, and Municipality Police in *Neve Sha'anan* serves as a constant reminder of migrant "illegality," and therefore "deportability." In the course of my fieldwork, I observed the Immigration Police raids for mass deportation in *Neve Sha'anan* even on *Shabbat*, when the Police unexpectedly closed off the streets in the neighborhood and raided shops, running random inspections. Because it has long been believed that *Shabbat* was a safe time for the undocumented, everyone was shocked by the raids.

It was during *Shabbat* that the majority of undocumented migrants appeared in the neighborhood. However, the scope of police raids was not limited to within the area. In December 2009 I participated in mass at St. Anthony Catholic church for my preliminary research. Located in Old Jaffa, the church has been known as a focal point for Filipino migrants to converse in Israel. During the mass, which was crowded with hundreds of Filipino migrants who stood between the benches and in empty spaces, the priest took attendance to check on the need for more chairs.

According to the priest, Immigration Police once raided the church on Saturday morning, and many Filipinos who could not find a way out were seriously injured because they were jostled in the crowd. At that time, most of the undocumented Filipino migrants inside were arrested. Around the same time, an African church near CBS, known as Redemption Power church, was also raided by Immigration Police. As these incidents occurred on *Shabbat*, *Shabbat* came to be believed no longer safe for those undocumented.

Another belief was also challenged. There had been a strong belief among Filipino migrants that Israeli police never caught Israel-born children and their parents who lacked legal status. In the late 1990s, the Israeli government recognized the increase of undocumented migrants and implemented deportation campaigns. In the beginning, the deportation campaign targeted men (Willen, 2007, p. 13), but it gradually enlarged its target to female migrants. According to many informants, some Filipino migrants intentionally got pregnant due to the belief and expectation that they could receive permanent residency. However, the Immigration Authority began to raid the neighborhood and arrested both mothers and their children, sending them to a detention facility.

It is not only in the public space that one encounters the Immigration Police. The Police also attempt to enter private houses of the migrants in the neighborhood. All the flats where I stayed for my fieldworks were frequently visited by the Immigration Police. Sometimes, the Immigration Police knocked on the door to enter or attempted to follow residents into the flat. However, the Immigration Police are not expected to break into private houses without the consent of its residents. In addition, it is not easy for them to recognize who lives in the flat where a number of people belong, or even who is undocumented in the flat.

Significantly, my informants claim that the Immigration Police cannot catch undocumented migrants successfully without the help of "reporters." They describe reporters as those who are once caught by the Immigration Police but discharged on the condition that they work for the Immigration Police by reporting the location of "illegal migrants." Amma, who says that she knows a reporter in *Neve Sha'anan*, describes how they work. For example, they put an empty bottle as an indicating mark in front of the flat where undocumented migrants reside so that the Immigration Police can make a sudden raid. Some of my flatmates pointed out a few Filipino men, who have no legal visa but are present in the neighborhood during weekdays without fear, whom they suspect might be reporters. However, the identities of the reporters are unknown.

The majority of my informants condemned the reporters for their "immoral" behavior, as they are paid USD 50 per case by the police "betraying" their co-ethnic fellows, as Amma expressed it. Because the reporters lie in everyday life without exposing their identity in order to detect "illegals" in *Neve Sha'anan*, most of my informants emphasize that reporters are even more dangerous than the Immigration Police. During my stay in Liza's flat, for this reason, my flatmates often cast a suspicious eye on their neighbors.

One of them was a man who always sat in front of a grocery store in the neighborhood. I was warned not to talk with him because he often tried to collect personal information on Filipino residents. It is clear that the daily presence of Immigration Police and reporters in the neighborhood is a threat to the foreign residents, particularly the undocumented migrants. In this way, *Neve Sha'anan* as a border space is separated from other part of the city and the stigmatization of the neighborhood as a "hide-out for illegal criminals" is enhanced. Although there is no fixed geographic line,

Neve Sha'anan's invisible borders can be clearly drawn from the everyday practices of surveillance and border control.

However, because the deportation campaign widely occurs throughout the country, many migrants live in a constant state of fear and uncertainty, living hidden lives. This is particularly true of those who overstay their visas and must create "shadow lives" (Chavez, 1994, 2007) under the pervasive threat of Immigration enforcement. Once, when I went to the laundry in *Neve Sha'anan*, I found a strange man instead of the Filipino man who usually worked there. Later I heard from that man that the Filipino man was arrested by the Immigration Police a few days prior. Such sudden disappearance of flatmates or neighbors was routine in the neighborhood. The migrants know that anyone might turn into an "illegal" and be deported suddenly. In addition, "illegal" migrants and "legal" migrants are not separated from each other but rather live together in the flat.

My informants told me that they could recognize who were Immigration Police even if they were in plain clothes. Joy elaborated on how undocumented migrants like her live in considerable fear of apprehension and deportation: "It is very difficult if you become a person with 'no visa.' I am afraid to go out. But life is going on. I am like a ghost." Upon losing her legal status, Joy changed all her ID names on *Facebook* and *Skype* because she believed that Immigration Police would detect her on the web and might locate her.

Her fear of being apprehended was so great that she didn't go out of her employer's house during the weekdays. As she worked as a reliever, she usually stayed inside the employer's house for a month and didn't go out until the legal care worker of the employer returned from her one-month vacation. For this reason, Joy sometimes asked me to visit her at her workplace and bring her what she needed such as international telephone cards, groceries, or cooked pork, and then paid me back.

In actuality, while many of the undocumented migrants are deported, others successfully "hide" and are employed on the black market as described. Constantly at risk of deportation, however, undocumented migrants attempt to keep a low profile. In this situation, invisibility is not simply imposed, but can also be a useful strategy. Whenever Joy felt a strong desire to go to *Neve Sha'anan*, she reserved a taxi to come back to her flat in spite of the high cost. According to Joy, the Immigration Police would not imagine that an "illegal" migrant moved by taxi.

Jimmy, an undocumented Filipino man in Jane's flat, worked as a reliever based on live-out conditions although his flatmates were always worried about his safety because they believed that it was very dangerous for "illegals" to work as live-out workers. He usually left the flat at 8 p.m. for work and returned the next morning. Given the risk of being exposed in everyday life, he attempted to dress up and disguise himself by attempting to look like an "Israeli office worker." He always wore a suit and carried a laptop bag because he believed that acting Israeli would protect him. His flatmates sometimes made fun of him because he was naïve. Despite his efforts at "passing," ultimately he was arrested on the street and eventually deported.

Significantly, it is also important to note that Filipino women who gave birth to a child in Israel experienced illegality in a different way. Grace's story is a useful backdrop. When I first met Grace in 2010, she was a single mother with a 2-year-old daughter living downstairs from Liza's flat. Before going out for work as a house cleaner every morning, Grace put her daughter in her room and locked it from outside. As her daughter was below 3 at that time, she was not accepted in the *Moadon* (daycare center) in the neighborhood.

It was only on *Shabbat* that her daughter went out of the room and could see the sun. Only after her daughter became five could Grace and her daughter go about in the neighborhood. Grace believed that undocumented migrants with a child at the age of five or more were relatively safe because the Immigration Police were reluctant to catch children and their parents. She always carried the birth certificate of her daughter, issued by the Philippine Embassy in Israel to show the Immigration Police when they asked for it.

She believed that the Immigration Police would not detain children because children were valued in the Jewish tradition. According to Grace, there were times when some undocumented migrants intentionally gave birth to a child, seeking opportunities for settlement. When I visited *Neve Sha'anan* again for my follow-up research in 2018, her daughter had turned seven. At that time, Grace was living in an one-room apartment near *Bialik-Rogozin* School, where children of refugees and migrant workers study together in integrative classes. Contrary to her wish, however, Israeli immigration control policies often expanded their targets to children without proper documents, and Grace felt anxiety about her future.

> I don't know how long we (my daughter and I) have to stay here. We don't know what will happen even tomorrow. Last year (2017) the situation was so bad. Too many Immigration (Police) here and there. The teachers in the school suggested that I leave Israel. They said, "It depends on you if you are going to your country or stay here. We cannot assure you [that you would not be deported with your daughter]." I couldn't send her to the Philippines because I don't have my parents there. They died when I

was young. And my daughter now speaks Hebrew. She was born here and is like an Israeli. How can she adapt to the Philippines if we return there?

The local mass media tends to criticize migrant women's requests for birthright citizenship and shows how it threatens the Jewish identity of the local society, calling undocumented children "anchor babies" (Chavez, 2017). Grace had hoped to receive permanent residence by virtue of her daughter, particularly when she heard that two sons of Richard, her neighbor, were granted permanent residence. The support by local teachers and NGO activists and the educational and clinical services from the municipality enable undocumented mothers like Grace to sustain their life in Israel. Nevertheless, Grace never received permanent residence during my project and continued living in fear with her daughter in the country where the deportation campaign operated targeting undocumented migrants and children.

Making Love in Liminal Phase

Although one of the main themes of the scholarly literature is the strained relations between migrant mothers and their children, some researchers pay attention to the impact of migration on marital relationships and sexuality (Arcinas, 1986; Constable, 2003; Margold, 1995; Pe-Pua, 2003; Pingol, 2010; Tsujimoto, 2014). According to these studies, physical separation between spouses has unfavorable effects often resulting in "broken families" (Rodriguez, 2002), allowing both migrants abroad and their spouses to engage in extramarital relationships, inevitably straining conjugal relationships.

Migrant women who are separated from their family due to overseas migration not only form transnational families, but they also have to reconstitute or reconfigure family relations in order to accommodate the realities of migration (Alicea, 1997; Avila, 2008; Zontini, 2010). In her research on cultural changes wrought by the feminization of Filipino overseas labor, Pingol (2010) notes that the marital relationship becomes precarious when couples are split, with either the wife being involved in an affair overseas, or the husband in the Philippines, or both.

During the 1980s, the Philippine media had already coined the term "Saudi Syndrome" to describe the anxieties of Filipino male workers who were employed in the Middle East and were worried about their wives' infidelity at home (Arcinas, 1986, p. 67). According to Gabriella (2001, p. 4), it is rare in Philippine society that women engage in extramarital affairs because if caught they are socially stigmatized and ostracized, whilst for married men it is quite acceptable to have a number of lovers. For example, "when the husband has an affair, it is explained in terms of the masculine sexual need; female infidelity, on the other hand, is considered a serious fault" (Pe-Pua, 2003, p. 171).

Recent studies, however, draw more attention to the engagement of female migrants in extramarital relationships as women increasingly participate in labor migration (Pingol, 2010; Pe-Pua, 2003; Tsujimoto, 2014). Due to legal constraints on family reunification, in which only the wife or the husband of a couple is allowed to apply for a care work job in Israel, the majority of my informants had arrived in Israel alone, leaving their spouses back in the Philippines.

Under these circumstances, the phenomenon of extra-marital affairs among OFWs is not a new one in Israel. While it is hard to provide exact statistical data, my fieldwork reveals that many migrants are involved in extramarital affairs, ranging from casual sex to relatively long-term pseudo-conjugal relationships in the absence of their spouses. Moreover, migrants' sexuality itself is not a great concern of the Israeli government unless it challenges nation-state borders by reproducing new generations (Kitiarsa, 2008, p. 598).

The majority of my informants are mothers who are typically in their thirties and forties, and their actual marital statuses are difficult to define: they can be identified as married, divorced, separated, widowed or single moms. All four apartments where I stayed for my fieldwork at different times accommodated an extra-marital couple. For instance, one of those flats had several couples, which comprised the majority of the flat residents; among 12 flatmates, eight persons were in couples. The majority of my informants describe extra-marital relationships as a dark side of Filipino lives abroad that they don't like to expose. However, extramarital relations have different implications for men and women among Filipinos, reflecting double standards which are more lenient toward male "offenders" but more intolerant of extramarital female sexual practices (Parreñas, 2001).

The specific conditions of transnational migration often provide grounds for migrants to reproduce or negotiate power and gender discourses inscribed in heteronormativity (Manalansan, 2006). The physical distance from their home country and from the prying eyes of local communities frees migrants from institutional and social structural constraints, allowing them to engage in extramarital relationships far from home. As Tsujimoto (2014) elucidates the extramarital relationships among Filipino workers in South Korea, transnational migration results in prolonged liminality through migrants' initiatives to pursue desired hetero-sexualities and the further endeavor to convert extramarital relationships into long-term intimacy.

At the same time, the account of Levy, a Filipino man, pinpoints the double moral standard for women in the *Neve Sha'anan*. When Levy came to visit Banessa's flat to meet Angela, Angela introduced me to him as someone conducting research about Filipino migrants in Israel. He directly brought up the issue of "infidelity" among Filipino women in Israel as a research topic for me. Levy himself, who was married, had a Filipina mistress in *Neve Sha'anan* but indignantly said, "If a single woman dates an Israeli man, I don't care. But if she is a married woman with children, I really feel ashamed for her."

Tom and Wilma are a couple in Liza's flat. Tom met Wilma when he lived in another flat where he first rented upon his arrival because some relatives of his wife also lived in that flat. However, after he started his relationship with Wilma, he rented a double-sized bed in Liza's flat to maintain his relationship with Wilma, while also maintaining his rent in the flat where the relatives of his wife lived. Although he and Wilma moved to Liza's flat, they still did not feel free. Tom, whose wife has a number of relatives in Israel, also had to be cautious whenever he came to *Neve Sha'anan* on weekends. For example, on Saturday afternoons he would first come to Liza's flat to spend half of his day-off with Wilma, and then on Sunday mornings he would go to the flat of his wife's aunt as if he had just arrived from his work. As such, Tom led a double life by renting different flats in *Neve Sha'anan* secretly.

According to Parreñas (2003), extramarital relationships among migrants are largely the result of loneliness and emotional distress resulting from migration. Parreñas (2003, p. 35) describes that "one government-mandated training workshop for outgoing female overseas contract workers warned participants not to fall into the temptation of the 'brother of homesickness ... home-sexness, and of the loneliness of being separated from their husbands.'" The separation from home and familiar relationships brings about a deep sense of loneliness among the migrant workers, requiring the migrants to cope with their emotional and sexual needs in the host societies.

This is the case of Ella, 33, a mother of three children who came to Israel in 2009 when her youngest son was 11 months, leaving all three of her sons under the care of her husband and his parents. When Ella arrived in Israel, she stayed together with her mother who was working as a care worker and helped her come to Israel. But after her mother went back to the Philippines, Ella moved into the flat where Gary, her third partner in Israel, had lived and began living with him, renting a double-sized bed. Ella met Gary in a daycare center where the girl she cares for regularly went. Ella and Gary soon began a relationship.

During their time in this flat, however, the other flatmates criticized their behavior as immoral. Ella explained that she had found flatmates staring at her and Gary in a disapproving manner since they engage in an extramarital relationship. As a result, the couple eventually moved out and found Liza's flat where several extramarital couples were already living. Ella and Gary occupied a small room with a double-sized bed together in Liza's flat. Ella began her relationship with Gary to alleviate the travails of her transnational life and to satisfy her desire for an intimate relationship. Ella explained to me how she entered into the adventurous intimate relationship with Gary:

> I do not love Gary. I just wanted to stay with someone together. That's it. I think by myself, what I am doing now is really bad. You know, I have lost my self-respect. Now it's very hard for me. The first year with him was good. There was an excitement because both of us were live-in [care workers]. Now no more excitement. I see him every night in the flat because both of us are live-out. I want to find something new in my life. Gary will be my last boyfriend in Israel.

As Ella stressed, "there are many Filipinos who have partners abroad." At the same time, it is noteworthy that such relationships are provisional. Several informants explain that many extramarital couples have an agreement from the outset that they will terminate their relationship when either of them leaves Israel. According to Ella, her relationship with Gary is valid only during their stay in Israel and they will not contact each other when they return to the Philippines. When Tom had to leave Israel because of the sudden death of his employer, his relationship with Wilma also ended. For this reason, several informants referred to such short-term relationships as "Ben-Gurion couples," meaning that such extramarital romances are maintained only in Israel and end when one party leaves the country through the Ben-Gurion Airport.

The majority of my informants, who have extramarital relationships, respond that they have no intention to divorce their spouses in the Philippines but plan to maintain such affairs only on a temporary basis while in Israel. However, Grace engaged in such relationship with the desire to have her own family. As her parents passed away long time ago, Grace said she always felt loneliness and wanted to marry when she graduated from college. After moving to Israel as a care worker, finally, she began an intimate relationship with Angelo, a Filipino man working in Israel, and gave birth to a daughter.

On a Friday night when I talked with Grace and Rosa, a mother of Angelo, in the flat, Rosa told me that Angelo had a wife in the Philippines, saying "I keep quiet because I am his mother. What can I do." As Angelo was a married man with two daughters, during his relationship with Grace, he still regularly sent remittances to his wife in the Philippines. After a year, however, Grace and Angelo were separated because Angelo began a relationship with another Filipino woman working in Israel. She also had a husband and a son in the Philippines.

It is also important to point out that while such relationships are provisional, they often result in the formation of a family or a single parent through childbirth in the host society. For instance, Wilma's relationship with Tom ended when Tom left Israel. Before long, Wilma found a new partner, Marco, a 45-year-old Filipino man, and moved to the flat where Marco lived. Although Marco had his wife and children in the Philippines, he maintained his relationship with Wilma and finally separated from his wife when Wilma got pregnant. Wilma and Marco had to decide if they would give birth to the child in Israel and live without documentation or whether they would send the baby alone back to the Philippines. Finally, they decided to go back to the Philippines and settled in Pampanga, Marco's hometown.

Several research projects further report that Filipina migrant workers often engage in a "tomboy" relationship as an unconventional strategy for coping with loneliness and sexual needs (Abesamis, 2000; Valerio, 2002). The term "tomboy" is used for females acting in the manner of men or lesbian women, while the term "*bakla*" is used for males acting in the manner of women. According to Valerio (2002, p. 63), six out of ten Filipina domestic workers in Hong Kong had extramarital affairs, while Abesamis (2000) shows that Filipina domestic workers in Hong Kong enter same-sex relationships as a form of "daily resistance" or "refusal to be dominated by oppressive forces and as a sign of resilience and creativity" or as a reaction to abusive husbands. In the Philippines, where only monogamous heterosexual relations are formally approved, extramarital ties, either hetero- or homosexual, are regarded as a form of moral deviance (Tsujimoto, 2014).

The intimate relationships among tomboys or *baklas*, and between heterosexual women and tomboys in the particular context of transnational migration, were observed also during my fieldwork in Israel. Negotiations of gender and sexuality among migrants tend to occur most intensely at borderlands. I often recognized those couples walking in the *Neve Sha'anan*

Street on weekends. During my stay in Liza's flat, sometimes tomboy or *bakla* couples visited us to look around the flat for renting. According to my informants, there are many Filipino migrants who practiced heterosexuality in the Philippines but changed their gender identity to a tomboy or *bakla* after they arrived in Israel, which is a country with a more liberal sexual standard and is far away from the Philippines.

Although the majority of my informants stressed that they were not prejudiced against queers, as in many societies heterosexual individuals often revealed disgust about queer identities and practices. For example, Amma said, "I have a friend from Pampanga, my hometown. She married in the Philippines and gave birth to a baby but is separated from her husband now. When she came to Israel, she met a Filipino tomboy, and they lived together. They are not in the Philippines, so they can do what they want to do. They are not afraid. But now she is pregnant with a man from the USA, while still living with the tomboy. I think she is crazy." As this comment implies, queer "couple" relationships among Filipino migrants are regarded as deviant in the migrant society.

An extramarital relationship reveals migrants' desire for sexual and intimate lives and the *Neve Sha'anan* neighborhood, which is located far away from most of their workplaces and from the Philippines, is an ideal site for practicing alternative sexualities. However, the bounded neighborhood is not a neutral place in which to conduct an affair. Migrants can encounter hometown friends or relatives in *Neve Sha'anan* as many of the Filipino migrant workers in Israel visit the neighborhood every weekend. For this reason, it is crucial for those who are in extramarital relationships to protect their privacy and freedom in the neighborhood where most of Filipino migrants are concentrated. It is within this context that the flat can be developed into a liminal space, ensuring a degree of autonomy. In the next section, I describe how the flat functions as a shelter for the migrants where they enjoy freedom and autonomy, escaping from the watching eyes of neighbors and Filipino society in Tel Aviv.

Paradox of Sheltering

Migrants employ spatial strategies against the defensive realities that surround them. They monitor their environments and protect their flat against the threatening environments through exclusionary practices, which emulate a feeling of ontological security. Migrants' attempts to shield the flat are two-fold: they regulate access through physical barriers and enforce a climate of anonymity. Through my examination, I reveal that the process of making a shelter strengthens the boundaries between inside and outside the flat, between us and them, but also creates paradoxical situations inside the enclosed space of flat, in which one's privacy and security are likely to be threatened by insiders even while internal solidarity is promoted.

Access Control Through Gating
Newman (1972, p. 3) describes a type of supportive living space, termed defensible space, as "a living residential environment which can be employed by inhabitants for the enhancement of their lives, while providing security for their families, neighbors, and friends." Such spaces have a clear indication of ownership, provide opportunities for surveillance, and define specific areas for different types of activities. In this theory, physical barriers communicate a clear message to outsiders to "keep out" in conjunction with symbolic barriers. For Newman, therefore, territoriality is a critical mechanism for creating the impermeable residential environment that defensible space advocates, with the fewest possible entry/exit points, making it well contained and easy to monitor and control.

Despite the hostile and precarious environments, migrants continuously shuttled between their workplace and flat every weekend to navigate their weekend lives. Under these circumstances, security was a major theme that ran through all the conversations with my informants, and the flat was at the heart of the issue. In reality, the only defense mechanism for the migrants is to retreat from the outside world to their flat and build a more controlled and safer unit by employing a range of territorial strategies and exclusionary practices. In this vein, the restricted access to the flat through physical barriers may play a particularly important role in the highly crowded conditions, by providing migrants with a system to control their shared space.

When I began my fieldwork in Janes' flat in 2010, I usually stayed in the flat during the daytime with Jimmy, a Filipino man in his late 40s, while Angela and Malou, live-out care workers, were out for work. Working as a care worker in Israel, Jimmy had remitted his whole salary back to his wife in the Philippines. But after a year he came to know that his wife ran away with a man, bringing all the money Jimmy sent with her. Shocked and disappointed at the news, Jimmy was not able to concentrate on his work. He said he lived like a dead man for a while, drinking alcohol every day without working. Finally, he was dismissed by his employer. At that time Jimmy began his relationship with Rosa, a Filipino woman in Jane's flat, and rented a veranda room to share with her. Since then, he has been undocumented and working over night as a reliever. However, nobody told me that Jimmy was undocumented because I was a stranger in the flat.

It was a Sunday evening when Immigration Police shouted to open the door that I recognized his legal status. Around 9 p.m. when most of the flatmates went back to their work, two Immigration Police knocked repeatedly on the door. Then, Jimmy and Jenny, another flatmate, rushed into my room and asked me to turn the light off. Finally, the police left after shutting down the electricity, and we fell asleep in the darkness. Through this, I came to know that those two flatmates did not have legal visas. Although the police left soon, we had to be caged in the room until the next morning. In the morning Jimmy and Jenny asked me to go out and check to see whether the police were still there. Across the street I made a gesture with my hands which signaled "no," and the two of them packed a backpack and ran somewhere at full speed. They temporarily stayed in their friends' flat, which was perceived as located in safer place in *Neve Sha'anan*, and came back after a few weeks.

As Jimmy worked as an undocumented reliever based on live-out conditions he was constantly at risk of deportation. All the flatmates were worried about his safety because they believed that it was very dangerous for "illegals" to work as live-out workers. He usually left the flat at 8 p.m. for work and returned the next morning. In practice, most of the undocumented workers were relievers based on a live-in pattern. But as mentioned earlier, Jimmy attempted to pass by dressing as an Israeli office worker. He was arrested nonetheless and eventually deported. This happened suddenly, and I didn't see him anymore. According to Rosa, Jimmy was directly sent to a detention facility and stayed there for a couple of weeks until he was deported to the Philippines. It was Rosa who arranged his stuff in the flat and shipped everything to Jimmy in the Philippines.

Such raids on flats often occurred during my fieldwork, but the police left, so arrests were unusual. However, it became dangerous if someone was unable to bear the fear and opened the door. The experience of Angela illustrates how the flat is defended by restrictive access regulation, creating a sense of territoriality. While Angela lived in Banessa's flat, she also rented a bed in Liza's flat only to get a right of access without participating in any communal activities. As a money lender, Angela loaned money to three persons in Liza's flat where her aunt, Joy, lived but she had difficulty getting it back. Angela was allowed to move into Liza's flat because John, the partner of Liza, was a debtor of Angela. Angela, who helped me move into Liza's flat, sometimes asked me if John was in the flat and then came to the flat to collect money from him. Angela explains:

My aunt, Joy, introduced John and some flatmates to me. Jennifer borrowed USD 1,500 from me but it took one year until she paid back. I always argued with Jennifer and two more people who lived in the flat about the debts. Finally, I moved into their flat and supervised them because I now had the "right to enter the flat."

After she got most of her money back, Angela stopped renting the flat. By paying rent, as seen above, Angela was given a key to open the gate, which gave her basic membership in the flat and the right to access inside. Every private house has its own gate, but it is impossible to remain impervious to the implication of the gate of a flat in *Neve Sha'anan* given that "gating" refers to a form of spatial fortification (Blakely & Snyder, 1997).

At first glance, the migrants' search for security and an inward-orientation can be read in the design of entrances. According to Watson and Gibson (1995), "gating" is emblematic of wider social systems of exclusion, domination and identity. Each flat has its own gate, an exclusionary spatial design that not only deters outsiders' incursions but also conveys a clear message to outsiders to "keep out." Typically, the entrance doors in the apartments, which are firmly locked throughout the week, are wide open only on weekends. Such a sanctuary-like character of the flat derives from the residents' desire for security and privacy, as a means of protection against an unfriendly and often hostile environment. In fact, such security is a key issue among the migrants who live in precarious and often hostile environments.

The importance of gating is most salient for undocumented migrants who resort to gating for their own security. The flat in *Neve Sha'anan* provides the only site of retreat and seclusion for them when they are between jobs. The physical presence of gates offers them the physical safety and security. For example, when Joy had to find a new flat, she came to search in *Neve Sh'anan* with me every Saturday. She said that she needed a strong door to protect herself from Immigration Police. Her main consideration for finding a flat was the existence of an iron door. According to Matan, a real estate broker in *Neve Sha'anan*, "Filipinas sometimes ask the landlord to install an iron gate. It's not strange here."

Although *Shabbat* is believed to be the only safe time when the Immigration Police are absent, Joy claims that it is still dangerous because there have been a series of surprise raids in the past and Immigration Police were everywhere. Nevertheless, most of the undocumented migrants continuously came back to *Neve Sha'anan* every weekend. For example, despite her sense of fear, every Friday at 3 p.m. Joy returned to Liza's flat where she belonged and left again on Saturday at 6 p.m. Every Friday morning Joy sent me a

SMS to ask if I saw Immigration Police in *Neve Sha'anan* before deciding if she would come to the flat on her day-off.

In practice, when Immigration Police raid the flats in *Neve Sha'anan*, gates serve as the only defense mechanism. In many cases the flats had undocumented migrants in them, and the gate was locked from both the inside and the outside in order to give the impression that the house was vacant. For example, when John, in Liza's flat, retreated to the flat when he overstayed his visa, he had to stay there for several months without going out until he found a reliever job. Over this period of time, when I would return to the flat every night, I had to call Liza to announce my arrival because John always locked the door from inside. Only after he removed the sofa which he used to block the door with and then unlatched the gate, was I able to enter the flat.

Several informants claim that it is most crucial not to open the door from inside when the Immigration Police come to the flat. As long as they do not open the gate from inside, they can be safe, but the moment that they open the door, they are caught by Immigration Police. Grace stresses that many of her neighbors were arrested because they opened the door under strain when the police smashed the door and shouted. Grace elaborated what she experienced. "Last time I saw through window the Immigration [Police] brought the man living downstairs to the police car. At that time police came to our flat also, but I didn't open the door. If you don't open, you are okay. I just stayed in the room. But the man downstairs, maybe he was afraid. I survived like that already three years."

Strategy of Secrecy

During my stay in Grace's flat, Joy once visited me to pick up her Dove soaps that she had asked me to buy for her. At the moment there were Grace and Pnina in the flat, so I introduced them to each other. I had expected that they would be glad to see other Filipinos, but I was obviously mistaken. They exchanged a few words in Tagalog. Although I could not understand what they said, I recognized that Grace and Pnina felt uncomfortable and were leery of Joy, a stranger. A few minutes later, Joy left the flat with her soaps. It was not the only case that I observed the migrants' attitudes towards outsiders of the flat. In the *Neve Sha'anan*, the boundary between insiders and outsiders was drawn based on the flat.

As noted above, the private residential space with its secured entrance is not freely accessible like a public place, creating physical and social segregation between flats. The flat is physically enclosed by the physical barriers such as entrance gates, which are operated by keys. Significantly, migrants' efforts to establish an isolated place in their flats through limiting access by outsiders derive from their desire for security and privacy against unfriendly and often hostile environments that surround them. To guard their own space of retreat and seclusion, however, spatial strategies against the defensive realities are practiced also within the flat, exercising tight control over the flat community in which they dwell by centering themselves on what they defined as the norm.

Private information of flatmates is routinely silenced in the flat. The story of John in Liza's flat best illustrates how security for undocumented migrants is guarded by flatmates through the tactic of concealment. When his employer for whom he had worked for 7 years as a live-in care workers passed away in 2012, John decided to overstay his visa and became undocumented. The fear of exposing his "illegality" to others forced him into a "habit of secrets and lies" (Kohli, 2006). For several months, John didn't reveal his situation even to his flatmates. However, because the flat is the only place where he could hide and survive, John finally recognized that he would have to let his flatmates know his current legal status. Although John continuously assured his flatmates that nothing happened to him, eventually he had to expose his legal status to all the flatmates for his own safety.

On a Saturday night, John called a meeting in the salon and confessed that he had become "illegal" and had concealed the fact out of fear. When I asked him why he decided to reveal his legal status at that moment, he responded, "Because there are a lot of reporters here, our neighbors. That's why we [Liza and John] kept secret. I tell flatmates now because I want them to be careful." As John did, those who become undocumented usually attempt to avoid more dangerous situations which might be caused by flatmates who are ignorant of their legal status and thus not cautious.

Whenever I moved into a flat for my fieldwork, my flatmates gave me specific precautions concerning the undocumented migrants in the flat: I was to carry my passport with me all the time; when I saw Immigration Police near the flat, I was not to try to come into the flat, but instead was to go somewhere else; and I must not open the door for the Immigration Police. According to Liza, Immigration Police usually follow those who don't carry a passport with them to their flat for a check, and in this case, there is no choice for the migrants but to open the gate of the flat.

My own experience also supports the critical role of flatmates in shielding the flat against Immigration Police. One evening I bumped into Immigration Police in the stairway inside the apartment building where I lived. As I hadn't carried my passport with me at that moment, the police intended to follow me to Liza's flat where Joy, an undocumented migrant, stayed inside.

Fortunately, the police found a "suspicious" man living on the second floor on the way to the flat, and I was able to get out of the building. Joy panicked when I told her this story. Although the police did not follow me to the flat to see my passport, they easily might have, thus endangering her.

Within the liminal space of the flat, the distinct categories of "legal" and "illegal" become blurry, challenging the hegemonic order. The majority of Filipino migrants in my study became "illegal" under various circumstances, in which they experience a range of situations on a continuum between "legal" and "illegal." The migrants clearly classify themselves either into "legal" or "illegal." However, the flat is an ambivalent zone where the categories of disorder and illegality are challenged. Within the flat, undocumented migrants are not a subject of exclusion. Rather, they are included and protected against the violence of the dominant society. In this light, the flat is constructed as a "deviant space" from the perspective of outside society.

Ella and Gary never walk together in *Neve Sh'anan* to avoid the risk of their relationship being detected by their relatives or neighbors from their hometowns. Instead, their relationship is bound to the flat where they live. Their small room is about 9 km² with a queen bed against wall. Their compartment room is tightly packed with a double bed, plastic dresser and carriers. In this cramped space, the framed photographs on the walls attracted my attention. Gary's and Ella's family pictures, including their spouses in the Philippines, are hung on the wall side by side. Sitting in front of the pictures, Gary often talks with his family through internet video calls, while Ella stays out of the way silently or sometimes goes out of the room so as not to overhear.

Although the private space of a flat with limited access harbors its residents' intimate relationships, they need the help of their flatmates who must conceal their transient romances. For instance, Jennifer concealed the extramarital relationship of Cora, her sister-in-law, while she stayed in Liza's flat with her. After Jennifer came to Israel in 2007, she lived with Cora who helped her to come to Israel. After they moved into Liza's flat together, Cora started a relationship with a Turkish man and rented a compartment room to stay with him. Although Jennifer sometimes expressed ambiguous feelings about Cora's relationship with the Turkish man, she responded to me about Cora's relationship with indifference and even provided a supporting excuse:

> I cannot say anything about her [extramarital] relationship. I cannot blame her because my brother had another girl in the Philippines and Cora knew it. But nothing happened. When Cora came back here to Israel, she also got a boyfriend. First, she got a Filipino man, and an Israeli old

man, and then the Turkish [man]. So I have no right to say, "why are you doing this." My flatmates told me, "Jennifer, it is good that you didn't tell your brother about Cora." I explained them I cannot blame her because it is my brother who did wrong first.

Liza also was able to maintain her relationship with John several years by virtue of her flatmates' secrecy. Liza's husband in the Philippines sometimes called Joy because Liza often did not answer the phone. According to Joy, Liza's husband sometimes asked her if Liza had an affair. Each time, Joy tried to ease his suspicions by telling a lie. Joy explained why she did not tell the truth to Liza's husband: "If he knows, there will be a trouble. Maybe he will kill her. I don't want to make any problem." At the same time, the relationship of Liza and John featured often in the gossip among flatmates, not because it deviated from expected norms of monogamous marriage but because it occurred while the wife of John was in Israel, even in the same flat. For this reason, many of the flatmates in Liza's flat criticized their relationship as "immoral."

As illustrated in the cases above, what comes to the fore in this imagery of the flat as safe shelter is a social existence that protects the migrants through anonymity in the well-guarded space. The maintenance of the established boundaries and the shelter function hinge on access control and secrecy among flatmates. Trying to secure themselves in their flat with visible physical markers and invisible surveillance, migrants seek to create a new type of community and space. As a consequence, the flat becomes a significant social unit, creating a greater distance between different social groups by excluding non-flatmates.

Ambiguity of Anonymous Space

The flat is a confined and bounded space, providing migrants with an experience of spatial isolation and suspension of time. The flat is a necessary environment for the temporary migrants who have adopted liminal identities, building an "imagined community." Migrants find temporary shelter in the flat wherein they can do what they are not supposed to do outside the flat. When they return to the Philippines and leave the flat, the "deviant" behaviors they may have engaged in are no longer a part of their lives. In this way, migrants can exert a certain degree of autonomy separating themselves from the hegemonic rules and discourses of the dominant societies, both in the Philippines and in Israel.

The issues of community and space among Filipino care workers can be located within a broader set of questions concerning identity and anonymity.

Simply being at a certain flat at particular times can be a key to presumed identity. However, to be integrated into the flat as insiders they need to contribute to making the flat anonymous through gating and secrecy. As Ponesse (2014, p. 316) points out, "because anonymity is a way of segregating an otherwise integrated self—of packaging the selves piecemeal for the world—anonymity involves a loss of visible integrity, and as such creates ambiguous identities." The formation of sharp boundaries between the inside and the outside of a flat molds the migrants' concept of self and other, invoking further parallel contrasts, including intimate and distant, safe and dangerous, same and different, freedom and repression.

Other than the "legal"/"illegal" status of insiders, their privacy, such as extramarital relationships, is also protected within the flat by virtue of other flatmates' secrecy. As long as the migrants keep such relationships only within the flat and remain unknown to outsiders, no one can trace their personal information and their private lives. Although *Neve Sha'anan* is located far away from their workplaces and the Philippines, the bounded neighborhood is not a neutral place in which to conduct an affair. Because they can encounter their hometown friends or relatives in *Neve Sha'anan*, they must make invisible their extramarital relationships, and their flat serves as the only place to do this far from the watchful eyes of other Filipino migrants, their employers, and their larger home community.

In that way, being part of a flat is critical in terms of immediate survival and finding safe shelter. This study showed how the flat becomes a vital component of a migrant identity, which provides grounds for activating a sense of belonging and security, and how the production of anonymity contributes to the making of the flat. There is a main principle that governs migrants' everyday practices in the flat, defining the proper ways of behaving: one must not reveal the private information of one's flatmates to outsiders. Both the sight of the flat and its anonymity convey exclusivity and boundaries, while generating feelings of belonging among insiders. Within the flat, migrants feel a special bond with their flatmates as they undertake collective action to build an anonymous space in order to accomplish their shared goals for a well-guarded space.

At the same time, the presumed private space obtains a dimension of public space. By residing in a constricted and restricted space apart from others, flatmates have little choice but to share their private lives and legal status inside the flat. While the anonymity enables the flatmates to enjoy their privacy and security against the hostile environment, it can be framed as a threat inside the flat where solidarities and identities are constantly and fluidly experienced, negotiated, and disrupted. Residents monitor their environments, "closely identifying those who do not belong," yet at the same time they are sheltered by the privacy made possible by their relationships inside the flat. In that way, the flat creates paradoxical situations inside the enclosed space of the flat, in which one's privacy and security are likely to be threatened by insiders even while internal solidarity is promoted.

Bibliography

Abesamis, M. (2000). *Women-loving-women: The experience of some Filipina domestic workers in Hong Kong* [originally titled *Romance and resistance: The experience of Filipina domestics in Hong Kong*]. Unpublished M.A. thesis. The Hague: Institute of Social Studies.

Alicea, M. (1997). A chambered Nautilus: The contradictory nature of Puerto Rican women's role in the social construction of a transnational community. *Gender & Society, 11*(5), 597–626. https://doi.org/10.1177/089124397011005005

Arcinas, F. R. (1986). *The Odyssey of the Filipino migrant workers to the Gulf Region.* Department of Sociology, University of the Philippines.

Avila, E. M. (2008). *Transnational motherhood and fatherhood: Gendered challenges and coping.* University of Southern California.

Blakely, E. J., & Snyder, M. G. (1997). *Fortress America: Gating communities in the United States.* Brookings Institution Press and Lincoln Institute of Land Policy, Washington, DC.

Bloch, A., & Schuster, L. (2005). At the extremes of exclusion: Deportation, detention and dispersal. *Ethnic and Racial Studies, 28*(3), 491–512. https://doi.org/10.1080/0141987042000337858

Chavez, L. R. (2007). The condition of illegality. *International Migration, 45*(3), 192–196. https://doi.org/10.1111/j.1468-2435.2007.00416.x

Chavez, L. R. (2017). A history of birth right citizenship. In *Anchor Babies and the Challenge of Birthright Citizenship* (pp. 42–54). Stanford University Press.

Constable, N. (2003). A transnational perspective on divorce and marriage: Filipina wives and workers. *Identities, 10*(2), 163–180. https://doi.org/10.1080/10702890304328

Coutin, S. B. (2000). *Legalizing moves: Salvadoran immigrants' struggle for U.S. Residency.* University of Michigan Press.

Coutin, S. B. (2005). Contesting criminality: Illegal immigration and the spatialization of legality. *Theoretical Criminology, 9*(1), 5–33. https://doi.org/10.1177/1362480605046658

De Genova, N. P. (2002). Migrant "illegality" and deportability in everyday life. *Annual Review of Anthropology, 31,* 419–447. https://doi.org/10.1146/annurev.anthro.31.040402.085432

De Genova, N. P. (2004). The legal production of Mexican/migrant "illegality." *Latino Studies*, *2*(2), 160–185. https://doi.org/10.1057/palgrave.list.8600085.

Friedlander, A. L. (2010). The state of Israel's approach to foreign workers and their families: A policy of ignoring aimed at segregation. In M. Shechory, S. Ben-David, & D. Seon, (Eds.), *Who pays the price?: Foreign workers, society, crime and the law* (pp. 137–150). Nova Science Publishers, Inc.

Gabriella, Q. (2001). *Gender based corruption in the Philippines*. Conference, the University of Sydney, December 13–15, 2001.

Hiemstra, N. (2010). Immigrant "illegality" as neoliberal governmentality in Leadville, Colorado. *Antipode*, *42*(1), 74–102. https://doi.org/10.1111/j.1467-8330.2009.00732.x

Isin, E. F., & Rygiel, K. (2007). Of other global cities: Frontiers, zones, camps. In H. Wimmen (Ed.), *Cities and globalization: Challenges for citizenship*. Saqi Books.

Kav LaOved. (2010). *Kav LaOved's (worker's hotline) Shadow report on the situation of female migrant workers in Israel*. Submitted to the Committee on the Elimination of All Forms of Discrimination against Women 48th Session, December 2010.

Kohli, R. K. S. (2006). The sound of silence: Listening to what unaccompanied asylum-seeking children say and do not say. *British Journal of Social Work*, *36*(5), 707–721. https://doi.org/10.1093/bjsw/bch305

Manalansan IV, M. F. (2006). Queer intersections: Sexuality and gender in migration studies. *International Migration Review*, *40*(1), 224–249. https://doi.org/10.1111/j.1747-7379.2006.00009.x

Margold, J. A. (1995). Narratives of masculinity and transnational migration: Filipino workers in the Middle East. In A. Ong & M. Z. Peletz (Eds.), *Bewitching women, pious men: Gender and body politics in Southeast Asia* (pp. 274–293). University of California Press.

Nathan, G. (2017). *The OECD expert group on migration SOPEMI annual report 2016–2017*. Research and Information Center, Israeli Parliament (Knesset).

Newman, O. (1972). *Creating defensible space*. Center for Urban Policy Research, Rutgers University.

Parreñas, R. S. (2000). *Servants of globalization: Women, migration and domestic work*. Stanford University Press.

Pe-pua, R. (2003). Wife, mother, and maid: The triple role of Filipino domestic workers in Spain and Italy. In N. Piper & M. Roces (Eds.), *Wife or worker?: Asian women and Migration* (pp. 157–180). Rowman & Littlefield Publishers, INC.

Pingol, A. (2010), Filipino women workers in Saudi: Making offerings for the here and now and hereafter. *The Asia Pacific Journal of Anthropology*, *11*(3–4), 394–409.

Ponesse, J. (2014). The ties that blind: Conceptualizing anonymity. *Journal of Social Philosophy*, *45*(3).

Porat, I., & Iecovich, E. (2010). Relationships between elderly care recipients and their migrant live-in home care workers in Israel. *Home Health Care Service Quarterly*, *29*(1), 1–21. https://doi.org/10.1080/01621424.2010.487035

Rodriguez, R. M. (2002). Migrant heroes: Nationalism, citizenship and the politics of Filipino migrant labor. *Citizenship Studies*, *6*(3), 341–356. https://doi.org/10.1080/1362102022000011658

Salter, M. B. (2007). Governmentalities of an airport: Heterotopia and confession. *International Political Sociology*, *1*(1), 49–d66. https://doi.org/10.1111/j.1749-5687.2007.00004.x

Tsujimoto, T. (2003). Church organization and its networks for the Filipino migrants: Surviving and empowering in Korea. In M. Tsuda (Ed.), *Filipino diaspora: Demography, social networks, empowerment and culture* (pp. 125–162). Philippine Migration Research Network (PMRN) and Philippine Social Science Council.

Tsujimoto, T. (2014). Negotiating gender dynamics in heteronormativity: Extramarital intimacy among migrant Filipino workers in South Korea. *Gender, Place & Culture*, *21*(6), 750–767. https://doi.org/10.1080/0966369X.2013.817965

Valerio, R. L. F. (2002). *Pagtitimpi at panggigigil: Sex and the migrant woman*. In E. Dizon-Anonuevo & A. T. Anonuevo (Eds.), *Coming home: Women, migration and re-integration* (pp. 60–69). Balikbayani Foundation, Inc. and Atikha Overseas Workers and Communities Initiative.

Watson, S., & Gibson, K. (1995). *Postmodern cities and spaces*. Blackwell.

Willen, S. (2007). Toward a critical phenomenon of "illegality": State power, criminalization, and abjectivity among undocumented migrant workers in Tel Aviv, Israel. *International Migration*, *45*(3), 8–38. https://doi.org/10.1111/j.1468-2435.2007.00409.x

Wonders, N. A. (2006). Global flows, semi-permeable borders and new channels of inequality. In S. Pickering & L. Weber (Eds.), *Borders, mobility and technologies of control* (pp. 63–86). Springer.

Yacobi, H. (2008). *Irregular migration to Israel: The sociopolitical perspective*. Cooperation project on the social integration of immigrants, migration, and the movement of persons (CARIM).

Zontini, E. (2010). Enabling and constraining aspects of social capital in migrant families: Ethnicity, gender and generation. *Ethnic and Racial Studies*, *33*(5), 816–831. https://doi.org/10.1080/01419870903254661

Conclusion: Creating an "Imagined Community" in Displacement

Abstract: This concluding chapter provides a comprehensive review of the book. Offering a repertoire of the Filipino migrants' own narratives, the ethnographic accounts represent migrant space as constructed by multiple agents and networks of complex connections. The flat provides an experience of spatial isolation and suspension of time that detaches migrants from the demands of reality in the host society, which shape the migrant space in relation to the wider social contexts. The spatial analysis of the flat contributes to migration scholarship by opening up avenues of analysis for space, communities, boundary-making and identities in trans-local contexts. I further demonstrate how the migrants exercise their agency by forming the flat as an escape route for freedom and autonomy, avoiding the pitfalls of binary notions of victimhood and agency, legal and illegal, formal and informal.

Keywords: migrant space, place-attachment, mobility, community, agency

The increasing flexibility and feminization of migration labor under neo-liberal globalization creates new patterns in the contemporary transnational world. With the growing demand for domestic work in many developed countries, the Philippine government has strongly responded to the changing global labor market and newly emerging employment opportunities by mobilizing its resources to capture a considerable part of the overseas labor market. Within the stratified global labor market, which facilitates the development of an institutionalized and commercialized migration industry, Filipino women migrate to more developed countries to be hired as low-paid domestic laborers. In these positions they move through diverse "survival circuits" (Sassen, 2002).

The majority of Filipino migrant workers I met in Israel had worked in different labor-importing countries, searching for a better life for their

---

Lim, Anna. *Filipino Care Workers in Israel: Migration, Trans-local Livelihoods and Space*. Amsterdam: Amsterdam University Press, 2025.
DOI: 10.5117/9789463720403_CONC

family and certainly for themselves. When they arrived in Israel as a care worker, after paying an exorbitant placement fee, they were placed in largely strange and unfriendly environment with their marginalized and precarious conditions as non-citizens and domestic laborers. Apart from institutional exclusion, the host society that forcibly marginalizes the migrants' incorporation within private households as live-in care workers places them in an ambiguous position as an "intimate Other." The in-betweens and temporariness of their experiences in Israeli society led to the creation of a distinctive social space, which is patterned within its own unique temporal and spatial orders.

Reflections on and Beyond Community and Boundaries

This book addresses the two major themes of space and community with reference to Filipino care workers in Israel and provides comprehensive insight into the dynamics of transnational labor migration. The flat where the migrants flock every weekend for their day-off provides an experience of spatial isolation from the mainstream society and from those to whom they give care, thus suspending time. Thereby, the flat detaches them from the demands of reality and offers opportunities for all sorts of new experiences with peers. While the Filipino migrants share national identity and status as working-class foreigners in Israel, their caretaking and migratory experiences are not usually shared. In the absence of their own family, flatmates replicate many of the rights and obligations usually associated with family ties, instilling a sense of insiderness that differentiates flatmates from non-flatmates, while binding migrants with different backgrounds into a flat.

The discussion of boundary-making among the migrants based on the flat makes a key contribution to understanding and destabilizing nationally bound conceptions of identity and community. In practice, the criticism of methodological nationalism is a crucial point for exploring what shapes the changing dynamics of cross-border mobility (Glick-Schiller & Salazar, 2013; Wimmer & Schiller, 2002). Methodological nationalism "confines the concept of society to the boundaries of nation-states and assumes the members of those states to share a common history and set of values, norms, social customs and institutions" (Glick-Schiller & Salazar, 2013, p. 191), consequently normalizing stasis.

This analysis disrupts traditional notions of place and community and provides useful insight into the construction and reconstruction of community in a translocal context. Experiences and accounts are not shared by the migrants who share a national identity due to the global dynamics in which migrants find themselves. As Glick-Schiller and Salazar (2013) suggest, a regime of mobility approach is neither confined by nor does it ignore nation and territory, but still gives more attention to the myriad ways in which people and their cultural practices are parts of multiple spatial networks within multiple intersecting scales (Yeates, 2013).

Interestingly enough, although the flat is imagined as a space of homogeneity and equality by the migrants, it becomes the source of differences and a site of intersecting and conflicting meanings, frustrating the utopic ideal of *communitas*. As a collective living space, at the same time, the flat promotes the emergence of a unique social structure and hierarchical order that together govern the community, producing different identities and meanings. In this notion, the flat is rather a fragmented space that encompasses incompatible differences and a space of hierarchy.

In this way, an important theme that recurs in this book is the issue of boundaries. In the making of the flat as a space with distinct functions, it is critical for the migrants to draw sharp boundaries between inside and outside based on the flat and sustain these. At the same time, the formation of flat community is significant for the temporary migrant workers beyond the economic advantage of shared accommodation. Sharp boundaries between the inside and the outside mold the migrants' concept of self and other, invoking further parallel contrasts, including intimate and distant, us and them, safe and danger, same and different, and freedom and repression.

Of significance, redrawing the boundaries of identity and community through the flat contributes to altering the meaning of hegemonic dichotomy for private and public and recreates the "inside." In the flat, the boundaries of the public and the private become blurred because migrants create a new "public realm" within due to their collective use of the space. Migrants flock to the flat every weekend, exemplifying public life flourishing in the privately owned space with its own organization and hierarchical structure. By subverting the relations of the public and private, the flat effectively unfolds the invisible aspects of the migrant lives in a way different from that which surrounds it.

This further poses issues for boundaries, questioning the binary categories between "legal" and "illegal," formal and informal, incorporation and exclusion. The categories of "legal" and "illegal," which are defined by the labor sovereigns, become blurry within the flat, even challenging these dominant designations. In the context of detection and deportation throughout the country, those migrants who lack legal visa status are considered subjects of "exclusion" and potential deportees. Within the ambivalent zone of the flat, however, the undocumented migrants are not subjects of exclusion. Rather, they are included and protected by flatmates. In that way, being part of a flat is critical in terms of immediate survival and finding safe shelter.

This study demonstrates how the flat becomes a vital component of a migrant identity, which provides grounds for activating a sense of belonging and security, and also how the production of anonymity contributes to the making of flat. Both the sight of the flat and its anonymity convey exclusivity and boundaries, while generating feelings of belonging among insiders. Within the flat, migrants feel a special bond with their flatmates as they undertake collective action to build an anonymous space in order to accomplish their shared goals for a well-guarded space.

At the same time, it is also important to note that solidarities and identities are constantly and fluidly experienced, negotiated, and disrupted. There is a main principle that governs migrants' everyday practices in the flat, defining the proper ways of behaving: one must not reveal the private information of one's flatmates to outsiders. Residents monitor their environments, "closely identifying those who do not belong," yet at the same time they are sheltered by the privacy made possible by their relationships inside the flat.

While the anonymity enables flatmates to enjoy their privacy and security against the hostile environment, it may be framed as a threat inside the flat. By residing in a constricted and restricted space apart from others, flatmates have little choice but to share their private lives and legal status inside the flat. In that way, the flat also creates paradoxical situations inside the enclosed space of the flat, in which one's privacy and security are likely to be threatened by insiders even while internal solidarity is promoted.

Intertwining Place Attachment and Mobility

This study also aligns with the growing body of research on transnational migrant space, underscoring the relevance of the migration research to broader discussions of space. Drawing on the place-making practices among the migrant care workers in Israel, this study shows not only the ways in which migrants organize their lives, but also conceptualizes the flat as constructed and experienced with the recognition of an increasingly interconnected transnational world, thereby underscoring the particular subjectivities of migrant workers. In this way, the structure of a flat signifies

CONCLUSION: CREATING AN "IMAGINED COMMUNITY" IN DISPLACEMENT

both migrants' marginality and challenging position, while also reflecting community and belonging.

Given the many regulations and circumscriptions placed on migrant life, it is important to address migrants' experiences, mobility, and complex social lives as productive in generating the flat and also as produced by the flat. Migrants further transform the flat into a shelter through spatial practices of access control and secrecy, wherein they can enjoy autonomy and security and turn their life around even if only temporarily. Importantly, the fortification of the flat is a spatial response to the defensive realities in which they are embedded. The meaning of the flat as a shelter takes shape in a "crime-ridden" urban context for migrants whose lives as lived outside the flat involve oppressive work conditions, constant surveillance by Immigration Police and Filipino reporters, and watchful eyes from the dominant society.

Furthermore, this study, taking up mobility and attachment as a lens of analysis, opens interesting avenues for understanding transnational migrant space, challenging the once sedentary paradigm of place. Although the flat is a space of exclusivity, which regulates outsiders' access, it is simultaneously an open space because migrants are able to negotiate the boundaries by entering and leaving. Once migrants get permission into a flat, they enjoy privileges as insiders within the fortified space where their privacy and security are protected. On the contrary, they become outsiders when they get out of the flat or return to the Philippines. Nonetheless, migrants constantly move out, searching for a better place for themselves, thus the flat is a transient place, an uncertain step in their journey, even when their destination is another flat, which becomes a new key point of departure and arrival.

In this scheme, the flat can be understood in terms of both place attachment and mobility, through which migrants come to experience the flat. The boundary of a flat is continually changing with its destruction and rebuilding. The practice of transfer is a major mechanism through which dynamics of the flat are driven, both by creating and disrupting the social ties of migrants. Therefore, migrants' mobility does not necessarily contradict the importance of place attachment (Gustafson, 2001). Rather, both concepts are integrated in the migrants' ordinary experiences and in the making of the flat as a distinct social space, in which a complex range of experiences and meanings are inscribed. Therefore, their mobility is crucial for understanding the construction of the flat, in which the disparate but mutually related themes of place attachment and disruption are necessarily integrated to create the role of the flat in imagining community.

Interplay of Migrant Agency and Structure

Finally, this book offers a comprehensive repertoire of migrant lives and migrants' own narratives, informing and informed by the subjectivities of migrants. This study shows how migrants are positioned in vulnerable and marginalized statuses but simultaneously demonstrates how migrants exercise their agency by forming the flat as an escape route for freedom and autonomy, avoiding the pitfalls of binary notions of victimhood and agency. Filipino migrant workers are incorporated into the Israeli society but marginalized and excluded via their constrained employment contexts as a result of their position as working-class foreigners and women. Nevertheless, they negotiate their position with consociates by practicing adaptive strategies in interactions in the flat and from that foundation with wider social fields.

I also provide a comprehensive look at the whole migration process, from the migrants' decision-making to their settlement in Israel, and even after that on the assumption that the recruitment process has great impact on migrant experiences and lives in the receiving society. State policies both in the Philippines and Israel play a crucial role in facilitating and shaping the migration flow. The existence of gender-specific job opportunities for migrant workers and the tendency of migration to sustain itself have produced male-dominated and female-dominated migratory linkages between certain countries. In this book, I demonstrate how the migrants realize their migration project within their limited migration and friendship circuits grounded in the flat. Illuminating the decision-making and the migratory processes, this book adds to our knowledge of emerging patterns of "serial labor migration" (Parreñas et al., 2019) or "stepwise international migration" (Paul, 2011).

I examine how Filipino migrant women who are unable to gain immediate entry into their preferred destination countries by low capital participate in the migration process, highlighting the key roles of the migrant workers. I provide detailed descriptions of migration flows from the Philippines to Israel, focusing on the linkages between state policies and the operations of the migration networks at a micro-level. I highlight the complementary roles of different actors, especially migrant workers, in sustaining self-perpetuating and self-serving "migration infrastructure" (Xiang & Lindquist, 2014), creating an informal sector within the Israeli migration scheme. The stories of migrant workers reveal that despite being trapped in legal regulatory frameworks, they are recognized as actors with agency by themselves, by consociates, and even by society as they blur the boundaries of formal and informal, legal and illegal, positioned workers and individuals with independent lives.

Bibliography

Glick-Schiller, N., & Salazar, N. B. (2013). Regimes of mobility across the globe. *Journal of Ethnic and Migration Studies, 39*(2), 183–200. https://doi.org/10.1080/1369183X.2013.723253

Gustafson, P. (2001). Roots and routes: Exploring the relationship between place attachment and mobility. *Environment and Behavior, 33*(5), 667–686. https://doi.org/10.1177/00139160121973188

Paul, A. M. (2011). Stepwise international migration: A multistage migration pattern for the aspiring migrant. *American Journal of Sociology, 116*(6), 1842–1886.

Parreñas, R. S., Silvey, R., Hwang, M. C., & Choi, C. A. (2019). Serial labor migration: Precarity and itinerancy among Filipino and Indonesian domestic workers. *International Migration Review, 53*(4), 1230–1258. https://doi.org/10.1177/0197918318804769

Sassen, S. (2002). Global cities and survival circuits. In J. A. Radway, K. Gaines, B. Shank, & P. V. Eschen (Eds.), *American studies: An anthology* (pp. 185–193). Wiley-Blackwell.

Wimmer, A., & Schiller, G.N. (2002). Methodological nationalism and beyond: Nation-state building, migration and the social sciences. *Global Networks, 2*(4), 301–334. https://doi.org/10.1111/1471-0374.00043

Xiang, B., & Lindquist, J. (2014). Migration infrastructure. *International Migration Review, 48*(1), 122–148. https://doi.org/10.1111/imre.12141

Yeates, N. (2013). Global care chains: A state-of-the-art review and future directions in care transnationalization research. *Global Networks, 12*(2), 135–154. https://doi.org/10.1111/j.1471-0374.2012.00344.x

Acknowledgements

This book is a product of my long-term ethnographic fieldwork. I am indebted to the Filipino migrants who gave me their valuable time and trusted me with their personal experiences. Without their contribution, this book would not exist. I would first like to express deep gratitude to prof. Adriana Kemp and prof. Ofra Goldstein-Gidoni of Tel Aviv University, for providing insightful feedback throughout the research process and encouraging me to publish my dissertation as a book. I extend my gratitude to prof. Myung-Seok Oh of Seoul National University for his invaluable guidance in my journey to becoming an anthropologist. Additionally, I would like to thank reviewers for all their valuable comments and suggestions, which helped me in improving the quality of my manuscript. And I am extremely grateful to the commissioning editors at AUP, Loretta Lou and Saskia Gieling. I would not be able to get my work done without their professional support and continual encouragement. Most of all, I am grateful to my family for their love and prayers.

Bibliography

Abesamis, M. (2000). *Women-loving-women: The experience of some Filipina domestic workers in Hong Kong* [originally titled *Romance and resistance: The experience of Filipina domestics in Hong Kong*]. Unpublished M.A. thesis. The Hague: Institute of Social Studies.

Aguilar, F. V. (2003). Global migrations, old forms of labor, and new transborder class relations. *Southeast Asian Studies, 41*(2), 137–161. https://doi.org/10.20495/tak.41.2_137

Alexander, M. (2003). *Host-stranger relations in Rome, Tel Aviv, Paris and Amsterdam: A comparison of local policies toward labour migrants*. Doctoral Thesis, University of Amsterdam, The Netherlands.

Alicea, M. (1997). A chambered Nautilus: The contradictory nature of Puerto Rican women's role in the social construction of a transnational community. *Gender & Society, 11*(5), 597–626. https://doi.org/10.1177/089124397011005005

Appadurai, A. (1995). The production of locality. In R. Fardon (Ed.), *Counterworks: Managing the diversity of knowledge* (pp. 204–225). New York. https://doi.org/10.4324/9780203450994

Appadurai, A. (1996). *Modernity at large: Cultural dimensions of globalization*. University of Minnesota Press.

Arat-Koc, S. (1989). In the privacy of our own home: Foreign domestic workers as solution to the crisis in the domestic sphere in Canada. *Studies in Political Economy, 28*(1), 33–58. https://doi.org/10.1080/19187033.1989.11675524

Arcinas, F. R. (1986). *The Odyssey of the Filipino migrant workers to the Gulf region*. Department of Sociology, University of the Philippines.

Armenta, A. (2009). Creating community: Latina nannies in a West Los Angeles park. *Qualitative Sociology, 32*, 279–292. https://doi.org/10.1007/s11133-009-9129-1

Aronson, J., & Neysmith, S. M. (1996). You are not just in there to do the work: Depersonalizing policies and the exploitation of home care workers' labor. *Gender & Society, 10*(1), 59–77. https://doi.org/10.1177/089124396010001005

Asis, M. (1992). The overseas employment program policy. In G. Battistella & A. Paganoni (Eds.), *Philippine labour migration: Impact and policy* (pp. 68–112). Scalabrini Migration Center.

Avila, E. M. (2008). *Transnational motherhood and fatherhood: Gendered challenges and coping*. University of Southern California.

Ayalon, L. (2009). Family and family-like interactions in households with round-the-clock paid foreign carers in Israel. *Ageing & Society, 29*(5), 671–686. https://doi.org/10.1017/S0144686X09008393

Ayalon, L., & Ohad, G. (2013). Live-in versus live-out home care in Israel: Satisfaction with services and care workers' outcomes. *The Gerontologist, 55*(4) 628–642. https://doi.org/10.1093/geront/gnt122

Babis, D. (2021). Digital mourning on Facebook: The case of Filipino migrant worker live-in caregivers in Israel. *Media, Culture & Society, 43*(3), 397–410. https://doi.org/10.1177/0163443720957550

Babis, D. (2022). Inclusion and beauty pageants? The Filipino migrant worker community in Israel. *Gender, Place & Culture, 29*(5), 625–648. https://doi.org/10.1080/0966369X.2021.1887090

Bakan, A. B., & Stasiulis, D. (1997). Foreign domestic worker policy in Canada and the social boundaries of modern citizenship. In A. B. Bakan & D. Stasiulis (Eds.), *Not one of the family: Foreign domestic workers in Canada* (pp. 29–52). University of Toronto Press.

Ball, R. E. (1997). The role of the state in the globalization of labour markets: The case of the Philippines. *Environment and Planning A: Economy and Space, 29*(9), 1603–1628. https://doi.org/10.1068/a291603

Ball, R. E. (2004). Divergent development, racialised rights: Globalised labour markets and the trade of nurses: The case of the Philippines. *Women's Studies International Forum, 27*(2), 119–133. https://doi.org/10.1016/j.wsif.2004.06.003

Barber, P. (2000). Agency in Philippine women's labour migration and provisional diaspora. *Women's Studies International Forum, 23*(4), 399–411. https://doi.org/10.1016/S0277-5395(00)00104-7

Barth, F. (1966). Models of social organization. Royal Anthropological Institute Occasional Paper, (23), London.

Batram, D. V. (1998). Foreign workers in Israel: History and theory. *International Migration Review, 32*(2), 303–325. https://doi.org/10.1177/019791839803200201

Ben-Peshat, M., & Sitton, S. (2011). Glocalized New Age spirituality: A mental map of the new Central Bus Station in Tel Aviv, deciphered through its visual codes and based on ethno-visual research. *Journal of Visual Literacy, 30*(2), 64–90. https://doi.org/10.1080/23796529.2011.11674690

Besley, T., Coate, S., & Loury, G. (1993). The economics of rotating savings and credit associations. *The American Economic Review, 83*(4), 792–810.

Blakely, E. J., & Snyder, M. G. (1997). *Fortress America: Gating communities in the United States.* Brookings Institution Press and Lincoln Institute of Land Policy, Washington, DC.

Bloch, A., & Schuster, L. (2005). At the extremes of exclusion: Deportation, detention and dispersal. *Ethnic and Racial Studies, 28*(3), 491–512. https://doi.org/10.1080/0141987042000337858

Biggart, N. W. (2001). Banking on each other: The situational logic of rotating savings and credit associations. *Advances in Qualitative Organization Research, 3*(1), 129–152.

Borris, E., & Parreñas, R. S. (2010). *Intimate labors: Cultures, technologies, and the politics of care*. Stanford Social Sciences.

Bourdieu, P. (1989). Social space and symbolic power. *Sociological Theory, 7*(1), 14–25. https://doi.org/10.2307/202060

Boyle, P. (2002). Population geography: Transnational women on the move. *Progress in Human Geography, 26*(4), 531–543. https://doi.org/10.1191/0309132502ph384pr

Brodsky, J., & Naon, D. (1993). Home care services in Israel-implications of the expansion of home care following implementation of the community long-term care insurance law. *Journal of Cross-Cultural Gerontology, 8*(4), 375–390. https://doi.org/10.1080/0141987042000337858

Brown, R. H. (2016). Multiple modes of care: Internet and migrant caregiver networks in Israel. *Global Networks, 16*(2), 237–256. https://doi.org/10.1111/glob.12112

Burawoy, M. (1998). The extended case method. *Sociological Theory, 16*(1), 4–33. https://doi.org/10.1111/0735-2751.00040

Carlos, M. R. (2010). *Filipino careworkers in ageing Japan: Trends, trajectories and policies*. A paper to be presented at the conference Migration: A World in Motion, 18–20. February 2010, University of Maastricht, Netherlands.

Castles, S., & Miller, M. J. (2003). *The age of migration*. Guilford Press.

Chammartin, G. M. (2005). Domestic workers: Little protection for the underpaid. *Migration Information Source*. Migration Policy Institute.

Charito, B., de Guzman, V., & Marchetti, S. (2012), *International migration and over-indebtedness: The case of Filipino workers in Italy*. Human settlements Working Paper, 36. International Institute for Environment and Development.

Chavez, L. R. (2007). The condition of illegality. *International Migration, 45*(3), 192–196. https://doi.org/10.1111/j.1468-2435.2007.00416.x

Chavez, L. R. (2017). A history of birth right citizenship. In *Anchor Babies and the Challenge of Birthright Citizenship* (pp. 42–54). Stanford University Press.

Choy, C. C. (2003). *Empire of care: Nursing and migration in Filipino American history*. Duke University Press.

Clifford, J. (1997). *Routes: Travel and translation in the late twentieth century*. Havard University Press.

Cohen, R. (1991). Women of color in white households: Coping strategies of live-in domestic workers. *Qualitative Sociology, 14*(2), 197–215. https://doi.org/10.1007/BF00992194

Coleman, J. S. (1990). *Foundations of social theory*. Harvard University Press.

Constable, N. (1997). *Maid to order in Hong Kong: Stories of Filipina workers*. Cornell University Press.

Constable, N. (2003). A transnational perspective on divorce and marriage: Filipina wives and workers. *Identities, 10*(2), 163–180. https://doi.org/10.1080/10702890304328

Constable, N. (2009). The commodification of intimacy: Marriage, sex, and reproductive labor. *Annual Review of Anthropology, 38*, 49–64. https://doi.org/10.1146/annurev.anthro.37.081407.085133

Coutin, S. B. (2000). *Legalizing moves: Salvadoran immigrants' struggle for U.S. residency*. University of Michigan Press.

Coutin, S. B. (2005). Contesting criminality: Illegal immigration and the spatialization of legality. *Theoretical Criminology, 9*(1), 5–33. https://doi.org/10.1177/1362480605046658

Cresswell, T. (2004). *Place: A short introduction*. Blackwell Publishing Ltd.

Cruz, G. T. (2008). Between identity and security: Theological implications of migration in the context of globalization. *Theological Studies, 69*(2), 357–375. https://doi.org/10.1177/004056390806900207

De Genova, N. P. (2002). Migrant 'illegality' and deportability in everyday life. *Annual Review of Anthropology, 31*, 419–447. https://doi.org/10.1146/annurev.anthro.31.040402.085432

De Genova, N. P. (2004). The legal production of Mexican/migrant "illegality." *Latino Studies, 2*(2), 160–185. https://doi.org/10.1057/palgrave.list.8600085

De Guzman, O. (2003). Overseas Filipino workers, labor circulation in Southeast Aisa, and the (mis)management of overseas migration programs. *Kyoto Review of Southeast Asia*, (4). Retrieved from http://kyotoreview.org/issue-4/overseas-filipino-workers-labor-circulation-in-southeast-asia-and-the-mismanagement-of-overseas-migration-programs

De Haas, H. (2010). The internal dynamics of migration processes: A theoretical inquiry. *Journal of Ethnic and Migration Studies, 36*(10), 1587–1617. https://doi.org/10.1080/1369183X.2010.489361

Doria, R. (2008). Absence at the dinner table: Loss of eating habits through Filipino generations. Unpublished manuscript. Downloaded from https://www.writing.ucsb.edu, University of California–Santa Barbara.

Drori, I. (2009). *Foreign workers in Israel: Global perspective*. SUNY Press.

Ebaugh, H. R., & Curry, M. (2000). Fictive kin as social capital in new immigrant communities. *Sociological Perspectives, 43*(2), 189–209. https://doi.org/10.2307/1389793

Ehrenreich, B., & Hochschild, A. R. (2003). *Global woman: Nannies, maids and sex workers in the new economy*. Henry Holt and Company.

Ellman, M., & Laacher, S. (2003). *Migrant workers in Israel: A contemporary form of slavery*. Euro-Mediterranean Human Rights Network (EMHRN), Copenhagen & Paris, June 2003. www.euromedrights.net.

Embree, J. F. (1939). *Suye Mura: A Japanese village*. University of Chicago Press.

Espiritu, Y. L. (2003). *Home bound: Filipino American lives across cultures, communities, and countries*. University of California Press.

Ezquerra, S. (2009). *The regulation of the south-north transfer of reproductive labor: Filipino women in Spain and the United States*. Ph.D. dissertation, University of Oregon.

Faist, T. (2000). *The volume and dynamics of international migration and transnational social spaces*. Oxford University Press.

Fenster, T., & Yacobi, H. (2005). Whose city is it? On urban planning and local knowledge in globalizing Tel Aviv-Jaffa. *Planning Theory & Practice*, 6(2), 191–211. https://doi.org/10.1080/14649350500137051

Friedlander, A. L. (2010). The state of Israel's approach to foreign workers and their families: A policy of ignoring aimed at segregation. In M. Shechory, S. Ben-David, & D. Seon (Eds.), *Who pays the price?: Foreign workers, society, crime and the law* (pp. 137–150). Nova Science Publishers, Inc.

Friedmann, J. (2007). Reflections on place and place-making in the cities of China. *International Journal of Urban and Regional Research*, 31(2), 257–279. https://doi.org/10.1111/j.1468-2427.2007.00726.x

Gabriella, Q. (2001). *Gender based corruption in the Philippines*. Conference, University of Sydney, December 13–15, 2001.

Garip, F. (2008). Social capital and migration: How do similar resources lead to divergent outcomes?. *Demography*, 45(3), 591–617. https://doi.org/10.1353/dem.0.0016

Gibson, K., Law, L. & McKay, D. (2001), Beyond heroes and victims: Filipina contract migrants, economic activism and class transformation. *International Feminist Journal of Politics*, 3(3), 365–386. https://doi.org/10.1080/14616740110078185

Gielis, R. (2009). A global sense of migrant places: Towards a place perspective in the study of migrant transnationalism. *Global Networks*, 9(2), 271–287. https://doi.org/10.1111/j.1471-0374.2009.00254.x

Gielis, R. (2011). The value of single-site ethnography in the global era: Studying transnational experiences in the migrant house. *Royal Geographical Society*, 43(3), 257–263. https://doi.org/10.1111/j.1475-4762.2011.01020.x

Glenn, E. N. (1992). From servitude to service work: Historical continuities in the racial division of paid reproductive labor. *Journal of Women in Culture and Society*, 18(1), 1–43.

Glick-Schiller, N., & Salazar, N. B. (2013). Regimes of mobility across the globe. *Journal of Ethnic and Migration Studies*, 39(2), 183–200. https://doi.org/10.1080/1369183X.2013.723253

Goffman, E. (1963). *Stigma: Notes on the management of spoiled identity*. Prentice-Hall.

Goffman, E. (1971). *The presentation of self in everyday life*. Anchor Books.

Golan, O., & Babis, D. (2019). Digital host national identification among Filipino temporary migrant workers. *Asian Journal of Communication*, 29(2), 164–180. https://doi.org/10.1080/01292986.2018.1541097

Goss, J., & Lindquist, B. (1995). Conceptualizing international labor migration: A structuration perspective. *International Migration Review*, 29(2), 317–351. https://doi.org/10.1177/019791839502900201

Granovetter, M. (1983). The strength of weak ties: A network theory revisited. *Sociological Theory, 1*, 201–233. https://doi.org/10.2307/202051

Granovetter, M. (1995). *Getting a job: A study of careers and contacts*. University of Chicago Press.

Guerrero, S. H. (2012). Gender and migration: Focus on Filipino women in international labor migration. *Review of Women's Studies, 10*(1/2), 275–298.

Guevarra, A. R. (2009). *Marketing dreams, manufacturing heroes: The transnational labor brokering of Filipino workers*. Rutgers University Press.

Gupta, A., & Ferguson, J. (1997). Beyond culture: Space, identity, and the politics of difference. In A. Gupta & J. Ferguson (Eds.), *Culture, power, place: Explorations in critical anthropology* (pp. 1–29). Duke University Press.

Gustafson, P. (2001). Roots and routes: Exploring the relationship between place attachment and mobility. *Environment and Behavior, 33*(5), 667–686. https://doi.org/10.1177/00139160121973188

Handa, S., & Kirton, C. (1999). The economics of rotating savings and credit associations: Evidence from the Jamaican "Partner." *Journal of Development Economics, 60*(1), 173–194. https://doi.org/10.1016/S0304-3878(99)00040-1

Harvey, D. (1990). Between space and time: Reflections on the geographical imagination. *Annals of the Association of American Geographers, 80*(3), 418–434. https://doi.org/10.1111/j.1467-8306.1990.tb00305.x

Hatuka, T. (2010). *Violent acts and urban space in contemporary Tel Aviv*. University of Texas Press.

Hawthorne, L. (2010). How valuable is two-step migration?: Labour market to outcomes for international student migrants to Australia. *Asian Pacific Migration Journal, 19*(1), 5–36. https://doi.org/10.1177/011719681001900102

Hernández-León, R. (2005). The migration industry in the Mexico–U.S. migratory system. *UCLA CCPR Population Working Papers.* http://www.paper.ccpr.ucla.edu/index.php/pwp/article/view/PWP-CCPR-2005-049

Hiemstra, N. (2010). Immigrant "illegality" as neoliberal governmentality in Leadville, Colorado. *Antipode, 42*(1), 74–102. https://doi.org/10.1111/j.1467-8330.2009.00732.x

Hochschild, A. R. (2000). Global care chains and emotional surplus value. In W. Hutton & A. Giddens (Eds.), *On the edge: Living with global capitalism* (pp. 130–146). Jonathan Cape.

Hondagneu-Sotelo, P. (2001). *Domestica: Immigrant workers cleaning and caring in the shadows of affluence*. University of California Press.

Hondagneu-Sotelo, P., & Avila, E. (1997). "I am here but I'm there": The meanings of Latina transnational motherhood. *Gender and Society, 11*(5), 548–71. https://doi.org/10.1177/089124397011005003

Hosoda, N. (2013). Kababayan solidarity? Filipino communities and class relations in United Arab Emirates cities. *Journal of Arabian Studies, 3*(1), 18–35. https://doi.org/10.1080/21534764.2013.802945

Huang, L., & Douglass, M. (2008). Foreign workers and spaces for community life: Taipei's little Philippines. In A. Daniere & M. Douglass (Eds.), *The politics of civic space in Asia* (pp. 67–87). Routledge.

Iecovich, E. (2007). Live-in and live-out homecare services and care recipient satisfaction. *Journal of Aging and Social Policy, 19*(2), 105–122.

Isin, E. F., & Rygiel, K. (2007). Of other global cities: Frontiers, zones, camps. In H. Wimmen (Ed.), *Cities and globalization: Challenges for citizenship*. Saqi Books.

Jackson, V. (2011). Belonging against the national odds: Globalisation, political security and Philippine migrant workers in Israel. *Global Society, 25*(1), 49–71. https://doi.org/10.1080/13600826.2010.522982

Kalir, B. (2009). Finding Jesus in the Holy Land and taking him to China: Chinese temporary migrant workers in Israel converting to evangelical Christianity. *Sociology of Religion, 70*(2), 130–156. https://doi.org/10.1093/socrel/srp027

Kalir, B. (2013). Moving subjects, stagnant paradigms: Can the "mobilities paradigm" transcend methodological nationalism?. *Journal of Ethnic and Migration Studies, 39*(2), 311–327. https://doi.org/10.1080/1369183X.2013.723260

Kapiszewski, A. (2006). Arab versus Asian migrant workers in the GCC countries. UN Population Division.

Kav LaOved (2008). *Illegal income from migrant workers*. Kav LaOved Information Sheet, February 2008. Kav LaOved.

Kav LaOved (2010). Kav LaOved's (worker's hotline). *Shadow report on the situation of female migrant workers in Israel*. Submitted to the Committee on the Elimination of All Forms of Discrimination against Women, 48th Session, December 2010.

Kav LaOved (2013). *Black money, Black labor: Collection of brokerage fees from migrant care workers in Israel*. Retrieved from https://www.kavlaoved.org.il/wp-content/uploads/sites/3/2014/05/Black-Money-Black-Labor.pdf

Kearney, M. (1995). The local and the global: The anthropology of globalization and transnationalism. *Annual Review of Anthropology, 24*(1), 547–565. https://doi.org/10.1146/annurev.an.24.100195.002555

Kemp, A. (2004). Labor migration and racialisation: Labor market mechanism and labour migration control policies in Israel. *Social Identities, 10*(2), 267–292. https://doi.org/10.1080/1350463042000227380

Kemp, A. (2007). Managing migration, reprioritizing national citizenship: Undocumented migrant workers' children and policy reforms in Israel. *Theoretical Inquiries in Law, 8*(2), 663–691. https://doi.org/10.2202/1565-3404.1164

Kemp, A. (2010). *Reforming policies on foreign workers in Israel*. OECD Social, Employment and Migration Working Papers No.103. OECD Publishing.

Kemp, A., & Kfir, N. (2016). Mobilizing migrant workers' rights in "non-immigration" countries: The politics of resonance and migrants' rights activism in Israel and Singapore. *Law & Society Review, 50*(1), 82–116. https://doi.org/10.1111/lasr.12179

Kemp, A., & Raijman, R. (2003). Christian Zionists in the holy hand: Evangelical churches, labor migrants, and the Jewish state. *Identities, 10*(3), 295–318. https://doi.org/10.1080/10702890390228883

Kemp, A., & Raijman, R. (2004). Tel Aviv is not foreign to you: Urban incorporation policy on labor migrants in Israel. *International Migration Review, 38*(1), 26–51. https://doi.org/10.1111/j.1747-7379.2004.tb00187.x

Kemp, A., & Raijman, R. (2014). Bringing in state regulations, private brokers, and local employers: A meso-level analysis of labor trafficking in Israel. *International Migration Review, 48*(3), 604–642. https://doi.org/10.1111/imre.12109

Kemp, A., Raijman, R., Resnik, J., & Gesser, S. S. (2000). Contesting the limits of political participation: Latinos and black African migrant workers in Israel. *Ethnic and Racial Studies, 23*(1), 94–119. https://doi.org/10.1080/014198700329141

Kitiarsa, P. (2008). Thai migrants in Singapore: State, intimacy and desire. *Gender, Place & Culture, 15*(6), 595–610. https://doi.org/10.1080/09663690802518495

Kofman, E. (1999). Female "birds of passage" a decade later: Gender and immigration in the European Union. *International Migration Review, 33*(2), 269–299. https://doi.org/10.1177/019791839903300201

Kohli, R. K. S. (2006). The sound of silence: Listening to what unaccompanied asylum-seeking children say and do not say. *British Journal of Social Work, 36*(5), 707–721. https://doi.org/10.1093/bjsw/bch305

Krase, J. (1979). *Stigmatized places, stigmatized people*: Crown Heights and Prospect-Lefferts Garddens.

Lagman, M. S. (2011). *Home-cooked food, basketball leagues, phone calls and cargo boxes as reflections of transnational intimacy and identity among Baltimore-based Filipinos*. International Conference on International Relations and Development (ICIRD), Bangkok, Thailand, May 2011.

Lan, P. (2003). Negotiating social boundaries and private zones: The micropolitics of employing migrant domestic workers. *Social Problems, 50*(4), 525–549. https://doi.org/10.1525/sp.2003.50.4.525

Law, L. (2001). Home cooking: Filipina migrant workers and geographies of the senses in Hong Kong. *Ecumene, 8*(3), 264–283. https://doi.org/10.1177/096746080100800302

Law, L. (2002). Defying disappearance: Cosmopolitan public spaces in Hong Kong. *Urban Studies, 39*(9), 1625–1645. https://doi.org/10.1080/00420980220151691

Lee, B., & LiPuma, E. (2002). Cultures of circulation: The imaginations of modernity. *Public Culture, 14*(1), 191–213. https://doi.org/10.1215/08992363-14-1-191

Lefebvre, H. (1991). *The production of space*. Wiley-Blackwell.

Levitt, P. (2001). *The transnational villagers*. University of California Press.

Liebelt, C. (2010). Domestic workers' struggles and pilgrimages for a cause in Israel. *The Asia Pacific Journal of Anthropology, 11*(3–4), 245–267. https://doi.org/10.1080/14442213.2010.511632

Liebelt, C. (2011). *Caring the "Holy Land": Filipina domestic workers in Israel*. Berghahn Books.

Liebelt, C. (2012). Consuming pork, parading the virgin and crafting origami in Tel Aviv: Filipina care workers' aesthetic formations in Israel. *Ethnos, 78*(2), 255–279. https://doi.org/10.1080/00141844.2012.655302

Light, I. (1996). Self-help solution to fight urban poverty. *The American Enterprise, 7*(4), 50–52.

Lim, A. (2015). Networked mobility in the migration industry: Transnational migration of Filipino care workers to Israel. *Asian Women, 31*(2), 85–118. https://doi.org/10.14431/aw.2015.06.31.2.85

Lim, L. L., & Oishi, N. (1996). International labor migration of Asian women: Distinctive characteristics and policy concerns. *Asian and Pacific Migration Journal, 5*(1), 85–116. https://doi.org/10.1177/011719689600500010

Lobel, O. (2001). Class and care: The roles of private intermediaries in the in-home care industry in the United States and Israel. *Harvard Journal of Law and Gender, 24*, 89–140.

Logan, J. R., Zhang, W. & Alba, R. D. (2002). Immigrant enclaves and ethnic communities in New York and Los Angeles. *American Sociological Review, 67*(2), 299–322. https://doi.org/10.2307/3088897

Longva, A. N. (1999). Keeping migrant workers in check: The kafala system in the Gulf. *Middle East Report*, (211), 20–22. Middle East Research and Information Project, Inc. www.jstor.org/stable/3013330.

Low, S., & Lawrence-Zuniga, D. (Eds.). (2003). *The anthropology of space and place*. Blackwell Publishers Ltd.

Mahler, S. J., & Pessar, P. R. (2006). Gender matters: Ethnographers bring gender from the periphery toward the core of migration studies. *Center for Migration Studies of New York, 40*(1), 28–63. https://doi.org/10.1111/j.1747-7379.2006.00002.x

Manalansan IV, M. F. (2006). Queer intersections: Sexuality and gender in migration studies. *International Migration Review, 40*(1), 224–249. https://doi.org/10.1111/j.1747-7379.2006.00009.x

Marcus, G. E. (1995). Ethnography in/of the world system: The emergence of multi-site ethnography. *Annual Review of Anthropology, 24*, 95–117. https://doi.org/10.1146/annurev.an.24.100195.000523

Margold, J. A. (1995). Narratives of masculinity and transnational migration: Filipino workers in the Middle East. In A. Ong & M. Z. Peletz (Eds.), *Bewitching women, pious men: Gender and body politics in Southeast Asia* (pp. 274–293). University of California Press.

Martin, P. (2007). Managing labor migration in the 21st century. *City & Society, 19*(1), 5–18. https://doi.org/10.1525/city.2007.19.1.5

Martin, P., Abella, M., & Midgley, E. (2004). Best practices to manage migration: The Philippines. *International Migration Review*, *38*(4). https://doi.org/10.1111/j.1747-7379.2004.tb00247.x

Mauss, M. (1990 [1925]). *The gift: The form and reason for exchange in archaic societies* (W. D. Halls, trans.). Routledge.

Massey, D. S. (1985). Ethnic residential segregation: A theoretical synthesis and empirical review. *Sociology and Social Research*, *69*, 315–350.

Massey, D. S. (1994). *Space, place and gender*. University of Minnesota Press.

Massey, D. S., Goldring, L. & Durand, J. (1994). Continuities in transnational migration: An analysis of nineteen Mexican communities. *American Journal of Sociology*, *99*(6), 1492–1533.

McDonnell, L. (2013). *The Balagan: Issues of crime and state interaction in South Tel Aviv*. African Refugee Development Center (ARDC), August 2013.

McKay, D. (2006). Translocal circulation: Place and subjectivity in an extended Filipino community. *The Asia Pacific Journal of Anthropology*, *7*(3), 265–78. https://doi.org/10.1080/14442210600979357

McKay, D. (2007). Sending dollars shows feeling: Emotions and economies in Filipino migration. *Mobilities*, *2*(2), 175–194. https://doi.org/10.1080/17450100701381532

Menachem, G. (2000). Jews, Arabs, Russians and foreigners in an Israeli city: Ethnic divisions and the restructuring economy of Tel Aviv, 1983–96. *International Journal of Urban and Regional Research*, *24*(3), 634–652. https://doi.org/10.1111/1468-2427.00269

Moors, A., Jureidini, R., Ozbay, F., & Sabban, R. (2009). Migrant domestic workers: A new public presence in the Middle East?. In S. Shami (Ed.), *Publics, politics and participation: Locating the public sphere in the Middle East and North Africa* (pp. 177–202). SSRC Books.

Morokvasic, M. (1984). Birds of passage are also women. *International Migration Review*, *18*(4), 886–907.
https://doi.org/10.1177/019791838401800040

Moukarbel, N. (2009). Not allowed to love?: Sri Lankan maids in Lebanon. *Mobilities*, *4*(3), 329–347. https://doi.org/10.1080/17450100903195409

Mundlak, G. (2008). Circular migration in Israel: Law's role in circularity and the ambiguities of the CM Strategy. *CARIM Analytic and Synthetic Notes* 2008/32. European University Institute.

Nagy, S. (1998). "This time I think I'll try a Filipina": Global and local influences on relations between foreign household workers and their employers in Doha, Qatar. *City & Society*, *10*(1), 83–103. https://doi.org/10.1525/city.1998.10.1.83

Nakash, O., Nagar, M., Shoshani, A., & Lurie, I. (2017). The association between perceived social support and posttraumatic stress symptoms among Eritrean and Sudanese male asylum seekers in Israel. *International Journal of Culture and Mental Health, 10*(3), 261–275. https://doi.org/10.1080/17542863.2017.1299190

Nathan, G. (2012). *The OECD expert group on migration (SOPEMI) report, immigration in Israel 2011–2012*. KRIF, Jerusalem, Israel.

Nathan, G. (2017). *The OECD expert group on migration SOPEMI annual report 2016–2017*. Research and Information Center, Israeli Parliament (Knesset).

Nathan, G. (2021). *The OECD expert group on migration SOPEMI annual report 2020–2021*. Research and Information Center, Israeli Parliament (Knesset).

Newman, O. (1972). *Creating defensible space*. Center for Urban Policy Research, Rutgers University.

Oishi, N. (2005). *Women in motion: Globalization, state policies, and labor migration in Asia*. Stanford University Press.

Olwig, K. F. (2009). A proper funeral: Contextualizing community among Caribbean migrants. *Journal of the Royal Anthropological Institute, 15*(3), 520–537. https://doi.org/10.1111/j.1467-9655.2009.01571.x

Pande, A. (2012). From "balcony talk" and "practical prayers" to illegal collectives: Migrant domestic workers and meso-level resistances in Lebanon. *Gender & Society, 26*(3), 382–405. https://doi.org/10.1177/0891243212439247

Parreñas, R. S. (2000). Migrant Filipina domestic workers and the international division of reproductive labor. *Gender & Society, 14*(4), 560–580. https://doi.org/10.1177/089124300014004005

Parreñas, R. S. (2001). *Servants of globalization: Women, migration and domestic work*. Stanford University Press.

Parreñas, R. S. (2003). The care crisis in the Philippines: Children and transnational families in the new global economy. In B. Ehrenreich & A. R. Hochschild (Eds.), *Global woman: Nannies, maids and sex workers in the new economy* (pp. 39–54). Metropolitan Books, Henry Holt and Company.

Parreñas, R. S. (2010). Homeward bound: The circular migration of entertainers between Japan and the Philippines. *Global Networks, 10*(3), 301–323. https://doi.org/10.1111/j.1471-0374.2010.00288.x

Parreñas, R. S., Silvey, R., Hwang, M. C., & Choi, C. A. (2019). Serial labor migration: Precarity and itinerancy among Filipino and Indonesian domestic workers. *International Migration Review, 53*(4), 1230–1258. https://doi.org/10.1177/0197918318804769

Paul, A. M. (2011). Stepwise international migration: A multistage migration pattern for the aspiring migrant. *American Journal of Sociology, 116*(6), 1842–1886.

Paz, A. I. (2016). Speaking like a citizen: Biopolitics and public opinion in recognizing non-citizen children in Israel. *Language & Communication, 48*, 18–27. https://doi.org/10.1016/j.langcom.2016.01.002

Paz, Y. (2011). *Ordered disorder: African asylum seekers in Israel and discursive challenges to an emerging refugee regime.* Research Paper No. 205, UNHCR. www.unhcr.org.

Pe-pua, R. (2003). Wife, mother, and maid: The triple role of Filipino domestic workers in Spain and Italy. In N. Piper & M. Roces (Eds.), *Wife or worker?: Asian women and migration* (pp. 157–180). Rowman & Littlefield Publishers, INC.

Peralta, M. T. S. (2004). *From where are you back home?: Ethnography of Filipino domestic workers spending Sundays at Satatue Square.* Ph.D. Thesis. The University of Southern California.

Pingol, A. (2010), Filipino women workers in Saudi: Making offerings for the here and now and hereafter. *The Asia Pacific Journal of Anthropology, 11*(3–4), 394–409.

Piper, N. (2003). Bridging gender, migration and governance: Theoretical possibilities in the Asian context. *Asian and Pacific Migration Journal, 12*(1–2), 21–48.

Piper, N., & Roces, M. (2003). Introduction: Marriage and migration in an age of globalization. In N. Piper & M. Roces (Eds.), *Wife or worker? Asian women and migration* (pp. 1–22), Rowman & Littlefield Publishers Inc.

Ponesse, J. (2014). The ties that blind: Conceptualizing anonymity. *Journal of Social Philosophy, 45*(3).

Porat, I., & Iecovich, E. (2010). Relationships between elderly care recipients and their migrant live-in home care workers in Israel. *Home Health Care Service Quarterly, 29*(1), 1–21. https://doi.org/10.1080/01621424.2010.487035

Pratt, G. (1999). From registered nurse to registered nanny: Discursive geographies of Filipina domestic workers in Vancouver, BC. *Economic Geography, 75*(3), 215–236.

Putnam, R. D. (2000). *Bowling alone.* Simon and Schuster.

Quassoli, F. (1999). Migrants in the Italian underground economy. *International Journal of Urban and Regional Research, 23*(2), 212–231. https://doi.org/10.1111/1468-2427.00192

Rafael, V. (1997). Your grief is our gossip: Overseas Filipinos and other spectral presences. *Public Culture, 9*(2), 267–291. https://doi.org/10.1215/08992363-9-2-267

Raijman, R., & Kemp, A. (2016). The institutionalization of labor migration in Israel. *Arbor, 192*(777), a289. http://dx.doi.org/10.3989/arbor.2016.777n1005

Raijman, R., & Kushnirovich, N. (2012). *Labor migration recruitment practices in Israel.* Final report for the Emek Hefer Ruppin Academic Center.

Rodman, M. C. (1992). Empowering place: Multilocality and multivocality. *American Anthropologist, 94*(3), 640–656. https://doi.org/10.1525/aa.1992.94.3.02a00060

Rodriguez, R. M. (2002). Migrant heroes: Nationalism, citizenship and the politics of Filipino migrant labor. *Citizenship Studies, 6*(3), 341–356. https://doi.org/10.1080/1362102022000011658

Romero, M. (1992). *Maid in the U.S.A.* Routledge.

Rosenhek, Z. (2003). The political dynamics of a segmented labour market: Palestinian citizens, Palestinians from the Occupied Territories and migrant workers in Israel. *Acta Sociologica*, *46*(3), 231–249.

Rosenhek, Z. (2006). Incorporating migrant workers into the Israeli labour market?. Cooperation project on the social integration of immigrants, migration, and the movement of persons. Robert Schuman Centre for Advanced Studies.

Rotbard, S. (2015). *White city, Black city: Architecture and war in Tel Aviv and Jaffa*. Pluto Press.

Sabar, G. (2010). Israel and the "Holy Land": The religio-political discourse of rights among African migrant labourers and African asylum seekers, 1990–2008. *African Diaspora*, *3*(1), 43–76.

Sabar, G., & Kanari, S. (2006). "I'm singing my way up": The significance of Music amongst African Christian migrants in Israel. *Studies in World Christianity*, *12*(2), 101–125. https://doi.org/10.1353/swc.2006.0017

Sabar, G., & Posner, R. (2013). Remembering the past and constructing the future over a communal plate: Restaurants established by African asylum seekers in Tel Aviv. *Food, Culture & Society*, *16*(2), 197–222. https://doi.org/10.2752/175174413X13589681351692

Sabban, R. (2004). Women migrant domestic workers in the United Arab Emirates. In S. Esim & M. Smith (Eds.), *Gender and migration in Arab States: The case of domestic workers* (pp. 86–107). International Labour Organization.

Salter, M. B. (2007). Governmentalities of an airport: Heterotopia and confession. *International Political Sociology*, *1*(1), 49–66. https://doi.org/10.1111/j.1749-5687.2007.00004.x

San Juan Jr., E. (2010). Overseas Filipino workers: The making of an Asian-pacific diaspora. *The Global South*, *3*(2), 99–129. https://doi.org/10.2979/gso.2009.3.2.99

Sandra, Z. (2009). *Lifelines: The networks of Filipina domestic workers in Beirut*. Thesis for MSc in International Development Studies, Lebanon. University of Amsterdam, Netherlands.

Santos, R. A. (1997). Filipino American children. In G. Johnson-Powell & J. Yamamoto (Eds.), *Transcultural child development: Psychological assessment and treatment*. John Wiley & Sons, Inc.

Sassen, S. (2000). Women's burden: Counter-geographies of globalization and the feminization of survival. *Journal of International Affairs*, 503–524. https://doi.org/10.1163/157181002761931378

Sassen, S. (2002). Global cities and survival circuits. In J. A. Radway, K. Gaines, B. Shank, & P. V. Eschen (Eds.), *American studies: An anthology* (pp. 185–193). Wiley-Blackwell.

Schnell, I., & Yoav, B. (2001). The sociospatial isolation of agents in everyday life spaces as an aspect of segregation. *Annals of the Association of American Geographers*, *91*(4), 622–636. https://doi.org/10.1111/0004-5608.00262

Shachar, A., & Felsenstein, D. (2002). Globalization processes and their impact on the structure of the metropolitan Tel Aviv area. In D. Felsenstein, E. W. Schamp, & A. Shachar (Eds.), *I emerging nodes in the global economy: Frankfrut and Tel Aviv Compared*. Springer.

Shapiro, M. (2013). *The politics of intimacy: An ethnography of illegalized migrant women and their undocumented children in Tel Aviv, Israel*. Ph.D. Thesis. York University.

Shurmer, P. (1971). Gift game. *New Society, 18*(492), 1242–1244.

Simmel, G. (1994). Bridge and door. *Theory, Culture and Society, 11*(1), 5–10. https://doi.org/10.1177/026327694011001002

Smart, J. E., Teodosio, V. A. & Jimenez, C. J. (1985). Filipino workers in the Middle East: Social profile and policy implications. *International Migration, 23*(1), 29–43. https://doi.org/10.1111/j.1468-2435.1985.tb00565.x

Smith, M. P. (1992). (2005). Transnational urbanism revisited. *Journal of Ethnic and Migration Studies, 31*(2), 235–244. https://doi.org/10.1080/1369183042000339909

Solomon, M. S. (2009). State-led migration, democratic legitimacy, and deterritorialization: The Philippines' labour export model. *European Journal of East Asian Studies, 8*(2), 275–300. https://doi.org/10.1163/156805809X12553326569759

Sri Tharan, C. T. (2009). *Gender, migration and social change: The return of Filipino women migrant workers*. Ph.D. Thesis. University of Sussex.

Stasiulis, D., & Bakan, A. (2005). *Negotiating citizenship: Migrant women in Canada and the global system*. University of Toronto Press.

St. John, G. (2001). Alternative cultural heterotopia and the liminoid body: Beyond Turner at ConFest. *The Australian Journal of Anthropology, 12*(1), 47–66. https://doi.org/10.1111/j.1835-9310.2001.tb00062.x

Stiell, B., & England, K. (1997). Domestic distinctions: Constructing difference among paid domestic workers in Toronto. *Gender, Place and Culture, 4*(3), 339–359. https://doi.org/10.1080/09663699725387

Sutton, D. E. (2000). Food and the senses. *Annual Review of Anthropology, 39*(1), 209–223. http://dx.doi.org/10.1146/annurev.anthro.012809.104957

Sutton, D. E. (2001). *Remembrance of repasts: An anthropology of food and memory*. Berg.

Szanton Blanc, C. (1996). Balikbayan: A Filipino extension of the national imaginary and of state boundaries. *Philippine Sociological Review, 44*(1–4), 178–193.

Tabuga, A. D., & Cabaero, C. C. (2021). Toward an inclusive social insurance coverage in the Philippines: Examining gender disparities. Research Paper Series No. 2021-06, Philippine Institute for Developmental Studies (PIDS).

Tsujimoto, T. (2003). Church organization and its networks for the Filipino migrants: Surviving and empowering in Korea. In M. Tsuda (Ed.), *Filipino diaspora: Demography, social networks, empowerment and culture* (pp. 125–162). Philippine Migration Research Network (PMRN) and Philippine Social Science Council.

Tsujimoto, T. (2014). Negotiating gender dynamics in heteronormativity: Extramarital intimacy among migrant Filipino workers in South Korea. *Gender, Place & Culture, 21*(6), 750–767. https://doi.org/10.1080/0966369X.2013.817965

Tyner, J. A. (1999). The global context of gendered labor migration from the Philippines to the United States. *American Behavioral Scientist, 42*(4), 671–689. https://doi.org/10.1177/00027649921954417

Tyner, J. A. (2000). Global cities and circuits of global labor: The case of Manila, Philippine. *Professional Geographer, 52*(1), 61–74. https://doi.org/10.1111/0033-0124.00205

Tyner, J. A. (2004). *Made in the Philippines: Gendered discourses and the making of migrants*. Routledge Curzon.

Valerio, R. L. F. (2002). *Pagtitimpi at panggigigil*: Sex and the migrant woman. In E. Dizon-Anonuevo & A. T. Anonuevo (Eds.), *Coming home: Women, migration and re-integration* (pp. 60–69). Balikbayani Foundation, Inc. and Atikha Overseas Workers and Communities Initiative.

Varia, N. (2011). "Sweeping changes?": A review of recent reforms on protections for migrant domestic workers in Asia and the Middle East. *Canadian Journal of Women and the Law, 23*(1), 265–287. https://doi.org/10.3138/cjwl.23.1.265

Watson, S., & Gibson, K. 1995. *Postmodern cities and spaces*. Blackwell.

Willen, S. (2003). Perspectives on labour migration in Israel. *Revue europeenne des migrations internationals, 19*(3), 243–262.

Willen, S. (2005). Birthing "invisible" children: State power, NGO activism, and reproductive health among "illegal migrant" workers in Tel Aviv, Israel. *Journal of Middle East Women's Studies, 1*(2), 55–88. https://doi.org/10.1215/15525864-2005-2003

Willen, S. (2007). Toward a critical phenomenon of "illegality": State power, criminalization, and abjectivity among undocumented migrant workers in Tel Aviv, Israel. *International Migration, 45*(3), 8–38. https://doi.org/10.1111/j.1468-2435.2007.00409.x

Wilson, K. L., & Martin, W. A. (1982). Ethnic enclaves: A comparison of the Cuban and Black economies in Miami. *The American Journal of Sociology, 88*(1), 135–160.

Wimmer, A., & Schiller, G. N. (2002). Methodological nationalism and beyond: Nation-state building, migration and the social sciences. *Global Networks, 2*(4), 301–334. https://doi.org/10.1111/1471-0374.00043

Wonders, N. A. (2006). Global flows, semi-permeable borders and new channels of inequality. In S. Pickering & L. Weber (Eds.), *Borders, mobility and technologies of control* (pp. 63–86). Springer.

Wu, P. (2010). How outsiders find home in the city: ChungShan in Taipei. In H. Jeffrey (Ed.), *Insurgent public space: Guerrilla urbanism and the remaking of contemporary cities* (pp. 134–146). Routledge.

Xiang, B., & Lindquist, J. (2014). Migration infrastructure. *International Migration Review, 48*(1), 122–148. https://doi.org/10.1111/imre.12141

Yacobi, H. (2008). *Irregular migration to Israel: The sociopolitical perspective.* Cooperation project on the social integration of immigrants, migration, and the movement of persons (CARIM).

Yacobi, H. (2010). "Let me go to the city": African asylum seekers, racialization and the politics of space in Israel. *Journal of Refugee Studies, 24*(1), 47–68. https://doi.org/10.1093/jrs/feq051

Yeates, N. (2013). Global care chains: A state-of-the-art review and future directions in care transnationalization research. *Global Networks, 12*(2), 135–154. https://doi.org/10.1111/j.1471-0374.2012.00344.x

Yeoh, B., & Huang, S. (1998). Negotiating public space: Strategies and styles of migrant female domestic workers in Singapore. *Urban Studies, 35*(3), 583–602. https://doi.org/10.1080/0042098984925

Yeoh, B., & Huang, S. (2000). Home and away: Foreign domestic workers and negotiations of diasporic identity in Singapore. *Women's Studies International Forum, 23*(4), 413–429. https://doi.org/10.1016/S0277-5395(00)00105-9

Zontini, E. (2010). Enabling and constraining aspects of social capital in migrant families: Ethnicity, gender and generation. *Ethnic and Racial Studies, 33*(5), 816–831. https://doi.org/10.1080/01419870903254661

Newspapers

Dona, W. (2010, July 8). Tel Aviv rabbis: Renting apartments to foreign workers violates Jewish law. *Ha'aretz.* https://www.haaretz.com/2010-07-08/ty-article/tel-aviv-rabbis-renting-apartments-to-foreign-workers-violates-jewish-law/0000017f-db9d-d856-a37f-ffddf2e80000

Toi, S. (2012, June 7). 52% of Israeli Jews agree: African migrants are "a cancer." *The Times of Israel.* https://www.timesofisrael.com/most-israeli-jews-agree-africans-are-a-cancer/

Yuval, A. (2005, June 6). Tel Aviv launches green plan to combat inner city drug-addict colonies. *Ha'aretz.* http://www.haaretz.com/print-edition/news/tel-aviv-launches-green-plan-to-combat-inner-city-drug-addict-colonies-1.160502

Ruth, S. (2003, Oct 15). Immigration police nab Foreign workers who did not go home. *Ha'aretz.* https://www.haaretz.com/2003-10-15/ty-article/immigration-police-nab-foreign-workers-who-did-not-go-home/0000017f-df0a-df7c-a5ff-df7a95320000

Websites

Asian Development Bank. (2009, December). *Remittances in Asia: Implications for the fight against poverty and the pursuit of economic growth.* https://www.adb.org/sites/default/files/publication/28397/economics-wp182.pdf

Bangko Sentral ng Pilipinas. (2020). Banko Sentral Pilipinas Dato. https://www.bsp.gov.ph/SitePages/Default.aspx

Kav LaOved. https://www.kavlaoved.org.il/en/caregivers-know-your-rights/

OECD. (2020). *International migration outlook 2021*. https://www.oecd-ilibrary.org/social-issues-migration-health/international-migration-outlook-2021_29f23e9d-en

Philippine Statistics Authority. (2021). *Survey on overseas Filipinos*. https://psa.gov.ph/content/2021-overseas-filipino-workers-final-results

Population and Immigration Authority. (2019). *Data on foreigners in Israel: Report*. https://www.gov.il/BlobFolder/reports/foreign_workers_status_2019/he/sum_2019.pdf

United Nations. (2020). *Mainstreaming ageing in Israel*. May 2020. United Nations Geneva. https://unece.org/sites/default/files/2021-03/Israel_CN_EN.pdf

Index

Agency   17, 19, 21, 22, 47, 194
Agent   17, 30, 39, 42, 45, 46, 52, 54–55, 56–60, 92–94, 126, 129–130, 151, 165, 189
Anonymity   29, 32, 157, 177, 183–184, 192
autonomy   22, 31, 71, 123, 136, 138–139, 143, 155, 157, 176, 183, 189, 193–194

ba'al habait   92, 109–110, 113, 117, 119–121, 124, 126–127, 130–131, 142–143, 148, 152
bakla   175–176
Bialik-Rogozin School   82, 111, 164, 170
binding system   15, 54, 63–64, 101, 158, 160
birthday party   14, 28, 32, 91, 132, 135–136, 144–151
boundaries   20, 22, 26, 31–32, 67, 71, 101, 108, 111, 118–119, 126, 131, 142, 149, 157, 164–165, 177, 183–184, 190–194
brokerage fee   39, 46, 48–54, 58–60, 92–94, 159–161

care worker   13–17, 19, 22–27, 31, 39–41, 43, 45–46, 48–61, 64, 66–71, 79, 89–93, 95–102, 107, 109, 111, 116, 122–126, 130, 137–139, 141–142, 144, 147, 152, 158–162, 164, 169, 173–174, 177, 181, 183, 190, 192
cargo   91, 98
Central Bus Station   13–14, 79–83, 167

day-off   15, 67, 71, 89–91, 95, 97, 100, 102, 109, 111, 123–126, 128, 132, 136, 139, 147, 173, 180, 190
deportation   65–66, 85, 87, 101, 157–158, 164–167, 169, 171, 178, 191
dinner gathering   118, 123, 136, 141–144
domestic workers   17, 19, 21–23, 41, 43–44, 47–50, 89, 137, 140, 175

elderly care   15, 62
employer   15, 17, 22, 24, 27–29, 52–54, 56–57, 60, 62–64, 67–71, 89–94, 100–102, 109, 119, 122–124, 136–138, 143, 157–161, 169, 174, 177, 181, 184
extramarital relationships   32, 122, 128, 157, 171–174, 176, 182, 184

Filipino migrant workers   26, 31, 39–40, 72, 119, 176, 189, 194
foreign workers   15–16, 31, 61–63, 65–67, 86

gating   177, 179, 184
gift   98–99, 144, 146–150

hierarchical order   31, 107, 116, 119–120, 191
holiday   31, 70, 116, 128, 144, 155

illegality   25, 32, 86, 157–158, 164, 167, 170, 181–182
Immigration Police   65, 85, 87, 118, 157, 164–170, 178–181, 193
informal economy   79–80, 95
internal solidarity   32, 142, 157, 177, 185, 192
Israel   13–16, 19–20, 23–31, 39–69, 79–83, 86, 88–90, 92–94, 96, 99–101, 108, 116, 119, 121–122, 124–126, 128, 133, 135, 137–138, 143–144, 151–152, 155, 157–164, 166–167, 170–177, 182–183, 189–190, 192, 194

Kav La'Oved   52, 59, 68, 82, 102, 162
Kosher   138

Levinsky Park   14, 82, 84, 87, 127, 142
live-in   15, 22, 27, 49, 67–71, 79, 89, 91–92, 95, 97, 102, 109–111, 113, 117, 119, 122–124, 126–128, 137–139, 141–142, 174, 178, 181, 190
live-out   27, 67, 70–71, 90, 100–102, 109–110, 113, 117–119, 122–124, 126–128, 130, 132, 146, 169–170, 174, 177–178

Mesila   66, 82
migration industry   39, 45, 52, 58, 189
mobility   19–20, 22, 25, 30–31, 45, 47, 52, 60, 64, 81, 107, 116, 125–126, 129–132, 160, 165, 189–193
moneylender   58–59, 145, 160

network   21–22, 24–25, 28, 31–32, 39, 52, 54, 57–59, 79, 89, 91–93, 95, 97, 100, 118, 125–126, 129–136, 140, 142, 1445–145, 147, 149–150, 152, 154–155, 159, 161, 189, 191, 194
Neve Sha'anan   13–16, 25–29, 31, 46, 63, 79–101, 108, 120, 125, 129–130, 133, 135, 139–140, 144, 151, 157–159, 161, 163–170, 173, 175–176, 178–180, 184
NGO   43, 58, 66, 82, 86, 160, 171

OFW   39–44, 48, 50–51, 172
Ovdim Zarim   15, 65

padala   99
paluwagan   32, 132, 135, 150–154
Philippines   154, 159–164, 167, 170–178, 182–184
place attachment   22, 31–32, 107, 119, 125, 132, 134–135, 155
place-making   13, 19, 21, 25, 192
POEA   43

recruitment process   26, 45, 53–56, 58–60, 92, 194
reciprocal exchanges   134, 136

reliever   101–103, 127, 161, 169, 178, 180
reporter   157, 168, 181, 193
rotate saving association   32, 135

settlement   31, 47, 79, 88–89, 91–92, 95, 107, 125–126, 159, 163, 167, 170, 194
Shabbat   14, 67, 79, 83, 95, 98, 102, 167, 170, 179
shelter   7, 176–177, 183–184
social capital   23, 39, 49, 58, 119, 130, 150–151, 155
social space   2, 20–22, 27, 114, 116, 125, 128–129
surveillance   64, 68, 158, 164–167, 169, 177, 183, 193

Tagalog   15, 91, 96, 141, 144, 150, 165, 180
Tel Aviv   10, 16, 19, 93–95, 108, 191, 204, 207
tomboy   175–176
transfer   59, 64, 98–99, 107, 117, 125–127, 129, 131–132, 193

undocumented migrants   23–25, 28–29, 65, 85, 87, 101, 110, 160–161, 165–171, 179–182, 192

weekend gathering   135, 152